Early English Dramatists

The

Dramatic Writings of

JOHN HEYWOOD

COMPRISING

The Pardoner and the Friar—The Four P.P.—
John the Husband, Tyb his wife, and Sir John the
Priest—Play of the Weather—Play of Love—
Dialogue concerning Witty and Witless—Note-Book
and Word-List

EDITED BY

JOHN S. FARMER

London
Privately Printed for Subscribers by the
EARLY ENGLISH DRAMA SOCIETY, 18 BURY STREET
BLOOMSBURY, W.C.

MCMV

Printing Statement:

Due to the very old age and scarcity of this book,
many of the pages may be hard to read due to the
blurring of the original text, possible missing pages,
missing text, dark backgrounds and other issues
beyond our control.

Because this is such an important and rare work, we
believe it is best to reproduce this book regardless of
its original condition.

Thank you for your understanding.

[Facsimile of woodcut portraits in *The Spider and the Flie* (ed. 1556) and in *Epigrams upon Proverbs* (ed. 1562) : see Note-Book.]

CONTENTS

A MERRY PLAY

BETWEEN THE PARDONER AND THE FRIAR, THE CURATE AND NEIGHBOUR PRATT

The Players:

A Pardoner   The Curate

A Friar   Neighbour Pratt

THE PARDONER AND
THE FRIAR

Friar. Deus hic, the Holy Trinity,
Preserve all that now here be !
Dear brethren, if ye will consider
The cause, why I am come hither,
Ye would be glad to know my intent:
For I come not hither for money nor for rent,
I come not hither for meat nor for meal,
But I come hither for your soul's heal :
I come not hither to poll nor to shave,
I come not hither to beg nor to crave,
I come not hither to gloss nor to flatter,
I come not hither to babble nor to clatter,
I come not hither to fable nor to lie,
But I come hither your souls to edify.
For we friars are bound the people to teach,
The gospel of Christ openly to preach,
As did the apostles by Christ their master sent,
To turn the people and make them to repent.
But since the apostles from heaven would not
We friars now must occupy their room. [come,
We friars are bound to search men's conscience,
We may not care for groats nor for pence,
We friars have professed wilful poverty,
No penny in our purse have may we ;
Knife nor staff may we none carry,

Except we should from the gospel vary.
For worldly adversity may we be in no sorrow,
We may not care to-day for our meat to-
    morrow,
Barefoot and barelegged must we go also:
We may not care for frost nor snow;
We may have no manner care, ne think
Nother for our meat nor for our drink;
But let our thoughts fro such things be as free
As be the birds that in the air flee.
For why our Lord, cleped sweet Jesus,
In the gospel speaketh to us thus:
Through all the world go ye, saith He,
And to every creature speak ye of me;
And show of my doctrine and cunning,
And that they may be glad of your coming.
If that you enter in any house anywhere,
Look that ye salute them, and bid my peace be
    there;
And if that house be worthy and elect,
Th'ilk peace there then shall take effect;
And if that house be cursed or pervert,
Th'ilk peace then shall to yourself revert.
And furthermore, if any such there be,
Which do deny for to receive ye,
And do despise your doctrine and your lore,
At such a house tarry ye no more;
And from your shoes scrape away the dust
To their reprefe; and I, both true and just,
Shall vengeance take of their sinful deed.
Wherefore, my friends, to this text take ye
Beware how ye despise the poor freres. [heed:
Which are in this world Christ's ministers;
But do them with an hearty cheer receive,
Lest they happen your houses for to leave;
And then God will take vengeance in His ire.

60 Wherefore I now, that am a poor friar,
Did inquire where any people were
Which were disposed the Word of God to hear;
And as I came hither, one did me tell
That in this town right good folk did dwell,
Which to hear the Word of God would be glad;
And as soon as I thereof knowledge had,
I hither hied me as fast as I might,
Intended by the grace of God Almighty,
And by your patience and supportation,
70 Here to make a simple collation;
Wherefore I require all ye in this prese[nce]
For to abide and give due audience.
But, first of all,
Now here I shall
To God my prayer make,
To give ye grace
All in this place
His doctrine for to take.
    [*And then kneeleth down the friar saying his*
    prayers, and in the meanwhile entereth the
    pardoner with all his relics, to declare what
    each of them been, and the whole power
    and virtue thereof.   [grace,
    Pard.   God and Saint Leonard send ye all his
50 As many as been assembled in this place!
Good devout people that here do assemble,
I pray God that ye may all well resemble
The image after which you are wrought,
And that ye save that Christ in you bought.
Devout Christian people, ye shall all wit,
That I am comen hither ye to visit;
Wherefore let us pray thus, ere I begin:
Our Saviour preserve ye all from sin,
And enable ye to receive this blessed pardon,
90 Which is the greatest under the sun:

Granted by the Pope in his bulls under lead,
Which pardon ye shall find, when ye are dead;
That offereth outher groats or else pence,
To these holy relics which, ere I go hence,
I shall here show in open audience,
Exhorting ye all to do to them reverence.
But first ye shall know well that I come from
Lo, here my bulls, all and some: [Rome;
Our liege Lord seal here on my patent
100 I bear with me my body to warrant;
That no man be so bold, be he priest or clerk,
Me to disturb of Christ's holy wark;
Nor have no disdain nor yet scorn
Of these holy relics which saints have worn.
First here I show ye of a holy Jew's hip
A bone—I pray you, take good keep
To my words and mark them well:
If any of your beasts' bellies do swell,
Dip this bone in the water that he doth take
110 Into his body, and the swelling shall slake;
And if any worm have your beasts stung,
Take of this water, and wash his tongue,
And it will be whole anon; and furthermore
Of pox and scabs, and every sore,
He shall be quite whole that drinketh of the well
That this bone is dipped in : it is truth that I tell.
And if any man, that any beast oweth,
Once in the week, ere that the cock croweth,
Fasting will drink of this well a draught,
120 As that holy Jew hath us taught,
His beasts and his stores shall multiply.
And, masters all, it helpeth well,
Though a man be foul in jealous rage,
Let a man with this water make his pottage,
And never more shall he his wife mistrist,
Though he in sooth the fault by her wist,

Or had she been taken with friars two or three.
And another holy relic may ye see :
He that his hand will put in this mitten,
130 He shall have increase of his grain,
That he hath sown, be it wheat or oats,
So that he offer pence or else groats,
And another holy relic eke here see ye may :
The blessed arm of sweet Saint Sunday;
And whosoever is blessed with this right hand,
Cannot speed amiss by sea nor by land.
And if he offereth eke with good devotion.
He shall not fail to come to high promotion.
And another holy relic here may ye see :
140 The great toe of the Holy Trinity;
And whosoever once doth it in his mouth take,
He shall never be diseased with the toothache;
Cancer nor pox shall there none breed :
This that I show ye is matter indeed.
And here is of our lady a relic full good : [hood,
Her bongrace which she ware, with her French
When she went out always for sun-burning :
Women with child which be in mourning
By virtue thereof shall be soon eased,
150 And of their travail full soon also released,
And if this bongrace they do devoutly kiss,
And offer thereto, as their devotion is.
Here is another relic eke, a precious one,
Of All-Hallows the blessed jaw bone,
Which relic without any fail
Against poison chiefly doth prevail;
For whomsoever it toucheth without doubt,
All manner venom from him shall issue out;
So that it shall hurt no manner wight.
160 Lo, of this relic the great power and might,
Which preserveth from poison every man !
Lo, of Saint Michael eke the brain-pan,

Whioh for the headache is a preservative
To every man or beast that beareth life;
And further it shall stand him in better stead,
For his head shall never ache, when that he is
    dead,
Nor he shall feel no manner grief nor pain,
Though with a sword one cleave it then a-twain;
But be as one that lay in a dead sleep. [creep,
Wherefore to these relics now come crouch and
But look that ye offering to them make,
Or else can ye no manner profit take.
But one thing, ye women all, I warrant you:
If any wight be in this place now,
That hath done sin so horrible, that she
Dare not for shame thereof shriven be,
Or any woman, be she young or old,
That hath made her husband cuckold:
Such folk shall have no power nor no grace
To offer to my relics in this place;
And whoso findeth herself out of such blame,
Come hither to me, on Christ's holy name.
And because ye
Shall unto me
Give credence at the full
Mine auctority
Now shall ye see
Lo, here the Pope's bull!

    [*Now shall the friar begin his sermon, and
      even at the same time the pardoner begin-
      neth also to show and speak of his bulls
      and auctorities come from Rome.*
    Friar. "Date et dabitur vobis:"
Good devout people, this place of Scripture—
    Pard. Worshipful masters, ye shall under-
    stand—
    Friar. Is to you that have no literature—

Pard. That Pope Leo the Tenth hath
    granted with his hand—
Friar. Is to say in our English tongue—
Pard. And by his bulls confirmed under
    lead—   [among—
Friar. As depart your goods the poor folk
Pard. To all manner people both quick and
    dead—   [again—
Friar. And God shall then give unto you
Pard. Ten thousand years and as many
    Lents of pardon—   [plain—
2c∂ *Friar.* This is the gospel, so is written
Pard. When they are dead, their souls for
    to guardon—   [largest wise—
Friar. Therefore give your alms in the
Pard. That will with their penny or alms
    deed—   [covetise!
Friar. Keep not your goods : fye, fye, on
Pard. Put to their hands to the good
    speed—   [able—
Friar. That sin with God is most abhomin-
Pard. Of the holy chapel of sweet Saint
    Leonard—   [damnable—
Friar. And is eke the sin that is most
Pard. Which late by fire was destroyed and
    marred—   [how—
2/° *Friar.* In Scripture eke but I say, sirs,
Pard. Ay, by the mass, one cannot hear—
Friar. What a babbling maketh yonder
    fellow !—   [frere—
Pard. For the babbling of yonder foolish
Friar. In Scripture eke is there many a
    place—   [to tell—
Pard. And also, masters, as I was about
Friar. Which showeth that many a man so
    far-forth lacketh grace—

Pard.   Pope Julius the Sixth hath granted
fair and well—

Friar.   That when to them God hath abun-
dance sent—   [pardon to them send—

Pard.   And doth twelve thousand years of

220 *Friar.*   They would distribute none to the
indigent—

Pard.   That ought to this holy chapel lend—

Friar.   Whereat God having great indigna-
tion—

Pard.   Pope Boniface the Ninth also—

Friar.   Punished these men after a divers
fashion—   [divers popes mo—

Pard.   Pope Julius, Pope Innocent, with

Friar.   As the gospel full nobly doth
declare—   [same—

Pard.   Hath granted to the sustaining of the

Friar.   How dives Epulus reigning in
welfare—   [every of you by name—

Pard.   Five thousand years of pardon to

230 *Friar.*   And on his board dishes delicate—

Pard.   And clean remission also of their
sin—   [gate—

Friar.   Poor Lazarus came begging at his

Pard.   As often times as you put in—

Friar.   Desiring some food his hunger to
relieve—   [coffer—

Pard.   Any money into the Pardoner's

Friar.   But the rich man nothing would him
give—

Pard.   Or any money up unto it offer—

Friar.   Not so much as a few crumbs of
bread—

Pard.   Or he that offereth penny or groat—

250 *Friar.*   Wherefore poor Lazarus of famine
straight was dead—

Pard. Or he that giveth the Pardoner a
  new coat—   [carry—
Friar. And angels his soul to heaven did
Pard. Or take of me other image or letter—
Friar. But now the rich man, of the con-
  trary—   [the better—
Pard. Whereby this poor chapel may fare
Friar. When he was dead, went to misery
  and pain.   [deed—
Pard. And (God wot) it is a full gracious
Friar. Wherefore evermore he shall re-
  main—   [your mede—
Pard. For which God shall quite you well
200 *Friar.* In brenning fire, which shall never
  cease—   [your will—
Pard. Now help our poor chapel, if it be
Friar. But I say, thou Pardoner, I bid thee
  hold thy peace !—   [still !—
Pard. And I say, thou friar, hold thy tongue
Friar. What, standest thou there all the
  day smattering !—
Pard. Marry, what standest thou there all
  the day clattering !—
Friar. Marry, fellow, I come hither to
  preach the Word of God,
Which of no man may be forbode ;
But heard with silence and good intent,
For why it teacheth them evident
270 The very way and path that shall them lead
Even to heaven's gates, as straight as any
  thread.   [ence,
And he that letteth the Word of God of audi-
Standeth accursed in the great sentence ;
And so art thou for interrupting me.
    Pard. Nay, thou art a cursed knave, and
    that shalt thou see ;

And all such that to me make interruption,
The Pope sends them excommunication
By his bulls here ready to be read,
By bishops and his cardinals confirmed;
280 And eke if thou disturb me any thing,
Thou art also a traitor to the king.   [seal,
For here hath he granted me under his broad
That no man, if he love his heal,
Should me disturb or let in any wise;   [spise,
And if thou dost the king's commandment de-
I shall make thee be set fast by the feet,
And, where thou saidst that thou art more meet
Among the people here for to preach,
Because thou dost them the very way teach,
290 How to come to heaven above:
Therein thou liest, and that shall I prove,
And by good reason I shall make thee bow,
And know that I am meeter than art thou.
For thou, when thou hast taught them once the
          way,   [or nay;
Thou carest not whether they come there, yea
But when that thou hast done altogether,
And taught them the way for to come hither,
Yet all that thou canst imagine
Is but to use virtue, and abstain fro sin.
300 And if they fall once, then thou canst no more:
Thou canst not give them a salve for their sore.
But these my letters be clean purgation,
Although never so many sins they have done.
But when thou hast taught them the way and
          all,   [a fall
Yet, ere they come there, they may have many
In the way, ere that they come thither
For why the way to heaven is very slidder.
But I will teach them after another rate,
For I shall bring them to heaven's gate,

310 And be their guides, and conduct all things,
And lead them thither by the purse-strings,
So that they shall not fall, though that they
    would.   [bold :
    Friar. Hold thy peace, knave, thou art very
Thou pratest, in faith, even like a Pardoner.
    Pard. Why despisest thou the Pope's
    minister?
Masters, here I curse him openly,
And therewith warn all this whole company
By the Pope's great auctority,
That ye leave him, and harken unto me;
For, till he be assoiled, his words take none
    effect,
320 For out of holy church he is now clean reject.
    Friar. My masters, he doth but jest and
    rave;
It forceth not for the words of a knave;
But to the Word of God do reverence,
And hear me forth with due audience.
Masters, I showed you ere while of alms-deed—
    Pard. Masters, this pardon which I showed
    you before—   [their need—
    Friar. And how ye should give poor folk at
    Pard. Is the greatest that ever was, sith
    God was bore—   [were done—
    Friar. And if of your parts that thing once
330   *Pard.* For why without confession or con-
    trition—   [retribution—
    Friar. Doubt not but God should give you
    Pard. By this shall ye have clean remis-
    sion—   [clared—
    Friar. But now further it ought to be de-
    Pard. And forgiven of the sins seven—
    Friar. Who be these poor folk, that should
have your reward—

Pard. Come to this pardon, if ye will come
    to heaven—   [speak and name?—
Friar. Who be those poor folk, of whom I
Pard. Come to this pardon, if ye will be in
    bliss—
Friar. Certes, we poor friars are the same—
340 *Pard.* This is the pardon, which ye cannot
    miss—
Friar. We friars daily take pain, I say—
Pard. This is the pardon, which shall men's
    souls win—   [pray—
Friar. We friars daily do both fast and
Pard. This is the pardon, the ridder of your
    sin—   [hour—
Friar. We friars travail and labour every
Pard. This is the pardon that purchaseth
    all grace—   [our Saviour—
Friar. We friars take pain for the love of
Pard. This is a pardon for all manner of
    trespass—
Friar. We friars also go on limitation—
350 *Pard.* This is the pardon, of which all mercy
    doth spring—   [nation—
Friar. For to preach to every Christian
Pard. This is the pardon, that to heaven
    shall ye bring—   [keep silence soon !—
Friar. But I say, thou Pardoner, thou wilt
Pard. Yea, it is like to be, when I have
    done !—   [thou, I say,
Friar. Marry, therefore the more knave art
That perturbest the Word of God, I say;
For neither thyself wilt hear God's doctrine,
Ne suffer other their ears to incline,
Wherefore our Saviour, in His holy Scripture,
360 Giveth thee thy judgment, thou cursed creature,
Speaking to thee after this manner :

" Maledictus qui audit verbum Dei negli-
    genter "—   [no audience,
Woe be that man, saith our Lord, that giveth
Or heareth the Word of God with negligence.
    Pard. Now thou hast spoken all, sir daw,
I care not for thee an old straw;
I had liever thou were hanged up with a rope,
Than I, that am come from the Pope,
And thereby God's minister, while thou
    standest and prate,
370 Should be fain to knock without the gate.
Therefore preach hardly thy bellyful,
But I nevertheless will declare the Pope's bull.
    Friar. Now, my friends, I have afore
    showed ye—   [clared—
    Pard. Now, my masters, as I have afore de-
    Friar. That good it is to give your charity—
    Pard. That pardoners from you may not be
    spared—   [told—
    Friar. And further I have at length to you
    Pard. Now hereafter shall follow and en-
    sue—   [should—
    Friar. Who be these people that ye receive
380   *Pard.* That followeth of pardons the great
    virtue—
    Friar. That is to say us friars poor—
    Pard. We pardoners for your souls be as
    necessary—
    Friar. That for our living must beg fro door
    to door—
    Pard. As is the meat for our bodies
    hungry—   [proper thing—
    Friar. For of our own proper we have no
    Pard. For pardons is the thing that
    bringeth men to heaven—   [giving—
    Friar. But that we get of devout people's

Pard. Pardons delivereth them fro the sins
    seven—   [and three—
Friar. And in our place be friars three score
370 *Pard.* Pardons for every crime may dis-
    pense—
Friar. Which only live on men's charity—
Pard. Pardon purchaseth grace for all
    offence—
Friar. For we friars wilful charity profess—
Pard. Yea, though he had slain both father
    and mother—   [nor less—
Friar. We may have no money nother more
Pard. And this pardon is chief above all
    other—   [care—
Friar. For worldly treasure we may nought
Pard. For who to it offereth groat or
    penny—   bodies bare—
Friar. Our souls must be rich and our
400 *Pard.* Though sins he had done never so
    many—   [behind—
Friar. And one thing I had almost left
Pard. And though that he had all his
    kindred slain—   [mind—
Friar. Which before came not to my
Pard. This pardon shall rid them from
    everlasting pain—   [thing—
Friar. And doubtless, it is none other
Pard. There is no sin so abhominable—
Friar. But when ye will give your alms and
    offering—
Pard. Which to remit this pardon is not
    able—
Friar. Look that ye distribute it wisely—
410 *Pard.* As well declareth the sentence of this
    letter—   [cry—
Friar. Not to every man that for it will

Pard. Ye cannot, therefore, bestow your
    money better—   [wise—
Friar. For if ye give your alms in that
Pard. Let us not here stand idle all the
    day—   [suffice—
Friar. It shall not both to them and us
Pard. Give us some money, ere that we go
    our way—
Friar. But I say, thou lewd fellow thou,
Haddest none other time to show thy bulls but
    now?
Canst not tarry and abide till soon,
420 And read them then, when preaching is done?
Pard. I will read them now, what sayest
    thou thereto?
Hast thou anything therewith to do?
Thinkest that I will stand and tarry for thy
    leisure?
Am I bound to do so much for thy pleasure?
Friar. For my pleasure? nay I would thou
    knowest it well :
It becometh the knave never a deal
To prate thus boldly in my presence,
And let the Word of God of audience.
Pard. Let the Word of God, quod a? nay
    let a whoreson drivel
430 Prate here all day, with a foul evil,
And all thy sermon goeth on covetise,
And biddest men beware of avarice ;   [thing,
And yet in thy sermon dost thou none other
But for alms stand all the day begging !
Friar. Leave thy railing, I would thee
    advise—   [be wise—
Pard. Nay, leave thou thy babbling, if thou
Friar. I would thou knowest it, knave, I
    will not leave a whit—

                       C

Pard. No more will I, I do thee well to
wit—

Friar. It is not thou shall make me hold my
peace—   [thinkest it for thy ease—

440 *Pard.* Then speak on hardly, if thou

Friar. For I will speak, whither thou wilt
or no—   [also—

Pard. In faith, I care not, for I will speak

Friar. Wherefore hardly let us both go to—

Pard. See which shall be better heard of us
two—   [ing pardoners—

Friar. What, should ye give ought to part-

Pard. What, should ye spend on these flattering liars—   [bold beggars—

Friar. What, should ye give ought to these

Pard. As be these babbling monks and
these friars—   [living—

Friar. Let them hardly labour for their

450 *Pard.* Which do nought daily but babble
and lie—   [giving—

Friar. It much hurteth them good men's

Pard. And tell you fables dear enough at a
fly—   [ful to wark—

Friar. For that maketh them idle and sloth-

Pard. As doth this babbling friar here
to-day—   [cark—

Friar. That for none other thing they will

Pard. Drive him hence, therefore, in the
twenty-devil way!—   [and cart—

Friar. Hardly they would go both to plough

Pard. On us pardoners hardly do your
cost—   [smart—

Friar. And if of necessity once they felt the

460 *Pard.* For why, your money never can be
lost—

Friar. But we friars be not in like estate—

Pard. For why, there is in our fraternity—
Friar. For our hands with such things we
may not maculate—   [there of be—
Pard. For all brethren and sistren that
Friar. We friars be not in like condition—
Pard. Devoutly song every year—
Friar. We may have no prebends ne ex-
hibition—   [there—
Pard. As he shall know well that cometh
Friar. Of all temporal service are we for-
bode—
470 *Pard.* At every of the five solemn feasts—
Friar. And only bound to the service of
God—   [good rest—
Pard. A mass and dirge to pray for the
Friar. And therewith to pray for every
Christian nation—   [sistren all—
Pard. Of the souls of the brethren and
Friar. That God witsafe to save them fro
damnation—
Pard. Of our fraternity in general—
Friar. But some of you so hard be of
heart—   [arrayed and dight—
Pard. With a hearse there standing well
Friar. Ye cannot weep, though ye full sore
smart—   [ning bright—
480 *Pard.* And torches and tapers about it bren-
Friar. Wherefore some man must ye hire
needs—   [ringing—
Pard. And with the bells eke solemnly
Friar. Which must intreat God for your
misdeeds—   [ing—
Pard. And priests and clerks devoutly sing-
Friar. Ye can hire no better, in mine
opinion—   [year—
Pard. And furthermore, every night in the
C 2

Friar. Than us God's servants, men of re-
   ligion—   [there—
Pard. Twelve poor people are received
Friar. And specially God heareth us poor
   friars—   [food—
Pard. And there have both harborow and
490 *Friar.* And is attentive unto our desires—
Pard. That for them is convenient and
   good—   [heard of our Lord—
Friar. For the more of religion the more
Pard. And furthermore, if there be any
   other—   [doth accord—
Friar. And that it so should, good reason
Pard. That of our fraternity be sister or
   brother—   [even he—
Friar. Therefore, doubt not, masters, I am
Pard. Which hereafter happen to fall in
   decay—   [charity—
Friar. To whom ye should part with your
Pard. And if ye then chance to come that
   way—   [alms take—
500 *Friar.* We friars be they that should your
Pard. Nigh unto our foresaid holy place—
Friar. Which for your soul's health do both
   watch and wake—   [space—
Pard. Ye shall there tarry for a month's
Friar. We friars pray, God wot, when ye
   do sleep—   [cost—
Pard. And be there found of the place's
Friar. We for your sins do both sob and
   weep—
Pard. Wherefore now, in the name of the
   Holy Ghost—
Friar. To pray to God for mercy and for
   grace—
Pard. I advise you all, that now here be—

510   *Friar.* And thus do we daily with all our
    whole place—
    Pard. For to be of our fraternity—
    Friar. Wherefore distribute of your tem-
    poral wealth—   [penny :—
    Pard. Fie on covetise! stick not for a
    Friar. By which ye may preserve your
    souls' health—   [many—
    Pard. For which ye may have benefits so
    Friar. I say, wilt thou not yet stint thy
    clap?
Pull me down the Pardoner with an evil hap!
    Pard. Master Friar, I hold it best
To keep your tongue, while ye be in rest—
520   *Friar.* I say, one pull the knave off his
    stool !   [fool !
    Pard. Nay, one pull the friar down like a
    Friar. Leave thy railing and babbling of
    friars,
Or, by Jis, I 'sh lug thee by the sweet ears !
    Pard. By God, I would thou durst presume
    to it !—   [to do it—
    Friar. By God, a little thing might make me
    Pard. And I shrew thy heart, and thou
    spare—   [thou slouch ;
    Friar. By God, I will not miss thee much,
And if thou play me such another touch,
I 'sh knock thee on the costard, I would thou it
    knew—   [Hew.''
530   *Pard.* '' Marry that I would see, quod blind
    Friar. Well, I will begin, and then let me
    see,
Whether thou darest again interrupt me,
And what thou would once to it say—
    Pard. Begin and prove, whether I will, yea
    or nay—

Friar. And to go forth, whereas I left right
    now—
Pard. Because some percase will think
    amiss of me—   [way how—
Friar. Our Lord in the gospel showeth the
Pard. Ye shall now hear the Pope's autho-
    rity.   [no lenger—
Friar. By Gog's soul, knave, I suffer thee
Pard. I say some good body lend me his
    hanger,
And I shall him teach by God Almighty,
How he shall another time learn for to fight!
I shall make that bald crown of his to look red;
I shall leave him but one ear on his head!
Friar. But I shall leave thee never an ear,
    ere I go:
Pard. Yea, whoreson friar, wilt thou soe—
                 [*Then they fight.*
Friar. Loose thy hands away from mine
    ears—   [my hairs:
Pard. Then take thou thy hands away from
Nay, abide, thou whoreson, I am not down yet;
I trust first to lay thee at my feet.   [bite?
Friar. Yea, whoreson, wilt thou scrat and
Pard. Yea, marry, will I, as long as thou
    dost smite—   [*Enter the Curate.*
Parson (or Curate). Hold your hands, a
    vengeance on ye both two,
That ever ye came hither to make this a-do!
To pollute my church, a mischief on you light!
I swear to you, by God Almight,
Ye shall both repent, every vein of your heart,
As sore as ye did ever thing, ere ye depart.
    Friar. Master Parson, I marvel ye will give
To this false knave in this audience   [licence
To publish his ragman-rolls with lies.

540

550

560

I desired him, i-wis, more than once or twice
To hold his peace, till that I had done;
But he would hear no more than the man in the
    moon—   [thou me?—
    Pard.   Why should I suffer thee more than
Master Parson gave me licence before thee;
And I would thou knowest it, I have relics here
Other manner stuff than thou dost bear.
I will edify more with the sight of it,
550 Than will all the prating of holy writ;
For that except that the preacher himself live
His predication will help never a dell,   [well,
And I know well that thy living is nought:
Thou art an apostate, if it were well sought.
An homicide thou art, I know well enough,
For myself knew where that thou slough
A wench with thy dagger in a couch:
And yet, as thou say'st in thy sermon, that no
    man shall touch.   [church!
    Parson.   No more of this wrangling in my
560 I shrew your hearts both for this lurch:
Is there any blood shed here between these
Thanked be God they had no staves   [knaves?
Nor edge-tools; for then it had been wrong.
Well, ye shall sing another song!
Neighbour Prat, come hither, I you pray—
    Prat.   Why, what is this nice fray?
    Parson.   I cannot tell you; one knave dis-
    dains another;   [the other.
Wherefore take ye the one, and I shall take
We shall bestow them there as is most con-
    venient;
570 For such a couple, I trow, they shall repent
That ever they met in this church here.
Neighbour, ye be constable; stand ye near,
Take ye that lay knave, and let me alone

With this gentleman; by God and by Saint
    John,
I shall borrow upon priesthood somewhat;
For I may say to thee, neighbour Prat,
It is a good deed to punish such, to the en-
    sample
Of such other, how that they shall mell
In like fashion, as these caitiffs do.   [do so,
600   *Prat.* In good faith, Master Parson, if ye
Ye do but well to teach them to beware.
    Pard. Master Prat, I pray ye me to spare;
For I am sorry for that that is done;
Wherefore I pray ye forgive me soon,
For that I have offended within your liberty;
And by my troth, sir, ye may trust me
I will never come hither more,
While I live, and God before.
    Prat. Nay, I am once charged with thee,
610 Wherefore, by Saint John, thou shalt not
    escape me,
Till thou hast scoured a pair of stocks.
    Parson. Tut, he weeneth all is but mocks!
Lay hand on him; and come ye on, sir friar,
Ye shall of me hardly have your hire;
Ye had none such this seven year,
I swear by God and by our lady dear.
    Pard. Nay, Master Parson, for God's
Intreat not me after that fashion;   [passion,
For, if ye do, it will not be for your honesty.
620 *Parson.* Honesty or not, but thou shall see,
What I shall do by and by:
Make no struggling, come forth soberly:
For it shall not avail thee, I say.   [straightway.
    Friar. Marry, that shall we try even
I defy thee, churl priest, and there be no more
    than thou.

I will not go with thee, I make God a vow.
We shall see first which is the stronger:
God hath sent me bones; I do thee not fear.
    Parson. Yea, by thy faith, wilt thou be
        there?
630 Neighbour Prat, bring forth that knave,
And thou, sir friar, if thou wilt algates rave.
    Friar. Nay, churl, I thee defy!
I shall trouble thee first;
Thou shalt go to prison by and by;
Let me see, now do thy worst!
    [*Prat with the Pardoner and the Parson with
      the Friar.*   [bour Prat,
    Parson. Help, help, neighbour Prat, neigh-
In the worship of God, help me somewhat!—
    Prat. Nay, deal as thou canst with that elf,
For why I have enough to do myself.
640 Alas! for pain I am almost dead;
The red blood so runneth down about my head.
Nay, and thou canst, I pray thee help me.
    Parson. Nay, by the mass, fellow, it will
      not be;   [spin;
I have more tow on my distaff than I can well
The cursed Friar doth the upper hand win.
    Friar. Will ye leave then, and let us in
      peace depart?   [with all our heart.
    Parson and Prat. Yea, by our lady, even
    Friar and Pard. Then adieu to the devil,
      till we come again.
    Parson and Prat. And a mischief go with
      you both twain!

Imprinted by Wyllyam Rastell the v. day of Apryll
the yere of our lorde M.CCCCC.XXXIII. Cum priuilegis.

𝕿𝖍𝖊 𝕻𝖑𝖆𝖞𝖊𝖗𝖘:

A PALMER

A PARDONER

A 'POTHECARY

A PEDLAR

¶ The playe called the foure PP

¶ A newe and a very mery enterlude of
A palmer.
A pardoner.
A potycary.
A pedler.

¶ Made by John Heewood

*[Facsimile of the Title-page of the copy of the edition of 1545
now in the British Museum: see Note Book.]*

The Play called the foure P.

¶ A very mery Enterlude of
a Palmer.
a Pardoner.
a Potecary.
a Pedler.

¶ Imprinted at Lon=
don at the long Shop adioyning vnto S.
Mildreds Churche in the Pul-
trie, by Iohn Alde.
Anno Domini. 1569. Septembris. 14.

[Facsimile of Title-page of ed. of 1569: see Note-Book.]

THE FOUR P.P.

Palmer. Now God be here; who keepeth
Now by my faith I cry you mercy; [this place?
Of reason I must sue for grace,
My rudeness showeth me so homely.
Whereof your pardon axed and won,
I sue you, as courtesy both me bind,
To tell this, which shall be begun,
In order as may come best in mind.
I am a Palmer, as ye see,
Which of my life much part have spent
In many a fair and far country.
As Pilgrims do of good intent.
At Jerusalem have I been
Before Christ's blessed sepulchre :
The mount of Calvary have I seen,
A holy place, you may be sure.
To Jehosaphat and Olivet
On foot, God wot, I went right bare :
Many a salt tear did I sweat,
Before thy carcase could come there.
Yet have I been at Rome also,
And gone the stations all a-row :
St Peter's shrine and many mo,
Than, if I told all, ye do know.
Except that there be any such,

That hath been there, and diligently
Hath taken heed, and marked much,
Then can they speak as much as I.
Then at the Rhodes also I was;
And round about to Amias.
At St Uncumber and St Trunnion;
At St Botoph and St Anne of Buxton.   [ark;
On the hills of Armenia, where I saw Noe's
With holy Job, and St George in Southwark;
At Waltham and at Walsingham;
And at the good rood of Dagenham;
At Saint Cornelys; at Saint James in Gales;
And at Saint Wenefrid's well in Wales;
At our Lady of Boston; at Saint Edmund's
     burgh;
And straight to Saint Patrick's Purgatory;
At Redburne, and at the blood of Hales,
Where pilgrims' pains right much avails;
At Saint David's, and at Saint Denis;
At Saint Matthew, and Saint Mark in Venice;
At Master John Shorn at Canterbury;
The great God of Catwade, at King Henry
At Saint Saviour's; at our lady of Southwell;
At Crome, at Willesden, and at Muswell;
At Saint Richard, and at Saint Rock;
And at Our Lady that standeth in the oak.
To these, with other many one,
Devoutly have I prayed and gone,
Praying to them to pray for me
Unto the blessed Trinity,
By whose prayers and my daily pain
I trust the sooner to obtain
For my salvation, grace, and mercy.
For be ye sure I think surely,
Who seeketh saints for Christ's sake,
And namely such as pain do take

On foot, to punish their frail body,
Shall thereby merit more highly
Than by anything done by man.   [can,
    Pard.   And when ye have gone as far as ye
For all your labour and ghostly intent,
Ye will come home as wise as ye went.
    Palmer.   Why, sir, despised ye pilgrimage?
    Pard.   Nay, fore God, sir, then did I rage;
I think ye right well occupied,
To seek these saints on every side.
Also your pain I not dispraise it;
But yet I discommend your wit:
And ere we go, even so shall ye,
If you in this will answer me.
I pray you show what the cause is,
Ye went all these pilgrimages?
    Palmer.   Forsooth, this life I did begin
To rid the bondage of my sin:
For which these saints rehearsed ere this
I have both sought and seen, i-wis;
Beseeching them to bear record
Of all my pain unto the Lord,
That giveth all remission,
Upon each man's contrition;
And by their good mediation,
Upon mine humble submission,
I trust to have in very deed
For my soul health the better speed.
    Pard.   Now is your own confession likely
To make yourself a fool quickly.
For I perceive ye would obtain
No other thing for all your pain,
But only grace your soul to save:
Now mark in this what wit ye have!
To seek so far, and help so nigh;
Even here at home is remedy;

For at your door myself doth dwell,
Who could have saved your soul as well;
As all your wide wandering shall do,
Though ye went thrice to Jericho.
Now since ye might have sped at home,
What have ye won by running at Rome?
    Palmer. If this be true that ye have moved,
Then is my wit indeed reproved.
But let us hear first what ye are?
    Pard. Truly I am a pardoner.   [true;
    Palmer. Truly a pardoner! that may be
But a true pardoner doth not ensue.
Right seldom is it seen, or never,
That truth and pardoners dwell together,
For be your pardons never so great,
Yet them to enlarge ye will not let
With such lies that ofttimes, Christ wot,
Ye seem to have that ye have not.
Wherefore I went myself to the self thing
In every place and without saying:
Had as much pardon there assuredly,
As ye can promise me here doubtfully.
Howbeit, I think ye do but scoff:
But if ye had all the pardon ye speak of,
And no whit of pardon granted
In any place where I have haunted:
Yet of my labour I nothing repent;
God hath respect how each time is spent;
And as in his knowledge all is regarded,
So by his goodness all is rewarded.
    Pard. By the first part of this last tale,
It seemeth ye came of late from the ale.
For reason on your side so far doth fail,
That ye leave reasoning, and begin to rail.
Wherein you forget your own part clearly,
For you be as untrue as I:

And in one point ye are beyond me,
For you may lie by authority,]
And all that have wandered so far,
That no man can be their controller.
And where you esteem your labour so much,
I say yet again my pardons are such,
That if there were a thousand souls on a heap,
I would bring them to heaven as good cheap.
As ye have brought yourself on pilgrimage,
In the least quarter of your voyage,
Which is far a side heaven, by God :
There your labour and pardon is odd.
With small cost and without any pain,
These pardons bring them to heaven plain ;
Give me but a penny or two pence,
And as soon as the soul departeth hence,
In half-an-hour, or threequarters at the most,
The soul is in heaven with the Holy Ghost.

    'Poth. Send ye any souls to heaven by
      water?

    Pard. If we do, sir, what is the matter?

    'Poth. By God, I have a dry soul should
      thither ;

I pray you let our souls go to heaven together,
So busy you twain be in soul's health ;
May not a 'pothecary come in by stealth?
Yes, that I will, by St Anthony,
And, by the leave of this company,
Prove ye false knaves both, ere we go,
In part of your saying, as this, lo !
Thou by thy travail thinkest heaven to get :
And thou by pardons and relics countest no let,
To send thine own soul to heaven sure ;
And all other whom thou list to procure.
If I took an action, then were they blank ;
For like thieves the knaves rob away my thank.

All souls in heaven having relief,
Shall they thank your crafts? nay, thank mine
No soul, ye know, entereth heaven-gate, [chief.
Till from the body he be separate :
And whom have ye known die honestly,
Without help of the 'pothecary?
Nay, all that cometh to our handling,
Except ye happen to come to hanging ;
That way perchance ye shall not mister
To go to heaven without a glister.
But be ye sure I would be woe,
If ye should chance to beguile me so.
As good to lie with me a-night,
As hang abroad in the moonlight.
There is no choice to flee my hand,
But, as I said, into the band.
Since of our souls the multitude
I send to heaven, when all is viewed,
Who should but I then altogether
Have thank of all their coming thither?
    Pard.   If ye killed a thousand in an hour's
      space,
When come they to heaven dying out of grace?
    'Poth.   If a thousand pardons about your
      necks were tied,
When come they to heaven, if they never died?
    Palmer.   Long life after good works indeed
Doth hinder man's receipt of mead ;
And death before one duty done,
May make us think we die too soon.
Yet better tarry a thing than have it ;
Than go too soon, and vainly crave it.   [tion,
    Pard.   The longer ye dwell in communica-
The less shall ye like this imagination.
For ye may perceive, even at the first chop,
Your tale is trapped in such a stop.

That at the least ye seem worse than we.
    'Poth. By the mass, I hold us nought all
       three.   [*Enter Pedlar.*
    Pedlar. By our lady, than have I gone
And yet to be here I thought it long.   [wrong;
    'Poth. Ye have gone wrong no whit,
I praise your fortune and your wit,
That can direct you so discreetly
To plant you in this company.
Thou a Palmer, and thou a Pardoner,
I a 'Pothecary.
    Pedlar. And I a Pedlar.
    'Poth. Now, on my faith, well watched;
Where the devil were we four hatched?
    Pedlar. That maketh no matter, since we be
      matched,
I could be merry if that I had catched
Some money for part of the ware in my pack.
    'Poth. What the devil hast thou there at
      thy back?   [every pedlar
    Pedlar. What! dost thou not know that
In all kind of trifles must be a meddler?
Specially in women's triflings;
Those use we chiefly above all things,
Which things to see, if ye be disposed,
Behold what ware here is disclosed!
This gear showeth itself in such beauty,
That each man thinketh it saith, *Come, buy me!*
Look where yourself can like to be chooser,
Yourself shall make price, though I be loser.
Is here nothing for my father Palmer?
Have ye not a wanton in a corner,
For all your walking to holy places?
By Christ, I have heard of as strange cases.
Who liveth in love, and love would win,
Even at this pack he must begin.
                      D 2

Wherein is right many a proper token,
Of which by name part shall be spoken :
Gloves, pins, combs, glasses unspotted,
Pomades, hooks, and laces knotted;
Brooches, rings, and all manner of beads;
Laces, round and flat, for women's heads;
Needles, thread, thimble, shears, and all such
    knacks,
Where lovers be, no such things lacks :
Sipers, swathbands, ribbons, and sleeve laces,
Girdles, knives, purses, and pincases.
    'Poth. Do women buy their pincases of you?
    Pedlar. Yea, that they do, I make God a
    vow.
    'Poth. So mot I thrive then for my part.
I beshrew thy knave's naked heart,
For making my wife's pincase so wide,
The pins fall out, they cannot abide :
Great pins she must have, one or other;
If she lose one, she will find another.
Wherein I find cause to complain :
New pins to her pleasure and to my pain !
    Pard. Sir, ye seem well-seen in women's
I pray you tell me what causeth this : [causes !
That women, after their arising,
Be so long in their apparelling?
    Pedlar. Forsooth, women have many lets,
And they be masked in many nets :
As frontlets, fillets, partlets, and bracelets;
And then their bonnets and their poignets :
By these lets and nets the let is such,
That speed is small when haste is much.
    'Poth. Another cause why they come not
    forward,
Which maketh them daily to draw backward;
And yet is a thing they cannot forbear;

The trimming and pinning up their gear;
Specially their fiddling with the tail-pin;
And when they would have it pricked in,
If it chance to double in the cloth,
Then be they wood, and sweareth an oath.
Till it stand right they will not forsake it,   [it.
Thus though it may not, yet would they make
But be ye sure they do but defer it;
For when they would make it, oft times mar it.
But prick them and pin them as nice as ye will,
And yet will they look for pinning still.
So that I durst hold with you a joint,
Ye shall never have them at a full point.
    Pedlar.   Let women's matters pass, and
        mark mine:
Whatever their points be, these points be fine.
Wherefore, if ye be willing to buy,
Lay down money, come, off quickly.
    Palmer.   Nay, by my troth, we be like friars;
We are but beggars, we be no buyers.   [mind.
    Pard.   Sir, ye may show your ware for your
But I think ye shall no profit find.   [cost,
    Pedlar.   Well, though this journey acquit no
Yet think I not my labour lost:
For, by the faith of my body,
I like full well this company.
Up shall this pack, for it is plain
I came not hither all for gain.
Who may not play one day in a week,
May think his thrift is far to seek.
Devise what pastime that ye think best,
And make ye sure to find me prest.
    'Poth.   Why, be ye so universal,
That ye can do whatsoever ye shall?
    Pedlar.   Sir, if ye list for to oppose me,
What I can do, then shall you see.

'*Poth.* Then tell me this : are you perfit in
  drinking?   [by thinking.
Pedlar. Perfit in drinking? as may be wished
'*Poth.* Then, after your drinking, how fall
  ye to winking?   [is tinking;
Pedlar. Sir, after drinking, while the shot
Some heads be swimming, but mine will be
    sinking,
And upon drinking my eyes will be pinking :
For winking to drinking is alway linking. [do;
  '*Poth.* Then drink and sleep you can well
But if ye were desired thereto,
I pray you tell me, can you sing?
  Pedlar. Sir, I have some sight in singing.
  '*Poth.* But is your breast any thing sweet?
  Pedlar. Whatever my breast be, my voice is
    meet.   [singing man.
  '*Poth.* That answer showeth you a right
Now what is your will, good father, then?
  Palmer. What helpeth will, where is no
    skill?   [will?
  Pard. And what helpeth skill, where is no
  '*Poth.* For will or skill, what helpeth it,
Where forward knave be lacking wit?
Leave off this curiosity.   [*sing.*
And who that list, sing after me. [*Here they*
  Pedlar. This liketh me well, so mot I thee.
  Pard. So help me God, it liketh not me.
Where company is met and well agreed,
Good pastime doth right well indeed.
But who can sit in daliance,
Men sit in such a variance?
As we were set, ere ye came in,
Which strife this man did first begin;
Alleging that such men as use
For love of God, and not refuse

On foot to go from place to place
A pilgrimage, calling for grace,
Shall in that pain with penitence
Obtain discharge of conscience :
Comparing that life for the best
Induction to your endless rest.
Upon these words our matter grew :
For if he could avow them true,
As good to be a gardener.
As for to be a pardoner.
But when I heard him so far wide,
I then approached and replied :
Saying this, that this indulgence,
Having the foresaid penitence,
Dischargeth man of all offence
With much more profit than this pretence.
I ask but twopence at the most ;
I-wis this is not very great cost,
And from all pain without despair,
My soul for to keep even in his chair,
And when he dieth, he may be sure
To come to heaven even at pleasure.
And more than heaven he cannot get,
How far soever he list to jet.
Then is his pain more than his wit,
To walk to heaven, since he may sit.
Sir, as we were in this contention,
In came this daw with his invention ;
Reviling us, himself avaunting,
That all the souls to heaven ascending
Are most bound to the 'pothecary,
Because he helpeth most men to die,
Before which death he saith indeed,
No soul in heaven can have his mede.
   Pedlar. Why, do 'pothecaries kill men?
   'Poth. By God, men say so, now and then.

Pedlar.   And I thought ye would not have
   mist
To make them live as long as ye list.
   'Poth.   As long as we list? nay, as long as
      they can.
   Pedlar.   So might we live without you then.
   'Poth.   Yea, but yet it is necessary
For to have a 'pothecary:
For when ye feel your conscience ready,
I can send you to heaven quickly.
Wherefore, concerning our matter here,
Above these twain I am best clear;
And if ye list to take me so,
I am content: you and no mo
Shall be our judge as in this case,
Which of us three shall take the best place.
   Pedlar.   I neither will judge thee best nor
For be ye blest or be ye curst,   [worst;
Ye know it is no whit my sleight
To be a judge in matters of weight.
It behoveth no pedlars nor proctors
To take on them judgment as doctors:
But if your minds be only set
To work for soul-health, ye be well met:
For each of you somewhat doth show,
That souls toward heaven by you do grow.
Then if ye can so well agree,
To continue together all three;
And all you three obey one will,
Then all your minds ye may fulfil.
As if ye came all to one man,
Who should go pilgrimage more than he can?
In that ye, Palmer, as deputy,
May clearly discharge him, parde;
And for all other sins once had contrition,
Your pardons giveth him full remission.

And then ye, Master 'Pothecary,
May send him to heaven by and by,   [prime,
    'Poth.   If he taste this box nigh about the
By the mass, he is in heaven ere evensong time.
My craft is such, that I can right well
Send my friends to heaven and myself to hell.
But, sirs, mark this man, for he is wise,
Who could devise such a device :
For if we three may be as one,
Then be we lords everychone;
Between us all could not be mist
To save the souls of whom we list.
But for good order, at a word,
Twain of us must wait on the third.
    'Poth.   And unto that I do agree,
For both you twain shall wait on me.
    Pard.   What chance is this, that such an elf
Command two knaves beside himself?
Nay, nay, my friend, that will not be;
I am too good to wait on thee.
    Palmer.   By our lady, and I would be loth
To wait on the better of you both.
    Pedlar.   Yet be ye sure for all this doubt,
This waiting must be brought about.
Men cannot prosper, wilfully led;
All things decay, where is no head.
Wherefore, doubtless, mark what I say,
To one of you three twain must obey.
And since ye cannot agree in voice,
Who shall be head, there is no choice
But to devise some manner thing,
Wherein ye all be like conning;
And in the same who can do best,
The other twain do make them prest,
In every thing of his intent,
Wholly to be at commandment.

And now have I found one mastery,
That ye can do indifferently;
And is nother selling nor buying,
But even on very lying.
And all ye three can lie as well,
As can the falsest devil in hell.
And though afore ye heard me grudge
In greater matters to be your judge,
Yet in lying I can some skill,
And if I shall be judge, I will.
And be you sure, without flattery,
Where my conscience findeth the mastery,
There shall my judgment straight be found,
Though I might win a thousand pound.
   Palmer.   Sir, for lying, though I can do it:
Yet am I loth for to go to it.
   Pedlar.   Ye have no cause for fear, be bold,
For ye may here lie uncontrolled.
And ye in this have good advantage,
For lying is your common usage.
And you in lying be well sped,
For all your craft doth stand in falsehood.
Ye need not care who shall begin;
For each of you may hope to win.
Now speak all three even as ye find:
Be ye agreed to follow my mind?
   Palmer.   Yea, by my troth, I am content.
   Pard.   Now, in good faith, and I assent.
   'Poth.   If I denied, I were a noddy;
For all is mine, by God's body,
                  [Here the 'Pothecary hoppeth.
   Palmer.   Here were a hopper to hop for the
   ring!
But, sir, this gear goeth not by hopping. [well,
   'Poth.   Sir, in this hopping I will hop so
That my tongue shall hop better than my heel:

Upon which hopping I hope, and not doubt it,
To hop so, that ye shall hop without it.
    Palmer. Sir, I will neither boast ne brawl.
But take such fortune as may fall :
And if ye win this mastery,
I will obey you quietly :
And sure I think that quietness
In any man is great riches
In any manner company,
To rule or be ruled indifferently.   [indeed,
  Pard. By that boast thou seemest a beggar
What can thy quietness help us at need?
If we should starve, thou hast not, I think,
One penny to buy us one pot of drink.
Nay, if riches might rule the roost,
Behold what cause I have to boast !
Lo, here be pardons half a dozen,
For ghostly riches they have no cousin.
And moreover to me they bring
Sufficient succour for my living.
And here be relics of such a kind,
As in this world no man can find,   [ing,
Kneel down all three, and when ye leave kiss-
Who list to offer shall have my blessing.
Friends, here shall ye see even anon
Of All-Hallows the blessed jaw-bone,
Kiss it hardily with good devotion.   [motion
    'Poth. This kiss shall bring us much pro-
Foh, by St Saviour, I never kissed a worse;
Ye were as good kiss All-Hallows' arse ;
For, by All-Hallows, yet me-thinketh,
That All-Hallows' breath stinketh.   [known :
    Palmer. Ye judge All-Hallows' breath un-
If any breath stink, it is your own.
      'Poth. I know mine own breath from All-
      Hallows,

Or else it were time to kiss the gallows.

Pard.   Nay, sirs, behold, here may ye see
The great toe of the Trinity :
Who to this toe any money voweth,
And once may roll it in his mouth,
All his life after, I undertake,
He shall never be vexed with the toothache.

'Poth.   I pray you turn that relic about :
Either the Trinity had the gout,
Or else, because it is three toes in one,
God made it as much as three toes alone. [this.

Pard.   Well, let that pass, and look upon
Here is a relic that doth not miss
To help the least as well as the most :
This is a buttock-bone of Pentecost.

'Poth.   By Christ, and yet for all your boast,
This relic hath beshitten the roast.   [whipper,

Pard.   Mark well this relic: here is a
My friends unfeigned : here is a slipper
Of one of the Seven Sleepers, be sure.
Doubtless this kiss shall do you great pleasure;
For all these two days it shall so ease you,
That none other savours shall displease you.

'Poth.   All these two days! nay, all these
two years ;
For all the savours that may come here
Can be no worse; for at a word
One of the seven sleepers trod in a turd.

Pedlar.   Sir, me-thinketh your devotion is
but small.

Pard.   Small! marry me-thinketh he hath
none at all.   [think?

'Poth.   What the devil care I what ye
Shall I praise relics, when they stink? [Turk.

Pard.   Here is an eye-tooth of the Great
Whose eyes be once set on this piece of work,

May happily lese part of his eyesight,
But not till he be blind outright.
    'Poth. Whatsoever any other man seeth,
I have no devotion unto Turks' teeth :
For although I never saw a greater,
Yet me-thinketh I have seen many better.
    Pard. Here is a box full of humble bees,
That stang Eve as she sat on her knees,
Tasting the fruit to her forbidden.
Who kisseth the bees within this hidden,
Shall have as much pardon of right,
As for any relic he kissed this night.   [heart.
    Palmer. Sir, I will kiss them with all my
    'Poth. Kiss them again, and take my part,
For I am not worthy : nay, let be :
Those bees that stung Eve shall not sting me.
    Pard. Good friends, I have yet here in this
Which on the drink at the wedding was [glass,
Of Adam and Eve undoubtedly.
If ye honour this relic devoutly,
Although ye thirst no whit the less,
Yet shall ye drink the more, doubtless :
After which drinking ye shall be as meet
To stand on your head as on your feet.
    'Poth. Yea, marry, now I can you thank ;
In presence of this—the rest be blank.
Would God this relic had come rather :
Kiss that relic well, good father.
Such is the pain that ye palmers take
To kiss the pardon-bowl for the drink sake.
O holy yeast, that looketh full sour and stale,
For God's body, help me to a cup of ale.
The more I behold thee, the more I thirst :
The oftener I kiss thee, the more like to burst.
But since I kiss thee so devoutly,
Hire me, and help me with drink, till I die.

What, so much praying and so little speed?
   Pard. Yea, for God knoweth when it is need
To send folks drink; but, by St Anthony,
I ween he hath sent you too much already.
   'Poth. If I have never the more for thee,
Then be thy relics no riches to me;
Nor to thyself, except they be
More beneficial than I can see.
Richer is one box of this triacle,
Than all thy relics, that do no miracle.
If thou hadst prayed but half so much to me,
As I have prayed to thy relics and thee,
Nothing concerning mine occupation,   [tion:
But straight should have wrought one opera-
And as in value I pass you an ace,
So here lieth much richness in little space.
I have a box of rhubarb here,
Which is as dainty as it is dear.
So help me God and halidom,
Of this I would not give a dram
To the best friend I have in England's ground,
Though he would give me twenty pound.
For though the stomach do it abhor,
It purgeth you clean from the choler;
And maketh your stomach sore to walter,
That ye shall never come to the halter.
   Pedlar. Then is that medicine a sovereign
       thing
To preserve a man from hanging.   [ye see,
   'Poth. If ye will taste but this crumb that
If ever ye be hanged, never trust me.
Here have I *diapompholicus,*
A special ointment, as doctors discuss,
For a fistula or for a canker:
This ointment is even shot-anchor;
For this medicine helpeth one and other,

Or bringeth them in case that they need no
Here is a *syrapus de Byzansis*,   [other.
A little thing is enough of this;
For even the weight of one scruple
Shall make you as strong as a cripple.
Here are others, as *diosfialios*,
Diagalanga and *sticados*,
Blanka, manna, diospoliticon,
Mercury sublime and *metridaticon*,
Pellitory and arsefetita;
Cassy and *colloquintita*.
These be the things that break all strife
Between man's sickness and his life.
From all pain these shall you deliver,
And set you even at rest for ever.
Here is a medicine no mo like the same,
Which commonly is called thus by name
Alikakabus or *Alkakengy*,
A goodly thing for dogs that be mangy.
Such be these medicines, that I can
Help a dog as well as a man.
Not one thing here particularly,
But worketh universally;
For it doth me as much good, when I sell it,
As all the buyers that taste it or smell it.
Now since my medicines be so special,
And in one operation so general,
And ready to work whensoever they shall,
So that in riches I am principal;
If any reward may entreat ye,
I beseech your maship be good to me,
And ye shall have a box of marmalade,
So fine that you may dig it with a spade.
   Pedlar.   Sir, I thank you; but your reward
Is not the thing that I regard:
I must and will be indifferent;

Wherefore proceed in your intent.
    'Poth.   Now if I wist this wish no sin,
I would to God I might begin.
    'Pard.   I am content that thou lie first.
    Palmer.   Even so am I; now say thy worst.
Now let us hear, of all thy lies,
The greatest lie thou mayst devise.
And in the fewest words thou can.
    'Poth.   Forsooth, ye be an honest man.
    ~~*Pedlar.*~~   There said ye much, but yet no lie.

Palmer (margin annotation)

    Pard.   Now lie ye both, by Our Lady.
Thou liest in boast of his honesty,
And he hath lied in affirming thee.
    'Poth.   If we both lie, and ye say true,
Then of these lies your part adieu !
And if ye win, make none avaunt,
For you are sure of one ill servant.
You may perceive by the words he gave,
He taketh your maship but for knave.
But who told truth or lied indeed,
That will I know, ere we proceed.
Sir, after that I first began
To praise you for an honest man,
When ye affirmed it for no lie :
Now, by your faith, speak even truly;
Thought ye your affirmation true?
    Palmer.   Yea, marry, for I would ye knew,
I think myself an honest man.   [then?
    'Poth.   What thought ye in the contrary
    Pard.   In that I said the contrary,
I think from truth I did not vary.
    'Poth.   And what of my words?
    Pard.   I thought ye lied.
    'Poth.   And so thought I, by God that died.
Now have you twain each for himself laid,
That none hath lied, but both true said :

And of us twain none hath denied,
But both affirmed that I have lied.
Now since both ye the truth confess,
How that I lied, do bear witness,
That twain of us may soon agree,
And that the lier the winner must be,
Who could provide such evidence,
As I have done in this pretence?
Me-thinketh this matter sufficient
To cause you to give judgment;
And to give me the mastery,
For ye perceive these knaves cannot lie.
  Palmer.   Though nother of us yet had lied,
Yet what we can do is untried;
For as yet we have devised nothing,
But answered you and given you hearing.
  Pedlar.- Therefore I have devised one way,
Whereby all three your minds may say,
For each of you one tale shall tell,
And which of you telleth most marvel,
And most unlikest to be true,
Shall most prevail, whatever ensue.
  'Poth.   If ye be set on marvelling,
Then shall ye hear a marvellous thing.
And though, indeed, all be not true,
Yet sure the most part shall be new.
I did a cure no longer ago,
But in *anno domini millesimo*,
On a woman young and so fair,
That never have I seen a gayer.
God save all women of that likeness.
This wanton had the falling sickness,
Which by descent came lineally,
For her mother had it naturally :
Wherefore this woman to recure,
It was more hard, ye may be sure.

E

But though I boast my craft is such,
That in such things I can do much:
How oft she fell were much to report;
But her head so giddy, and her belly so short,
That, with the twinkling of an eye,
Down would she fall even by and by.
But ere she would arise again,
I showed much practice much to my pain.
For the tallest man within this town
Could not with ease have broken her swoon.
Although for life I did not doubt her,
Yet I did take more pains about her,
Than I would take with my own sister.
Sir, at the last I gave her a glister:
I thrust a tampion in her tewell,
And bade her keep it for a jewel;
But I knew there it was too heavy to carry,
That I sure was it would not tarry:
For where gunpowder is once fired,
The tampion will no lenger be hired:
Which was well seen in time of this chance,
For when I had charged this ordnance,
Suddenly, as it had thundered,
Even at a clap loosed her bombard.
Now mark, for here beginneth the revel:
This tampion flew ten long mile level,
To a fair castle of lime and stone,
For strength I know not such a one,
Which stood upon a hill full high,
At foot whereof a river ran by,
So deep, till chance had it forbidden,
Well might the Regent there have ridden.
But when this tampion at this castle did light,
It put the castle so fair to flight,
That down they came each upon other,
No stone left standing, by God's mother!

But rolled down so fast the hill
In such a number, and so did fill
From bottom to brim, from shore to shore,
This foresaid river so deep before,
That who list now to walk thereto,
May wade it over and wet no shoe.
So was this castle laid wide open,
That every man might see the token.
But in a good hour may these words be spoken
After the tampion on the walls was wroken,
And piece by piece in pieces broken.
And she delivered with such violence
Of all her inconvenience,
I left her in good health and lust;
And so she doth continue, I trust.

    Pedlar. Sir, in your cure I can nothing tell;
But to your purpose ye have said well.

    Pard. Well, sir, then mark what I can say.
I have been a pardoner many a day,
And done greater cures ghostly
Than ever he did bodily.
Namely this one, which ye shall hear,
Of one departed within this seven year,
A friend of mine, and likewise I
To her again was as friendly :
Who fell so sick so suddenly,
That dead she was even by and by,
And never spake with priest nor clerk,
Nor had no whit of this holy work;
For I was thence, it could not be,
Yet heard I say she asked for me.
But when I bethought me how this chanced,
And that I have to heaven avanced
So many souls to me but strangers,
And could not keep my friend from dangers,
But she to die so dangerously,

                        E 2

For her soul-health especially;
That was the thing that grieved me so,
That nothing could realise my woe,
Till I had tried even out of hand,
In what estate her soul did stand.
For which trial, short tale to make,
I took this journey for her sake.
Give ear, for here beginneth the story:
From hence I went to Purgatory,
And took with me this gear in my fist,
Whereby I may do there what I list.
I knocked and was let in quickly:
But, Lord, how low the souls made curtesy;
And I to every soul again
Did give a beck them to retain,
And asked them this question then,
If that the soul of such a woman
Did late among them there appear?
Whereto they said, she came not here.
Then feared I much it was not well;
Alas, thought I, she is in hell;
For with her life I was so acquainted,
That sure I thought she was not sainted.
With this it chanced me to sneeze;
Christ help, quoth a soul that lay for his fees.
Those words, quoth I, thou shalt not lese;
Then with these pardons of all degrees
I paid his toll and set him so quit,
That straight to heaven he took his flight,
And I from thence to hell that night,
To help this woman, if I might;
Not as who saith by authority,
But by the way of entreaty.
And first to the devil that kept the gate
I came, and spake after this rate:
All hail, sir devil, and made low curtesy:

Welcome, quoth he thus smilingly.
He knew me well, and I at last
Remembered him since long time past:
For, as good hap would have it chance,
This devil and I were of old acquaintance;
For oft, in the play of Corpus Christi,
He hath played the devil at Coventry.
By his acquaintance and my behaviour,
He showed to me right friendly favour,
And to make my return the shorter,
I said to this devil: Good master porter,
For all old love, if it lie in your power,
Help me to speak with my lord and your.
Be sure, quoth he, no tongue can tell,
What time thou couldst have come so well:
For as on this day Lucifer fell,
Which is our festival in hell.
Nothing unreasonable craved this day,
That shall in hell have any nay.
But yet beware thou come not in,
Till time thou may thy passport win.
Wherefore stand still, and I will wit,
If I can get thy safe-conduit.
He tarried not, but shortly got it
Under seal, and the Devil's hand at it,
In ample wise, as ye shall hear;
Thus it began: Lucifer,
By the power of God, chief devil of hell,
To all the devils that there do dwell
And every of them, we send greeting,
Under strait charge and commanding,
That they aiding and assistant be
To such a Pardoner, and named me,
So that he may at liberty
Pass safe without any jeopardy,
Till that he be from us extinct,

And clearly out of hell's precinct.
And his pardon to keep in safeguard,
We will they lie in the porter's ward.
Given in the furnace of our palace,
In our high court of matters of malice,
Such a day and year of our reign.
God save the devil, quoth I, amain.
I trust this writing to be sure:
Then put thy trust, quod he, in ure,
Since thou art sure to take no harm.
This devil and I walked arm in arm
So far, till he had brought me thither,
Where all the devils of hell together
Stood in array in such apparel,
As for that day there meetly fell.
Their horns well-gilt, their claws full clean,
Their tails well-kempt, and, as I ween,
With sothery butter their bodies anointed;
I never saw devils so well appointed.
The master-devil sat in his jacket,
And all the souls were playing at racket.
None other rackets they had in hand,
Save every soul a good firebrand:
Wherewith they played so prettily,
That Lucifer laughed merrily;
And all the residue of the fiends
Did laugh thereat full well like friends.
But of my friend I saw no whit,
Nor durst not ask for her as yet.
Anon all this rout was brought in silence,
And I by an usher brought in presence
Of Lucifer; then low, as well I could,
I kneeled, which he so well allowed,
That thus he becked, and, by St Anthony,
He smiled on me well-favouredly,
Bending his brows as broad as barn-doors,

Shaking his ears as rugged as burrs;
Rolling his eyes as round as two bushels;
Flashing the fire out of his nosthrils;
Gnashing his teeth so vaingloriously,
That me-thought time to fall to flattery,
Wherewith I told, as I shall tell:
O pleasant picture! O prince of hell!
Feutred in fashion abhominable,
And since that is inestimable
For me to praise thee worthily.
I leave of praise, as unworthy
To give thee praise, beseeching thee
To hear my suit, and then to be
So good to grant the thing I crave;
And, to be short, this would I have:
The soul of one which hither is flitted,
Delivered hence, and to me remitted.
And in this doing, though all be not quit,
Yet in some part I shall deserve it,
As thus: I am a pardoner,
And over souls as controller,
Thorough out the earth my power doth stand,
Where many a soul lieth on my hand,
That speed in matters as I use them,
As I receive them or refuse them.
Whereby what time thy pleasure is,
I shall requite any part of this,
The least devil here that can come thither,
Shall choose a soul and bring him hither.
Ho, ho! quoth the devil, we are well pleased;
What is his name thou wouldst have eased?
Nay, quoth I, be it good or evil,
My coming is for a she devil.
What callst her, quoth he, thou whoreson?
Forsooth, quoth I, Margery Corson.
Now, by our honour, said Lucifer,

No devil in hell shall withhold her;
And if thou wouldest have twenty mo,
Wert not for justice, they should go.
For all we devils within this den
Have more to do with two women,
Than with all the charge we have beside;
Wherefore, if thou our friend will be tried,
Apply thy pardons to women so,
That unto us there come no mo.
To do my best I promised by oath;
Which I have kept, for, as the faith goeth,
At this day to heaven I do procure
Ten women to one man, be sure.
Then of Lucifer my leave I took,
And straight unto the master-cook
I was had into the kitchen,
For Margery's office was therein.
All things handled there discreetly,
For every soul beareth office meetly:
Which might be seen to see her sit
So busily turning of the spit.
For many a spit here hath she turned,
And many a good spit hath she burned:
And many a spitful hot hath roasted,
Before the meat could be half roasted,
And ere the meat were half-roasted indeed,
I took her then fro the spit with speed.
But when she saw this brought to pass,
To tell the joy wherein she was!
And of all the devils, for joy how they
Did roar at her delivery!
And how the chains in hell did ring.
And how all the souls therein did sing;
And how we were brought to the gate,
And how we took our leave thereat,
Be sure lack of time suffereth not

To rehearse the twentieth part of that,
Wherefore, this tale to conclude briefly,
This woman thanked me chiefly,
That she was rid of this endless death,
And so we departed on Newmarket-heath.
And if that any man do mind her,
Who lists to seek her, there shall he find her.
　　Pedlar.　Sir, you have sought her wonders
And where ye found her as ye tell,　　　　[well,
To hear the chance ye had in hell,
I find ye were in great peril.
　　Palmer.　His tale is all much perilous;
But part is much more marvellous:
As where he said the devils complain,
That women put them to such pain.
Be their conditions so crooked and crabbed,
Frowardly fashioned, so wayward and wrabbed.
So far in division, and stirring such strife,
That all the devils be weary of their life.
This in effect he told for truth.
Whereby much marvel to me ensueth,
That women in hell such shrews can be,
And here so gentle, as far as I see.
Yet have I seen many a mile,
And many a woman in the while.
Not one good city, town, or borough
In Christendom, but I have been thorough,
And this I would ye should understand,
I have seen women five hundred thousand:
And oft with them have long time tarried.
Yet in all places where I have been,
Of all the women that I have seen,
I never saw nor knew in my conscience
Any one woman out of patience.
　　'*Poth.*　By the mass, there is a great lie.
　　Pard.　I never heard a greater, by our Lady.

Pedlar.   A greater! nay, know ye any so
    great?
Palmer.   Sir, whether that I lose or get,
For my part judgment shall be prayed.
    Pard.   And I desire, as he hath said.
    'Poth.   Proceed, and ye shall be obeyed.
    Pedlar.   Then shall not judgment be delayed,
Of all these three, if each man's tale
In Paul's Churchyard were set on sale,
In some man's hand that hath the sleight,
He should sure sell these tales by weight;
For as they weigh, so be they worth,
But which weigheth best, to that now forth.
Sir, all the tale that ye did tell
I bear in mind, and yours as well:
And as ye saw the matter meetly,
So lied ye both well and discreetly;
Yet were your lies with the least, trust me;
For if ye had said ye had made flee
Ten tampions out of ten women's tails,
Ten times ten mile to ten castles or jails,
And filled ten rivers ten times so deep,   [keep;
As ten of that which your castle-stones did
Or if ye ten times had bodily
Fet ten souls out of purgatory;
And ten times so many out of hell:
Yet, by these ten bones, I could right well,
Ten times sooner all that believed,
Than the tenth part of that he hath meved.
    'Poth.   Two knaves before one lacketh two
    knaves of five:
Then one, and then one, and both knaves alive.
Then two, and then two, and three at a cast,
Thou knave, and thou knave, and thou knave
    at last.
Nay knave, if ye try me by number,

I will as knavishly you accumber
Your mind is all on your privy tithe,
For all in ten me-thinketh your wit li'th.
Now ten times I beseech him that high sits,
Thy wife's ten commandments may search thy
    five wits.
Then ten of my turds in ten of thy teeth,
And ten on thy nose, which every man seeth;
And twenty times ten this wish I would
That thou hadst been hanged at ten year old:
For thou goest about to make me a slave.
I will thou know that I am a gentle knave.
And here is another shall take my part. [heart,
   Pard. Nay, first I beshrew your knave's
Ere I take part in your knavery:
I will speak fair, by our lady.
Sir, I beseech your maship to be
As good as ye can be unto me.
   Pedlar. I would be glad to do you good,
And him also, be he ever so wood;
But doubt you not I will now do
The thing my conscience leadeth me to.
Both your tales I take for impossible,
Yet take I his farther incredible.
Not only the thing itself alloweth it,
But also the boldness thereof avoweth it.
I know not where your tale to try;
Nor yours, but in hell or purgatory.
But his boldness hath faced a lie,
That may be tried even in this company.
As if ye list to take this order,
Among the women in this border, [oldest,
Take three of the youngest, and three of the
Three of the hottest, and three of the coldest,
Three of the wisest, and three of the shrewdest,
Three of the chastest, and three of the lewdest

Three of the lowest, and three of the highest,
Three of the farthest, and three of the nighest,
Three of the fairest, and three of the maddest,
Three of the foulest, and three of the saddest,
And when all these threes be had asunder
Of each three, two justly by number
Shall be found shrews, except this fall,
That ye hap to find them shrews all.
Himself for truth all this doth know,
And oft hath tried some of this row;
And yet he sweareth by his conscience,
He never saw woman break patience.
Wherefore, considered with true intent,
His lie to be so evident,
And to appear so evidently,
That both you affirmed it a lie;
And that my conscience so deeply
So deep hath sought this thing to try,
And tried it with mind indifferent;
Thus I award by way of judgment :
Of all the lies ye all have spent,
His lie to be most excellent.   [equity
    Palmer. Sir, though ye were bound of
To do as ye have done to me,
Yet do I thank you of your pain,
And will requite some part again.
    Pard. Marry, sir, ye can no less do,
But thank him as much as it cometh to;
And so will I do for my part.
Now a vengeance on thy knave's heart,
I never knew a pedlar a judge before,
Nor never will trust pedling knave more.
What doest thou there, thou whoreson noddy?
    'Poth. By the mass, learn to make cour-
        tesy :
Courtesy before, and courtesy behind him,

And then on each side, the devil blind him!
Nay, when ye have it perfitly,
Ye shall have the devil and all of courtesy:
But it is not soon learned, gentle brother,
One knave to make courtesy to another.
Yet when I am angry, that is the worst,
I shall call my master knave at the first.

    Palmer. Then would some master perhaps
But, as for me, ye need not doubt ye; [clout ye,
For I had liever be without ye,
Than have such business about ye.

    'Poth. So help me God, so were ye better;
What, should a beggar be a jetter?
It were no whit your honesty
To have us twain jet after ye.

    Pard. Sir, be your sure he telleth you true,
If we should wait, this would ensue:
It would be said, trust me at a word,
Two knaves made courtesy to the third. [mind,

    Pedlar. Now, by my troth, to speak my
Since they be so loth to be assigned,
To let them lose I think it best.
And so shall ye live the better in rest.

    Palmer. Sir, I am not on them so fond,
To compel them to keep their bond;
And since ye list not to wait on me,
I clearly of waiting do discharge ye.

    Pard. Marry, sir, I heartily thank you.

    'Poth. And likewise I, to God I vow.

    Pedlar. Now be ye all even as ye began;
No man hath lost, nor no man hath wan.
Yet in the debate wherewith ye began,
By way of advice I will speak as I can.
I do perceive that pilgrimage
Is chief the thing ye have in usage;
Whereto in effect, for the love of Christ,

Ye have, or should have been enticed :
And who so doth with such intent,
Doth well declare his time well-spent.
And so do ye in your pretence,
If ye procure thus indulgence
Unto your neighbours charitably,
For love of them in God only.
All this may be right well applied
To show you both well occupied :
For though ye walk not both one way,
Yet walking thus, this dare I say,
That both your walks come to one end ;
And so for all that do pretend
By aid of God's grace to ensue
Any manner kind of virtue ;
As some great alms for to give :
Some, in wilful poverty to live :
Some, to make highways and such like works,
And some to maintain priests and clerks
To sing and pray for soul departed :
These, with all other virtues well marked,
Although they be of sundry kinds,
Yet be they not used with sundry minds.
But as God only doth all those move,
So every man only for his love,
With love and dread obediently
Worketh in these virtues uniformly.
Thus every virtue, if we list to scan,
Is pleasant to God and thankful to man.
And who that, by grace of the Holy Ghost,
To any one virtue is moved most,
That man by that grace that one apply,
And therein serve God most plentifully,
Yet not that one so far wide to wrest :
So liking the same, to mislike the rest.
For who so wresteth, his work is in vain ;

And even in that case I perceive you twain :
Liking your virtue in such wise,
That each other's virtue ye do despise.
Who walketh this way for God, would find him,
The farther they seek him, the farther behind
One kind of virtue to despise another,   [him.
Is like as the sister might hang the brother.
      'Poth.   For fear lest such perils to me might
I thank God I use no virtue at all.   [fall,
      Pedlar.   That is of all the very worst way ;
For more hard it is, as I have heard say,
To begin virtue where none is pretended,
Than where it is begun, th' abuse to be
How be it, ye be not all to begin,   [mended.
One sign of virtue ye are entered in :
As this, I suppose ye did say true,
In that ye said ye use no virtue.
In the which words I dare well report,
You are well beloved of all this sort,
By your railing here openly
At pardons and relics so lewdly.
      'Poth.   In that I think my fault not great ;
For all that he hath I know counterfeit.
      Pedlar.   For his and all other that ye know
         feigned,
You be not counselled nor constrained
To any such thing in any such case,
To give any reverence in any such place.
But where ye doubt, the truth not knowing,
Believing the best, good may be growing,
In judging the best, no harm at the least ;
In judging the worst, no good at the best.
But best in these things it seemeth to me,
To make no judgment upon ye ;
But as the church doth judge or take them,
So do ye receive or forsake them.

And so be you sure ye cannot err,
But may be a fruitful follower.
   'Poth. Go ye before, and as I am true man,
I will follow as fast as I can.   [well,
   Pard. And so will I, for he hath said so
Reason would we should follow his counsel.
   Palmer. Then to our reason God give us
     his grace,
That we may follow with faith so firmly
His commandments, that we may purchase
His love, and so consequently
To believe his church fast and faithfully;
So that we may, according to his promise,
Be kept out of error in any wise.
And all that hath scaped us here by negligence,
We clearly revoke and forsake it;
To pass the time in this without offence,
Was the cause why the Maker did make it;
And so we humbly beseech you to take it,
Beseeching our Lord to prosper you all
In the faith of his Church Universal.

Imprynted at London in Fletestrete at the sygne of the George, by Wyllyam Myddylton.

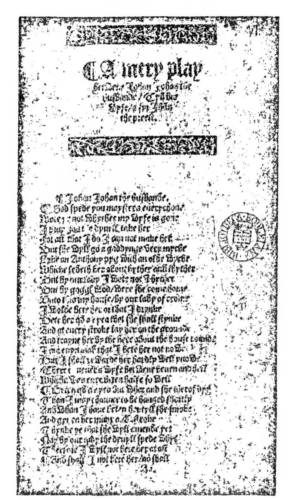

[Facsimile of the Title-page of the Bodleian Copy:
see Note-Book.]

F

A MERRY PLAY

Between JOHN JOHN, *the husband*, TYB, *his wife*,
and SIR JOHN, *the priest*

John John, the Husband. God speed you,
    masters, every one,
Wot ye not whither my wife is gone?
I pray God the devil take her,
For all that I do I can not make her,
But she will go a gadding very much
Like an Antony pig with an old witch,
Which leadeth her about hither and thither;
But, by our lady, I wot not whither.
But, by Gog's blood, were she come home
Unto this my house, by our lady of Crome,
I would beat her or that I drink.
Beat her, quotha? yea, that she shall stink!
And at every stroke lay her on the ground,
And train her by the hair about the house
I am even mad that I beat her not now, [round.
But I shall reward her, hard[e]ly, well ynowe;
There is never a wife between heaven and hell
Which was ever beaten half so well.   [of die?
  Beaten, quotha? yea, but what and she there-
Then I may chance to be hanged shortly.
And when I have beaten her till she smoke,
And given her many a c. stroke,
Think ye that she will amend yet?

Nay, by our lady, the devil speed whit!
Therefore I will not beat her at all.
  And shall I not beat her? no shall?
When she offendeth and doth amiss,
And keepeth not her house, as her duty is?
Shall I not beat her, if she do so?
Yes, by Cock's blood, that shall I do;
I shall beat her and thwack her, I trow,
That she shall beshit the house for very woe.
  But yet I think what my neighbour will say
        then,   [John? "
He will say thus: "Whom chidest thou, John
"Marry," will I say! "I chide my curst wife,
The veriest drab that ever bare life,
Which doth nothing but go and come,
And I can not make her keep her at home."
Then I think he will say by and by, [hardly."
"Walk her coat, John John, and beat her
But then unto him mine answer shall be,
"The more I beat her the worse is she:
And worse and worse make her I shall."
  He will say then, "beat her not at all."
"And why?" shall I say, "this would be wist,
Is she not mine to chastise as I list?"
  But this is another point worst of all,
The folks will mock me when they hear me
But for all that, shall I let therefore   [brawl;
To chastise my wife ever the more,
And to make her at home for to tarry?
Is not that well done? yes, by Saint Mary,
That is a point of an honest man
For to beat his wife well now and then.
  Therefore I shall beat her, have ye no dread!
And I ought to beat her, till she be stark dead.
And why? by God, because it is my pleasure,
And if I should suffer her, I make you sure,

Nought should prevail me, nother staff nor
    waster,
Within a while she would be my master.
    Therefore I shall beat her by Cock's mother,
Both on the tone side and on the tother,
Before and behind; nought shall be her boot,
From the top of the head to the sole of the foot.
    But, masters, for God's sake, do not entreat
For her, when that she shall be beat;
But, for God's passion, let me alone,
And I shall thwack her that she shall groan :
Wherefore I beseech you, and heartily you
And I beseech you say me not nay,   [pray,
But that I may beat her for this ones;
And I shall beat her, by Cock's bones,
That she shall stink like a pole-cat;
But yet, by Gog's body, that need not,
For she will stink without any beating,
For every night once she giveth me an heating;
From her issueth such a stinking smoke,
That the savour thereof almost doth me choke.
But I shall beat her now, without fail;
I shall beat her top and tail,
Head, shoulders, arms, legs, and all,
I shall beat her, I trow that I shall;
And, by Gog's body, I tell you true,
I shall beat her till she be black and blue.
    But where the devil trow ye she is gone?
I hold a noble she is with Sir John;
I fear I am beguiled alway,
But yet in faith I hope well nay;
Yet I almost enrage that I ne can
See the behaviour of our gentlewoman.
And yet, I think, thither as she doth go
Many an honest wife goeth thither also,
For to make some pastime and sport.

But then my wife so oft doth thither resort
That I fear she will make me wear a feather.
But yet I need not for to fear nether,
For he is her gossip, that is he.
　　But abide a while, yet let me see,
Where the devil hath our gossipry begone?
My wife had never child, daughter nor son.
　　Now if I forbid her that she go no more,
Yet will she go as she did before,
Or else will she choose some other place;
And then the matter is in as ill case.
　　But in faith all these words be in waste,
For I think the matter is done and past;
And when she cometh home she will begin to
　　chide,   [side;
But she shall have her payment stick by her
For I shall order her, for all her brawling,
That she shall repent to go a catterwauling.
　　　　　　　　　　　　　　　[Enter Tyb.
　　Tyb.　Why, whom wilt thou beat, I say,
　　thou knave?
　　John.　Who, I, Tyb? none, so God me save.
　　Tyb.　Yes, I heard thee say thou wouldst
　　one beat.　　　　　　　　　[Thames Street,
　　John.　Marry, wife, it was stockfish in
Which will be good meat against Lent.
Why, Tyb, what hadst thou thought that I had
　　meant?　　　　　　　　　　　　　　[ing.
　　Tyb.　Marry, me thought I heard the bawl-
Wilt thou never leave this wawlyng?
How the devil dost thou thy self behave?
Shall we ever have this work, thou knave?
　　John.　What! wife, how sayst thou? was it
　　well guessed of me
That thou wouldst be come home in safety,
As soon as I had kindled a fire?

Come warm thee, sweet Tyb, I thee require.
  Tyb. O, John John, I am afraid, by this
That I shall be sore sick this night.   [light,
  John [aside]. By Cock's soul, now, I dare
    lay a swan
That she comes now straight from Sir John;
For ever when she hath fetched of him a lick,
Then she comes home, and saith she is sick.
  Tyb. What sayst thou?
  John. Marry, I say,
It is mete for a woman to go play
Abroad in the town for an hour or two.
  Tyb. Well, gentleman, go to, go to!
  John. Well, let us have no more debate.
  Tyb [aside]. If he do not fight, chide, and
Brawl and fare as one that were frantic, [rate,
There is nothing that may him like.
  John [aside]. If that the parish priest, Sir
Did not see her now and then,   [John,
And give her absolution upon a bed,
For woe and pain she would soon be dead.
  Tyb. For God's sake, John John, do thee
Many a time I am ill at ease.   [not displease,
What thinkest now, am not I somewhat sick?
  John [aside]. Now would to God, and sweet
    Saint Dyryk,
That thou wert in the water up to the throat,
Or in a burning oven red hot,
To see an I would pull thee out.   [doubt.
  Tyb. Now, John John, to put thee out of
Imagine thou where that I was
Before I came home.
  John. My percase,
Thou wast praying in the Church of Poules
Upon thy knees for all Christian souls.
  Tyb. Nay.

John.   Then if thou wast not so holy,
Show me where thou wast, and make no lie?
   Tyb.   Truly, John John, we made a pie,
I and my gossip Margery,
And our gossip the priest, Sir John,
And my neighbour's youngest daughter Anne;
The priest paid for the stuff and the making,
And Margery she paid for the baking.
   John.   By Cock's lylly woundis, that same
      is she,
That is the most bawdy hence to Coventry.
   Tyb.   What say you?
   John.   Marry, answer me to this:
Is not Sir John a good man?
   Tyb.   Yes, that he is.
   John.   Ha, Tyb! if I should not grieve thee,
I have somewhat whereof I would meve thee.
   Tyb.   Well, husband! now I do conject
That thou hast me somewhat in suspect;
But, by my soul, I never go to Sir John
But I find him like an holy man,
For either he is saying his devotion,
Or else he is going in procession.
   John [aside].   Yea, round about the bed doth
      he go,
You two together, and no mo;
And for to finish the procession,
He leapeth up and thou liest down.
   Tyb.   What sayst thou?
   John.   Marry, I say he doth well,
For so ought a shepherd to do, as I heard tell,
For the salvation of all his fold.
   Tyb.   John John!
   John.   What is it that thou would?
   Tyb.   By my soul I love thee too too,
And I shall tell thee, or I further go,
The pie that was made, I have it now here,

And therewith I trust we shall make good
    cheer.
    John. By Cock's body that is very happy.
    Tyb. But wotest who gave it?
    John. What the devil reck I?   [then
    Tyb. By my faith, and I shall say true,
The Devil take me, and it were not Sir John.
    John. O hold thy peace, wife, and swear no
    more,
But I beshrew both your hearts therefore [tion
    Tyb. Yet peradventure, thou hast suspec-
Of that was never thought nor done.
    John. Tush, wife, let all such matters be,
I love thee well, though thou love not me :
But this pie doth now catch harm,
Let us set it upon the hearth to warm.
    Tyb. Then let us eat it as fast as we can.
But because Sir John is so honest a man,
I would that he should thereof eat his part.
    John. That were reason, I thee ensure.
    Tyb. Then, since that it is thy pleasure,
I pray thee then go to him right,
And pray him come sup with us to night.
    John [*aside*]. Shall he come hither? by
    Cock's soul I was a-curst
When that I granted to that word first !
But since I have said it, I dare not say nay,
For then my wife and I should make a fray;
But when he is come, I swear by God's mother,
I would give the devil the tone to carry away
    Tyb. What sayst?   [the tother.
    John. Marry, he is my curate, I say,
My confessor and my friend alway,
Therefore go thou and seek him by and by,
And till thou come again, I will keep the pie.
    Tyb. Shall I go for him? nay, I shrew me
    then !

Go thou, and seek, as fast as thou can,
And tell him it.
   John.   Shall I do so?
In faith, it is not meet for me to go.
   Tyb.   But thou shalt go tell him, for all that.
   John.   Then shall I tell him, wotest [thou]
   what?
That thou desirest him to come make some
   cheer.   [sup here.
   Tyb.   Nay, that thou desirest him to come
   John.   Nay, by the rood, wife, thou shalt
   have the worship
And the thanks of thy guest, that is thy gossip.
   Tyb [*aside*].   Full oft I see my husband will
   me rate,
For this hither coming of our gentle curate.
   John.   What sayst, Tyb? let me hear that
   Tyb.   Marry, I perceive very plain [again.
That thou hast Sir John somewhat in suspect;
But by my soul, as far as I conject,
He is virtuous and full of charity.
   John [*aside*].   In faith, all the town knoweth
   better, that he
Is a whoremonger, a haunter of the stews,
An hypocrite, a knave, that all men refuse;
A lier, a wretch, a maker of strife,   [wife.
Better than they know that thou art my good
   Tyb.   What is that, that thou hast said?
   John.   Marry, I would have the table set and
In this place or that, I care not whither. [laid,
   Tyb.   Then go to, bring the trestles hither.
Abide a while, let me put off my gown!
But yet I am afraid to lay it down,
For I fear it shall be soon stolen.   [stolen.
   John.   And yet it may lie safe enough un-
   Tyb.   It may lie well here, and I list,—

But, by Cock's soul, here hath a dog pist;
And if I should lay it on the hearth bare,
It might hap to be burned, or I were ware,
Therefore I pray you [*probably turning to one
    of the audience*], take ye the pain
To keep my gown till I come again.
    But yet he shall not have it, by my fay,
He is so near the door, he might run away;
But because that ye [*another in the audience*]
    be trusty and sure
Ye shall keep it, and it be your pleasure;
And because it is arrayed at the skirt,
While ye do nothing, scrape of the dirt.
    John. Lo, now am I ready to go to Sir John,
And bid him come as fast as he can.
    Tyb. Yea, do so without any tarrying.
But I say, hark ! thou hast forgot one thing ;
Set up the table, and that by and by.
Now go thy ways.
    John. I go shortly ;
But see your candlesticks be not out of the way.
    Tyb. Come again, and lay the table I say ;
What ! me thinks, ye have soon done !
    John. Now I pray God that his malediction
Light on my wife, and on the bald priest.
    Tyb. Now go thy ways and hie thee ! seest?
    John. I pray to Christ, if my wish be no
        sin,   [comes in.
That the priest may break his neck, when he
    Tyb. Now come again.
    John. What a mischief wilt thou, fool !
    Tyb. Marry, I say, bring hither yonder
        stool.
    John. Now go to, a little would make me
For to say thus, a vengeance take thee !
    Tyb. Now go to him, and tell him plain,

That till thou bring him, thou wilt not come
    again.   [stand.
  John.   This pie both burn here as it doth
  Tyb.   Go, wash me these two cups in my
    hand.   [face !
  John.   I go, with a mischief light on thy
  Tyb.   Go, and bid him hie him apace,
And the while I shall all things amend.
  John.   This pie burneth here at this end.
Understandest thou?
  Tyb.   Go thy ways, I say.
  John.   I will go now, as fast as I may.
  Tyb.   How, come once again : I had forgot;
Look, and there be any ale in the pot.
  John.   Now a vengeance and a very mischief
Light on the peel'd priest, and on my wife,
On the pot, the ale, and on the table,
The candle, the pie, and all the rabble,
On the trestles, and on the stool;
It is much ado to please a curst fool.
  Tyb.   Go thy ways now, and tarry no more,
For I am a hungered very sore.
  John.   Marry, I go.
  Tyb.   But come once again yet;
Bring hither that bread, lest I forget it.
  John.   I-wis it were time for to turn
The pie, for I-wis it doth burn.   [patter,
  Tyb.   Lord ! how my husband now doth
And of the pie still doth clatter.
Go now, and bid him come away;
I have bid thee an hundred times to-day.
  John.   I will not give a straw, I tell you
If that the pie wax could again.   [plain,
  Tyb.   What ! art thou not gone yet out of
    this place?   [space :
I had went thou hadst been come again in the

But, by Cock's soul, and I should do the right,
I should break thy knave's head to-night.
  John.   Nay, then if my wife be set a chiding,
It is time for me to go at her bidding.
There is a proverb, which true now proveth,
He must needs go that the devil driveth.
                   [*Exit to the house of the priest.*
How master curate, may I come in
At your chamber door, without any sin.
  Sir John the Priest.   Who is there now that
      would have me?
What! John John! what news with thee?
  John.   Marry, Sir, to tell you shortly,
My wife and I pray you heartily,
And eke desire you with all our might,
That ye would come and sup with us to-night.
  Sir J.   Ye must pardon me, in faith I ne
      can.
  John.   Yes, I desire you, good Sir John,
Take pain this once; and, yet at the least,
If ye will do nought at my request,
Yet do somewhat for the love of my wife.
  Sir J.   I will not go, for making of strife.
But I shall tell thee what thou shalt do,
Thou shalt tarry and sup with me, or thou go.
  John.   Will ye not go then? why so?
I pray you tell me, is there any disdain,
Or any enmity, between you twain?   [me,
  Sir J.   In faith to tell thee, between thee and
She is as wise a woman as any may be;
I know it well; for I have had the charge
Of her soul, and searched her conscience at
      large.
I never knew her but honest and wise,
Without any evil, or any vice,
Save on fault, I know in her no more,

And because I rebuke her, now and then, there-
    fore,
She is angry with me, and hath me in hate;
And yet that that I do, I do it for your wealth.
    John.   Now God yield it you, good master
And as ye do, so send you your health, [curate,
Ywys I am bound to you a pleasure.   [ture,
    Sir J.   Yet thou thinkest amiss, peradven-
That of her body she should not be a good
    woman,
But I shall tell thee what I have done, John,
For that matter; she and I be sometime aloft,
And I do lie upon her, many a time and oft,
To prove her, yet could I never espy
That ever any did worse with her than I. [nine,
    John.   Sir, that is the least care I have of
Thanked be God, and your good doctrine;
But if it please you, tell me the matter,
And the debate between you and her.   [secret.
    Sir J.   I shall tell thee, but thou must keep
    John.   As for that, Sir, I shall not let.
    Sir J.   I shall tell thee now the matter
    plain,—
She is angry with me and hath me in disdain
Because that I do her oft entice
To do some penance, after mine advice,
Because she will never leave her wrawlyng,
But alway with thee she is chiding and brawl-
    ing;
And therefore I know, she hateth [my] pre-
    sence.   [ence.
    John.   Nay, in good faith, saving your rever-
    Sir J.   I know very well, she hath me in hate.
    John.   Nay, I dare swear for her, master
[*Aside*] But, was I not a very knave? [curate:
I thought surely, so God me save,

That he had loved my wife, for to deceive me,
And now he quitteth himself; and here I see
He doth as much as he may, for his life,
To styn[te] the debate between me and my
     wife.   [ill,
   Sir J.   If ever she did, or though[t] me any
Now I forgive her with m[y] free will;
Therefore, John John, now get thee home
And thank thy wife, and say I will not come.
   John.   Yet, let me know, now, good Sir
Where ye will go to supper then.   [John,
   Sir J.   I care not greatly and I tell thee.
On Saturday last, I and two or three
Of my friends made an appointment,
And against this night we did assent
That in a place we would sup together;
And one of them said, [s]he would bring thither
Ale and bread; and for my part, I
Said, that I would give them a pie,
And there I gave them money for the making;
And another said, she would pay for the bak-
And so we purpose to make good cheer [ing;
For to drive away care and thought.
   John.   Then I pray you, Sir, tell me here,
Whither should all this gear be brought?
   Sir J.   By my faith, and I should not lie,
It should be delivered to thy wife, the pie.
   John.   By God! it is at my house, standing
     by the fire.   [quire.
   Sir J.   Who bespake that pie? I thee re-
   John.   By my faith, and I shall not lie,
It was my wife, and her gossip Margerie,
And your good masship, called Sir John,
And my neighbour's youngest daughter Anne;
Your masship paid for the stuff and making,
And Margery she paid for the baking.

Sir J.   If thou wilt have me now, in faith I
will go.   [do so,
John.   Yea, marry, I beseech your masship
My wife tarrieth for none but us twain;
She thinketh long or I come again.   [presence,
Sir J.   Well now, if she chide me in thy
I will be content, and take [it] in patience.
John.   By Cock's soul, and she once chide,
Or frown, or lour, or look aside,   [heave,
I shall bring you a staff as much as I may
Then beat her and spare not; I give you good
To chastise her for her shrewd varying. [leave
          [They return to John's house.
Tyb.   The devil take thee for thy long tarry-
Here is not a whit of water, by my gown, [ing!
To wash our hands that we might sit down;
Go and hie thee, as fast as a snail,
And with fair water fill me this pail.
John.   I thank our Lord of his good grace ҳ
That I cannot rest long in a place.
Tyb.   Go, fetch water, I say, at a word,
For it is time the pie were on the board;
And go with a vengeance, and say thou art
          prayed.
Sir J.   Ah! good gossip! is that well said?
Tyb.   Welcome, mine own sweetheart,
We shall make some cheer or we depart.
John.   Cock's soul, look how he approach-
          eth near
Unto my wife: this abateth my cheer. [*Exit.*
Sir J.   By God, I would ye had heard the
          trifles,
The toys, the mocks, the fables, and the niffles,
That I made thy husband to believe and think!
Thou mightest as well into the earth sink,
As thou couldst forbear laughing any while.

Tyb.   I pray thee let me hear part of that
      wile.   [can.
Sir J.   Marry, I shall tell thee as fast as I
But peace, no more—yonder cometh thy good
      man.   [*Re-enter John.*
John.   Cock's soul, what have we here?
As far as I saw, he drew very near
Unto my wife.
Tyb.   What, art come so soon?
Give us water to wash now—have done.
         [*Then he bringeth the pail empty.*
John.   By Cock's soul, it was, even now,
      full to the brink,
But it was out again or I could think;
Whereof I marvelled, by God Almight,
And then I looked between me and the light
And I spied a clift, both large and wide.
Lo, wife! here it is on the tone side.
Tyb.   Why dost not stop it?
John.   Why, how shall I do it?
Tyb.   Take a little wax.
John.   How shall I come to it?   [say,
Sir J.   Marry, here be two wax candles, I
Which my gossip Margery gave me yesterday.
Tyb.   Tush, let him alone, for, by the rood,
It is pity to help him, or do him good.
Sir J.   What! John John, canst thou make
      no shift?
Take this wax, and stop therewith the clift.
John.   This wax is as hard as any wire.
Tyb.   Thou must chafe it a little at the fire.
John.   She that bought thee these wax
      candles twain,
She is a good companion certain.
Tyb.   What, was it not my gossip Margery?
Sir J.   Yes, she is a blessed woman surely.

                                    G

Tyb. Now would God I were as good as
For she is virtuous, and full of charity.   [she,
    John [*aside*]. Now, so God help me; and by
        my holydom,   [Rome.
She is the errantest baud between this and
    Tyb. What sayst?
John. Marry, I chafe the wax,
And I chafe it so hard that my fingers cracks.
But take up this pie that I here turn;
And it stand long, i-wis it will burn.   [say.
    Tyb. Yea, but thou must chafe the wax, I
    John. Bid him sit down, I thee pray—
Sit down, good Sir John, I you require.   [fire,
    Tyb. Go, I say, and chafe the wax by the
While that we sup, Sir John and I.   [the pie?
    John. And how now, what will ye do with
Shall I not eat thereof a morsel?   [well,
    Tyb. Go and chafe the wax while thou art
And let us have no more prating thus.
    Sir J. Benedicite.
    John. Dominus.
    Tyb. Now go chafe the wax, with a mis-
        chief.   [sweet wife!
    John. What! I come to bless the board,
It is my custom now and then.
Much good do it you, Master Sir John.
    Tyb. Go chafe the wax, and here no longer
        tarry.   [gatory
    John [*aside*]. And is not this a very pur-
To see folks eat, and may not eat a bit?
By Cock's soul, I am a very woodcock.
This pail here, now a vengeance take it!
Now my wife giveth me a proud mock!
    Tyb. What dost?
    John. Marry, I chafe the wax here,
And I imagine to make you good cheer,

[*Aside.*] That a vengeance take you both as
For I know well I shall not eat a bit.   [ye sit,
But yet, in faith, if I might eat one morsel,
I would think the matter went very well.
    Sir J. Gossip, John John, now much good
      do it you.
What cheer make you, there by the fire?
    John. Master parson, I thank you now;
I fare well enow after mine own desire.
    Sir J. What dost, John John, I thee re-
      quire?
    John. I chafe the wax here by the fire.
    Tyb. Here is good drink, and here is a
      good pie.
    Sir J. We fare very well, thanked be our
      lady.   [wax that is hard,
    Tyb. Look how the cuckold chafeth the
And for his life, dareth not look hitherward.
    Sir J. What doth my gossip?
    John. I chafe the wax—   [cracks;
[*Aside.*] And I chafe it so hard that my fingers
And eke the smoke putteth out my eyes two:
I burn my face, and ray my clothes also,
And yet I dare not say one word,
And they sit laughing yonder at the board.
    Tyb. Now, by my troth, it is a pretty jape, |
For a wife to make her husband her ape.
Look of John John, which maketh hard shift
To chafe the wax, to stop therewith the clift.
    John [*aside*]. Yea, that a vengeance take ye
      both two,
Both him and thee, and thee and him also;
And that ye may choke with the same meat
At the first morsel that ye do eat.
    Tyb. Of what thing now dost thou clatter,
John John? or whereof dost thou patter?
                   G 2

John.   I chafe the wax, and make hard shift
To stop herewith of the pail the rift.
      Sir J.   So must he do, John John, by my
            father kin,
That is bound of wedlock in the yoke.
      John [*aside*].   Look how the peel'd priest
            crammeth in;
That would to God he might therewith choke.
      Tyb.   Now, Master Parson, pleaseth your
            goodness
To tell us some tale of mirth or sadness,
For our pastime, in way of communication.
      Sir J.   I am content to do it for our recrea-
And of three miracles I shall to you say. [tion,
      John.   What, must I chafe the wax all day,
And stand here, roasting by the fire?   [desire!
      Sir J.   Thou must do somewhat at thy wife's
I know a man which wedded had a wife,
As fair a woman as ever bare life,
And within a sennight after, right soon
He went beyond sea, and left her alone,
And tarried there about a seven year;   [cheer,
And as he came homeward he had a heavy
For it was told him that she was in heaven.
But, when that he comen home again was,
He found his wife, and with her children seven,
Which she had had in the mean space;
Yet had she not had so many by three
If she had not had the help of me.
Is not this a miracle, if ever were any,   [many
That this good wife should have children so
Here in this town, while her husband should be
Beyond the sea, in a far country.
      John.   Now, in good sooth, this is a won-
            derous miracle,
But for your labour, I would that your tackle

Were in a scalding water well sod.   [God.
   Tyb.   Peace, I say, thou lettest the word of
   Sir J.   Another miracle eke I shall you say,
Of a woman, which that many a day
Had been wedded, and in all that season
She had no child, nother daughter nor son;
Wherefore to Saint Modwin she went on pil-
   grimage,
And offered there a live pig, as is the usage
Of the wives that in London dwell;
And through the virtue thereof, truly to tell,
Within a month after, right shortly,
She was delivered of a child as much as I.
How say you, is not this miracle wonderous?
   John.   Yes, in good sooth, sir, it is marvel-
But surely, after mine opinion,   [lous;
That child was nother daughter nor son.
For certainly, and I be not beguiled,
She was delivered of a knave child.
   Tyb.   Peace, I say, for God's passion,
Thou lettest Sir John's communication.
   Sir J.   The third miracle also is this:
I knew another woman eke y-wys,   [after
Which was wedded, and within five months
She was delivered of a fair daughter,
As well formed in every member and joint,
And as perfect in every point   [th' end.
As though she had gone five months full to
Lo! here is five months of advantage.   [mend;
   John.   A wonderous miracle! so God me
I would each wife that is bound in marriage,
And that is wedded here within this place,
Might have as quick speed in every such case.
   Tyb.   Forsooth, Sir John, yet for all that
I have seen the day that puss, my cat,
Hath had in a year kittlins eighteen.

John.   Yea, Tyb, my wife, and that have I
    seen.   [pie?
But how say you, Sir John, was it good, your
The devil the morsel that thereof eat I.
By the good lord this is a piteous work—
But now I see well the old proverb is true :
That parish priest forgetteth that ever he was
But, Sir John, doth not remember you   [clerk !
How I was your clerk, and holpe you mass to
    sing?
And held the basin alway at the offering?
He never had half so good a clerk as I !
But, notwithstanding all this, now our pie
Is eaten up, there is not left a bit,
And you two together there do sit,
Eating and drinking at your own desire,
And I am John John, which must stand by the
    fire
Chafing the wax, and dare none other wise do.
    Sir J.   And shall we alway sit here still, we
That were too much.   [two?
    Tyb.   Then rise we out of this place.
    Sir J.   And kiss me then in the stead of
    grace;
And farewell leman and my love so dear.
    John.   Cock's body, this wax it waxeth cold
    again here;—
But what ! shall I anon go to bed,
And eat nothing, nother meat nor bread?
I have not be wont to have such fare.   [are,
    Tyb.   Why ! were ye not served there as ye
Chafing the wax, standing by the fire?
    John.   Why, what meat gave ye me, I you
    require?   [heartily,
    Sir J.   Wast thou not served, I pray thee
Both with the bread, the ale, and the pie?

John.   No, sir, I had none of that fare.

Tyb.   Why! were ye not served there as ye
Standing by the fire chafing the wax?   [are,

John.   Lo, here be many trifles and knacks—
By Cock's soul, they ween I am other drunk or
    mad.   [had?

Tyb.   And had ye no meat, John John? no

John.   No, Tyb my wife, I had not a whit.

Tyb.   What, not a morsel?

John.   No, not one bit;
For hunger, I trow, I shall fall in a sowne.

Sir J.   O, that were pity, I swear by my

Tyb.   But is it true?   [crown.

John.   Yea, for a surety.

Tyb.   Dost thou lie?

John.   No, so mote I thee!

Tyb.   Hast thou had nothing?

John.   No, not a bit.

Tyb.   Hast thou not drunk?

John.   No, not a whit.

Tyb.   Where wast thou?

John.   By the fire I did stand.

Tyb.   What didst?

John.   I chafed this wax in my hand,
Whereas I knew of wedded men the pain
That they have, and yet dare not complain;
For the smoke put out my eyes two,
I burned my face, and rayed my clothes also,
Mending the pail, which is so rotten and old,
That it will not skant together hold;
And sith it is so, and since that ye twain
Would give me no meat for my sufficiance,
By Cock's soul I will take no longer pain,
Ye shall do all yourself, with a very vengeance,
For me, and take thou there thy pail now,
And if thou canst mend it, let me see how.

Tyb.   A ! whoreson's knave ! hast thou
   broke my pail?
Thou shalt repent, by Cock's lylly nail.
Reach me my distaff, or my clipping shears :
I shall make the blood run about his ears.
   John.   Nay, stand still, drab, I say, and
   come no near,
For by Cock's blood, if thou come here,
Or if thou once stir toward this place,   [face.
I shall throw this shovel full of coals in thy
   Tyb.   Yea ! whoreson drivel ! get thee out
   of my door.   [priest's whore.
John.   Nay ! get thou out of my house, thou
Sir J.   Thou liest, whoreson cuckold, even
   to thy face.   [evil grace.
John.   And thou liest, peel'd priest, with an
Tyb.   And thou liest.
John.   And thou liest, Sir.
Sir J.   And thou liest again.
John.   By Cock's soul, whoreson priest,
   thou shalt be slain ;
Thou hast eat our pie, and give me nought,
By Cock's blood, it shall be full dearly bought.
   Tyb.   At him, Sir John, or else God give
   thee sorrow.   [Saint George to borrow.
John.   And have at your whore and thief,
   [*Here they fight by the ears a while, and then
   the priest and the wife go out of the place.*
John.   A ! sirs ! I have paid some of them
   even as I list,
They have borne many a blow with my fist,
I thank God, I have walked them well,
And driven them hence.   But yet, can ye tell
Whither they be gone? for by God, I fear me,
That they be gone together, he and she,
Unto his chamber, and perhaps she will,

Spite of my heart, tarry there still,
And, peradventure, there, he and she
Will make me cuckold, even to anger me;
And then had I a pig in the worse panyer,
Therefore, by God, I will hie me thither
To see if they do me any villainy :
And thus fare well this noble company.

FINIS.

Imprinted by Wyllyam Rastell
the xii day of February
the yere of our Lord
MCCCC and xxxIII
Cum privilegio

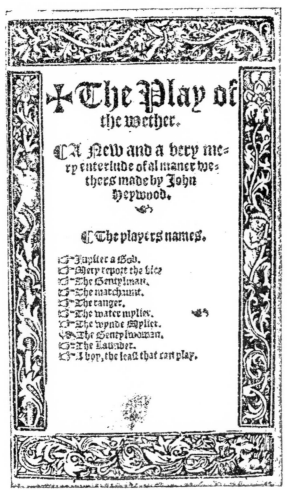

✠ The Play of the wether.

¶ A new and a very merry enterlude of al maner wethers made by John Heywood.

¶ The players names.

- ☞ Jupiter a God.
- ☞ Mery reporte the vice
- ☞ The Gentylman.
- ☞ The marchaunt.
- ☞ The ranger.
- ☞ The water myller.
- ☞ The wynde Myller.
- ☞ The Gentylwoman.
- ☞ The Launder.
- ☞ A boy, the leaft that can play.

[Facsimile Title-page of the Copy now in the Bodleian: see Note-Book.]

The Players' Names:

JUPITER, A GOD
MERRY REPORT, THE VICE
THE GENTLEMAN
THE MERCHANT
THE RANGER
THE WATER-MILLER
THE WIND-MILLER
THE GENTLEWOMAN
THE LAUNDER
A BOY, THE LEAST THAT CAN PLAY

THE PLAY OF THE WEATHER

Jupiter. Right far too long, as now, were to recite   [reigned,
The ancient estate wherein our self hath
What honour, what laud, given us of very
    right,
What glory we have had, duly unfeigned,
Of each creature, which duty hath constrained;
For above all gods, since our father's fall,
We, Jupiter, were ever principal.
If ye so have been, as truth it is indeed,
Beyond the compass of all comparison,
Who could presume to show, for any meed,
So that it might appear to human reason,
The high renown we stand in at this season?
For, since that heaven and earth were first
    create,
Stood we never in such triumphant estate
As we now do, whereof we will report
Such part as we see meet for time present,
Chiefly concerning your perpetual comfort,
As the thing self shall prove in experiment,
Which highly shall bind you, on knees lowly
    bent,
Solely to honour our highness, day by day.

(93)

And now to the matter give ear, and we shall
    say.
Before our presence, in our high parliament,
Both gods and goddesses of all degrees
Hath late assembled, by common assent,
For the redress of certain enormities,
Bred among them, through extremities
Abused in each to other of them all,
Namely, to purpose, in these most special :
Our foresaid father Saturn, and Phebus,
Eolus and Phebe, these four by name,
Whose natures, not only, so far contrarious,
But also of malice each other to defame,
Have long time abused, right far out of frame,
The due course of all their constellations,
To the great damage of all earthly nations :
Which was debated in place said before;
And first, as became, our father most ancient,
With beard white as snow, his locks both cold
    and hoar,
Hath entered such matter as served his intent,
Lauding his frosty mansion in the firmament,
To air and earth as thing most precious,
Purging all humours that are contagious.
Howbeit, he allegeth that, of long time past,
Little hath prevailed his great diligence,
Full oft upon earth his fair frost he hath cast,
All things hurtful to banish out of presence.
But Phebus, intending to keep him in silence,
When he hath laboured all night in his powers,
His glaring beams marreth all in two hours.
Phebus to this made no manner answering,
Whereupon they both then Phebe defied,
Each for his part laid in her reproving [tried;
That by her showers superfluous they have
In all that she may their powers be denied;
Whereunto Phebe made answer no more

Than Phebus to Saturn had made before.
Anon upon Eolus all these did flee,
Complaining their causes, each one a-row,
And said, to compare, none was so evil as he;
For, when he is disposed his blasts to blow,
He suffereth neither sunshine, rain nor snow.
They each against other, and he against all
    three,—
Thus can these four in no manner agree! [ing,
Which seen in themself, and further consider-
The same to redress was cause of their as-
And, also, that we, evermore being, [semble;
Beside our puissant power of deity,
Of wisdom and nature so noble and so free,
From all extremities the mean dividing,
To peace and plenty each thing attempering,
They have, in conclusion, wholly surrendered
Into our hands, at much as concerning
All manner weathers by them engendered,
The full of their powers, for term everlasting,
To set such order as standeth with our pleas-
    ing,
Which thing, as of our part, no part required,
But of all their parts right humbly desired,
To take upon us.   Whereto we did assent.
And so in all things, with one voice agreeable,
We have clearly finished our foresaid parlia-
    ment,   [stable,
To your great wealth, which shall be firm and
And to our honour far inestimable;
For since their powers, as ours, added to our
    own,   [known?
Who can, we say, know us as we should be
But now, for fine, the rest of our intent,
Wherefore, as now, we hither are descended,
Is only to satisfy and content

All manner people which have been offended
By any weather meet to be amended,
Upon whose complaints, declaring their grief,
We shall shape remedy for their relief.
 And to give knowledge for their hither resort
We would this afore proclaimed to be,
To all our people, by some one of this sort
 [*one of the audience*],
Whom we list to choose here amongst all ye.
Wherefore each man advance, and we shall see
Which of you is most meet to be our cryer.
               [*Here entereth Merry Report.*
 Merry Report.   Brother [*to attendant*], hold
  up your torch a little higher !
Now, I beseech you, my lord, look on me first.
I trust your lordship shall not find me the
  worst.   [proachest so nigh?
 Jupiter. Why! what art thou that ap-
 Merry Report. Forsooth, and please your
  lordship, it is I.   [what I?
 Jupiter. All that we know very well, But
 Merry Report. What I? Some say I am I
But, what manner I so ever be I,   [per se I.
I assure your good lordship, I am I.
 Jupiter. What manner man art thou, show
  quickly.   [dwelleth hereby.
 Merry Report. By god, a poor gentleman,
 Jupiter. A gentleman! Thyself bringeth
  witness nay,
Both in thy light behaviour and array.
But what art thou called where thou dost
  resort?   [Merry Report.
 Merry Report. Forsooth, my lord, master
 Jupiter. Thou art no meet man in our busi-
  ness,
For thine appearance is of too much lightness.

Merry Report.   Why, cannot your lordship
   like my manner
Mine apparel, nor my name nother?
   Jupiter.   To nother of all we have devotion.
   Merry Report.   A proper likelihood of pro-
Well, then, as wise as ye seem to be, [motion !
Yet can ye see no wisdom in me.
But since ye dispraise me for so light an elf,
I pray you give me leave to praise myself :
And, for the first part, I will begin
In my behaviour at my coming in,
Wherein I think I have little offended,
For, sure, my courtesy could not be amended ;
And, as for my suit your servant to be,
Might ill have been missed for your honesty ;
For, as I be saved, if I shall not lie,
I saw no man sue for the office but I !
Wherefore if ye take me not or I go,
Ye must anon, whether ye will or no.
And since your intent is but for the weathers,
What   skills   our   apparel   to   be   frieze   or
   feathers?
I think it wisdom, since no man forbade it,
With this to spare a better—if I had it !
And, for my name, reporting alway truly,
What hurt to report a sad matter merrily?
As, by occasion, for the same intent,
To a certain widow this day was I sent,
Whose husband departed without her witting,
A special good lover and she his own sweeting !
To whom, at my coming, I cast such a figure,
Mingling the matter according to my nature,
That when we departed, above all other things,
She thanked me heartily for my merry tidings !
And if I had not handled it merrily,
Perchance she might have taken it heavily ;

H

But in such fashion I conjured and bound her,
That I left her merrier than I found her! [fort
What man may compare to show the like com-
That daily is showed by me, Merry Report?
And, for your purpose, at this time meant,
For all weathers I am so indifferent,
Without affection, standing so upright,
Sunlight, moonlight, starlight, twilight, torch-
     light,   [lightning, thunder,
Cold, heat, moist, dry, hail, rain, frost, snow,
Cloudy, misty, windy, fair, foul, above head or
    under,
Temperate or distemperate, whatever it be,
I promise your lordship, all is one to me.
    Jupiter. Well, son, considering thine in-
        differency,
And partly the rest of thy declaration,
We make thee our servant and immediately
Well will thou depart and cause proclamation,
Publishing our pleasure to every nation,
Which thing once done, with all diligence,
Make thy return again to this presence,
Here to receive all suitors of each degree;
And such as to thee may seem most meetly,
We will thou bring them before our majesty,
And for the rest, that be not so worthy,
Make thou report to us effectually,
So that we may hear each manner suit at large.
Thus see thou depart and look upon thy
    charge!   [lady be with ye!
    Merry Report. Now, good my lord god, our
Friends, a fellowship, let me go by ye!
Think ye I may stand thrusting among you
    there?
Nay, by god, I must thrust about other gear!
    [*Merry Report goeth out. At the end of this*

stave the god hath a song played in his
throne or Merry Report come in.
Jupiter. Now, since we have thus far set
forth our purpose,
A while we will withdraw our godly presence,
To embold all such more plainly to disclose,
As here will attend, in our foresaid pretence.
And now, according to your obedience,
Rejoice ye in us with joy most joyfully,
And we ourself shall joy in our own glory!
  [Jupiter here shut out from view. Merry
      Report cometh in.
  Merry Report. Now, sirs, take heed! for
      here cometh god's servant!
Avaunt! carte[r]ly caitiffs, avaunt!
Why, ye drunken whoresons, will it not be?
By your faith, have ye nother cap nor knee?
Not one of you that will make curtesy
To me, that am squire for god's precious body?
Regard ye nothing mine authority?
No welcome home! nor where have ye be?
Howbeit, if ye axed, I could not well tell,
But sure I think a thousand mile from hell,
And on my faith, I think, in my conscience,
I have been from heaven as far as heaven is
      hence,
At Louvain, at London and in Lombardy,
At Baldock, at Barfold, and in Barbary,
At Canterbury, at Coventry, at Colchester,
At Wandsworth and Welbeck, at Westchester,
At Fulham, at Faleborne, and at Fenlow,
At Wallingford, at Wakefield, and at Wal-
      thamstow,
At Taunton, at Tiptree and at Tottenham,
At Gloucester, at Guildford and at Gotham,

At Hertford, at Harwich, at Harrow-on-the
    hill,
At Sudbury, Southampton, at Shooter's Hill,
At Walsingham, at Witham, and at Warwick,
At Boston, at Bristow and at Berwick,
At Gravelyn, at Gravesend, and at Glaston-
    bury,   [bury.
Ynge Gyngiang Jayberd the parish of Buts-
The devil himself, without more leisure,
Could not have gone half thus much, I am
    sure !   [choose;
But, now I have warned them, let them even
For, in faith, I care not who win or lose.
    [*Here the gentleman before he cometh in
       bloweth his horn.*
    Merry Report.   Now, by my troth, this was
       a goodly hearing.
I went it had been the gentlewoman's blowing !
But it is not so, as I now suppose,
For women's horns sound more in a man's
    nose.   [everyone.
    Gentleman.   Stand ye merry, my friends,
    Merry Report.   Say that to me and let the
       rest alone !
Sir, ye be welcome, and all your meyny.
    Gentleman.   Now, in good sooth, my friend,
       god a mercy !
And since that I meet thee here thus by chance,
I shall require thee of further acquaintance,
And briefly to show thee, this is the matter.
I come to sue to the great god Jupiter
For help of things concerning my recreation,
According to his late proclamation.
    Merry Report.   Marry, and I am he that this
       must speed.
But first tell me what be ye indeed.

Gentleman. Forsooth, good friend, I am a
   gentleman.   [saint Anne !
Merry Report. A goodly occupation, by
On my faith, your maship hath a merry life.
But who maketh all these horns, yourself or
   your wife?
Nay, even in earnest, I ask you this question.
   Gentleman. Now, by my troth, thou art a
      merry one.   [never one sad,
   Merry Report. In faith, of us both I think
For I am not so merry but ye seem as mad !
But stand ye still and take a little pain,
I will come to you, by and by, again.
Now, gracious god, if your will so be,
I pray ye, let me speak a word with ye
   Jupiter. My son, say on ! Let us hear thy
      mind   [suitor even here behind,
   Merry Report. My lord, there standeth a
A Gentleman, in yonder corner,
And, as I think, his name is Master Horner
A hunter he is, and cometh to make you sport.
He would hunt a sow or twain out of this sort.
      [*Here he pointeth to the women.*
   Jupiter. Whatsoever his mind be, let him
      appear.
   Merry Report. Now, good master Horner,
      I pray you come near.
   Gentleman. I am no horner, knave ! I will
      thou know it,   [when ye did blow it,
   Merry Report. I thought ye had [been], for
Heard I never whoreson make horn so go.
As lief ye kist mine arse as blow my hole so !
Come on your way, before the God Jupiter,
And there for yourself ye shall be suitor.
   Gentleman. Most mighty prince and god of
      every nation,

Pleaseth your highness to vouchsafe the hear-
    ing   [tion,
Of me, which, according to [y]our proclama-
Doth make appearance, in way of beseeching,
Not sole for myself, but generally
For all come of noble and ancient stock,
Which sort above all doth most thankfully
Daily take pain for wealth of the common flock,
With diligent study alway devising
To keep them in order and unity,
In peace to labour the increase of their living,
Whereby each man may prosper in plenty.
Wherefore, good god, this is our whole desir-
    ing,
That for ease of our pains, at times vacant,
In our recreation, which chiefly is hunting,
It may please you to send us weather pleasant,
Dry and not misty, the wind calm and still.
That after our hounds journeying so merrily,
Chasing the deer over dale and hill,
In hearing we may follow and to comfort the
    cry.   [whole request,
    Jupiter. Right well we do perceive your
Which shall not fail to rest in memory,
Wherefore we will ye set yourself at rest,
Till we have heard each man indifferently,
And we shall take such order, universally,
As best may stand to our honour infinite,
For wealth in common and each man's singular
    profit.   [be the name
    Gentleman.   In heaven and earth honoured
Of Jupiter, who of his godly goodness
Hath set this matter in so goodly frame, [less.
That every wight shall have his desire, doubt-
And first for us nobles and gentlemen,
I doubt not, in his wisdom, to provide

Such weather as in our hunting, now and then,
We may both teyse and receive on every side.
Which thing, once had, for our said recreation,
Shall greatly prevail you in preferring our
    health   [tion,
For what thing more needful than our preserva-
Being the weal and heads of all common
    wealth?   [whose head be you?
    Merry Report.   Now I beseech your maship,
    Gentleman.   Whose head am I?   Thy head.
What sayst thou now?   [so god me help!
    Merry Report.   Nay, I think it very true,
For I have ever been, of a little whelp,
So full of fancies, and in so many fits,
So many small reasons, and in so many wits,
That, even as I stand, I pray God I be dead,
If ever I thought them all meet for one head.
But since I have one head more than I knew,
Blame not my rejoicing,—I love all things new.
And sure it is a treasure of heads to have store :
One feat can I now that I never could before.
    Gentleman.   What is that?
    Merry Report.   By god, since ye came
    hither,
I can set my head and my tail together.
This head shall save money, by Saint Mary,
From henceforth I will no 'pothecary;
For at all times, when such things shall mister
My new head shall give mine old tail a glister.
And, after all this, then shall my head wait
Upon my tail, and there stand at receipt.
Sir, for the rest I will not now move you,
But, if we live, ye shall smell how I love you.
And, sir, touching your suit here, depart, when
    it please you
For be ye sure, as I can I will ease you.

Gentleman.   Then give me thy hand.   That
   promise I take.
And if for my sake any suit thou do make,
I promise thy pain to be requited
More largely than now shall be recited.
   Merry Report.   Alas, my neck! God's pity,
   where is my head?
By Saint Eve, I fear me I shall be dead.
And if I were, methink it were no wonder,
Since my head and my body is so far asunder,
             [Entereth the Merchant.
Master parson, now welcome by my life!
I pray you, how doth my mistress, your wife?
   Merchant.   Sir, for the priesthood and wife
   that ye allege
I see ye speak more of dotage than knowledge.
But let pass, sir, I would to you be suitor
To bring me, if ye can, before Jupiter.
   Merry Report.   Yes, Marry, can I, and will
   do it indeed.   *[Goes to Jupiter.*
Tarry, and I shall make way for your speed.
In faith, good lord, if it please your gracious
   godship,   [ship,
I must have a word or twain with your lord-
Sir, yonder is another man in place,
Who maketh great suit to speak with your
   grace.   [by.
Your pleasure once known, he cometh by and
   Jupiter.   Bring him before our presence, son,
   hardly.   [I not find ye?
   Merry Report.   Why! where be you? shall
Come away, I pray god, the devil blind ye!
   Merchant.   Most mighty prince and lord of
   lords all,
Right humbly beseecheth your majesty
Your merchantmen through the world all,

That it may please you, of your benignity,
In the daily danger of our goods and life,
First to consider the desert of our request,
What wealth we bring the rest, to our great
    care and strife,
And then to reward us as ye shall think best.
What were the surplusage of each commodity,
Which groweth and increaseth in every land,
Except exchange by such men as we be?
By way of intercourse, that lieth on our hand
We fraught from home, things whereof there
    is plenty;   [scant.
And home we bring such things as there be
Who should afore us merchants accompted be?
For were not we, the world should wish and
    want
In many things, which now shall lack rehearsal.
And, briefly to conclude, we beseech your high-
That of the benefit proclaimed in general [ness
We may be partakers, for common increase,
'Stablishing weather thus, pleasing your grace,
Stormy, nor misty, the wind measurable.
That safely we may pass from place to place,
Bearing our sails for speed most vailable;
And also the wind to change and to turn,
East, West, North and South, as best may be
In any one place not too long to sojourn, [set,
For the length of our voyage may lose our
    market.
    Jupiter. Right well have ye said, and we
    accept it so,
And so shall we reward you ere we go hence.
But ye must take patience till we have heard
That we may indifferently give sentence. [mo,
There may pass by us no spot of negligence,
But justly to judge each thing, so upright

That each man's part may shine in the self
      right.   [ye should be sworn,
    Merry Report. Now, sir, by your faith, if
Heard ye ever god speak so, since ye were
      born?
So wisely, so gently his words be showed!
    Merchant. I thank his grace. My suit is
      well bestowed.
    Merry Report. Sir, what voyage intend ye
      next to go?
    Merchant. I trust or mid-Lent to be to Scio.
    Merry Report. Ha, ha! Is it your mind to
      sail at Scio?
Nay, then, when ye will, byr lady, ye may go,
And let me alone with this. Be of good cheer!
Ye may trust me at Scio as well as here.
For though ye were fro me a thousand mile
      space,
I would do as much as ye were here in place,
For, since that from hence it is so far thither,
I care not though ye never come again hither.
    Merchant. Sir, if ye remember me, when
      time shall come,
Though I requite not all, I shall deserve some.
                        [*Exit Merchant.*
    Merry Report. Now, fare ye well, and God
      thank you, by saint Anne,   [man;
I pray you, mark the fashion of this honest
He putteth me in more trust, at this meeting
      here,
Than he shall find cause why, this twenty year.
                  [*Here entereth the Ranger.*
    Ranger. God be here, now Christ keep this
      company!   [very scantly!
    Merry Report. In faith, ye be welcome, even
Sir, for your coming what is the matter?

Ranger. I would fain speak with the god
    Jupiter.   [do this—
Merry Report. That will not be, but ye may
Tell me your mind. I am an officer of his.
    Ranger. Be ye so? Marry, I cry you mercy.
Your mastership may say I am homely.
But since your mind is to have reported
The cause wherefore I am now resorted,
Pleaseth your mastership it is so.
I come for myself and such other mo,
Rangers and keepers of certain places,
As forests, parks, purlieus and chases
Where we be charged with all manner game.
Small is our profit and great is our blame.
Alas! For our wages, what be we the near?
What is forty shillings, or five mark, a year?
Many times and oft, where we be flitting,
We spend forty pence apiece at a sitting.
Now for our vantage, which chiefly is windfall.
That is right nought, there bloweth no wind at
    all,
Which is the thing wherein we find most grief,
And cause for my coming to sue for relief,
That the god, of pity, all this thing knowing,
May send us good rage of blustering and blow-
And, if I cannot get god to do some good, [ing,
I would hire the devil to run through the wood,
The roots to turn up, the tops to bring under.
A mischief upon them, and a wild thunder!
    Merry Report. Very well said, I set by your
    charity
As much, in a manner, as by your honesty.
I shall set you somewhat in ease anon.
Ye shall put on your cap, when I am gone.
For, I see, ye care not who win or lose,
So ye may find means to win your fees.

Ranger. Sir, as in that, ye speak as it
    please ye.
But let me speak with the god, if it may be.
I pray you, let me pass ye.
    Merry Report. Why, nay, sir! By the
    mass, ye—
    Ranger. Then will I leave you even as I
    found ye.   [here hath bound ye.
    Merry Report. Go when ye will. No man
    [*Here entereth the Water-miller and the
    Ranger goeth out.*
    Water-miller. What the devil should skyl,
    though all the world were dumb,
Since all our speaking we never be heard?
We cry out for rain, the devil speed drop will
We water-millers be nothing in regard. [come.
No water have we to grind at any stint,
The wind is so strong the rain cannot fall,
Which keepeth our milldams as dry as a flint.
We are undone, we grind nothing at all,
The greater is the pity, as thinketh me.
For what availeth to each man his corn,
Till it be ground by such men as we be?
There is the loss, if we be forborne.
For, touching ourselves, we are but drudges,
And very beggars save only our toll,
Which is right small and yet many grudges
For grist of a bushel to give a quart bowl.
Yet, were not reparations, we might do well.
Our millstones, our wheel with her cogs, and
    our trindle
Our floodgate, our millpool, our water wheel,
Our hopper, our extre, our iron spindle,
In this and much more so great is our charge,
That we would not reck though no water were,
Save only it toucheth each man so large,

And each for our neighbour Christ biddeth us
    care.   [hither,
Wherefore my conscience hath pricked me
In this to sue, according to the cry,
For plenty of rain to the god Jupiter
To whose presence I will go even boldly.
   Merry Report. Sir, I doubt nothing your
But I fear me ye lack capacity,   [audacity,
For, if ye were wise, ye might well espie,
How rudely ye err from rules of courtesy.
What! ye come in reveling and reheating,
Even as a knave might go to a bear-baiting!
   Water-miller. All you bear record what
    favour I have!
Hark, how familiarly he calleth me knave!
Doubtless the gentleman is universal!   [call
But mark this lesson, sir. You should never
Your fellow knave, nor your brother whoreson;
For nought can ye get by it, when ye have
    done.   [fellow to me,
   Merry Report. Thou art nother brother nor
For I am God's servant, mayst thou not see?
Would ye presume to speak with the great
    god?
Nay, discretion and you be too far odd!
By'r lady, these knaves must be tied shorter.
Sir, who let you in? Spake ye with the porter?
   Water-miller. Nay, by my troth, nor with
    no nother man.
Yet I saw you well, when I first began.
How be it, so help me god and holydam,
I took you but for a knave, as I am.
But, marry, now, since I know what ye be,
I must and will obey your authority.
And if I may not speak with Jupiter
I beseech you be my solicitor.

Merry Report. As in that, I will be your
I perceive you be a water-miller. [well-willer.
And your whole desire, as I take the matter,
Is plenty of rain for increase of water.
The let whereof, ye affirm determinately,
Is only the wind, your mortal enemy. [aloft,
  Water-miller. Truth it is, for it bloweth so
We never have rain, or, at the most, not oft.
Wherefore, I pray you, put the god in mind
Clearly for ever to banish the wind.
              [*Here entereth the Wind-miller.*
  Wind-miller. How! Is all the weather
    gone or I come?
For the passion of God, help me to some.
I am a wind-miller, as many mo be.
No wretch in wretchedness so wretched as we!
The whole sort of my craft be all marred at
    once,
The wind is so weak it stirreth not our stones,
Nor scantly can shatter the shitten sail
That hangeth shattering at a woman's tail.
The rain never resteth, so long be the showers,
From time of beginning till four-and-twenty
    hours;
And, end when it shall, at night or at noon,
Another beginneth as soon as that is done.
Such revel of rain ye know well enough,
Destroyeth the wind, be it never so rough,
Whereby, since our mills become to still stand-
    ing,
Now may we wind-millers go even to hanging.
A miller! with a murrain and a mischief!
Who would be a miller? As good be a thief!
Yet in time past, when grinding was plenty,
Who were so like God's fellows as we? [meal.
As fast as God made corn, we millers made

Which might be best forborn for common
weal?
But let that gear pass, for I fear our pride
Is cause of the care which God doth us provide.
Wherefore I submit me, intending to see
What comfort may come by humility.
And, now, at this time, they said in the cry,
The god is come down to shape remedy.
   Merry Report. No doubt, he is here, even
    in yonder throne.
But in your matter he trusteth me alone,
Wherein, I do perceive by your complaint,
Oppression of rain doth make the wind so
   faint,
That ye wind-millers be clean cast away. [say.
   Wind-miller. If Jupiter help not, it is as ye
But, in few words to tell you my mind round,
Upon this condition I would be bound,
Day by day to say our lady's psalter,
That in this world were no drop of water,
Nor never rain, but wind continual,
Then should we wind-millers be lords over all.
   Merry Report. Come on and assay how you
    twain can agree—
A brother of yours, a miller as ye be!
   Water-miller. By mean of our craft we may
    be brothers,
But whilst we live shall we never be lovers.
We be of one craft, but not of one kind,
I live by water and he by the wind.
       [Here Merry Report goeth out.
And, sir, as ye desire wind continual,
So would I have rain evermore to fall,
Which two in experience, right well ye see,
Right selde, or never, together can be.
For as long as the wind ruleth, it is plain,

Twenty to one ye get no drop of rain;
And when the element is too far oppressed,
Down cometh the rain and setteth the wind at
      rest.
By this, ye see, we cannot both obtain.
For ye must lack wind, or I must lack rain.
Wherefore I think good, before this audience,
Each for ourself to say, or we go hence;
And whom is thought weakest, when we have
      finished,
Leave off his suit and content to be banished.
    Wind-miller. In faith, agreed! but then,
      by your licence,
Our mills for a time shall hang in suspense.
Since water and wind is chiefly our suit,
Which best may be spared we will first dispute.
Wherefore to the sea my reason shall resort,
Where ships by means of wind try from port to
      port,
From land to land, in distance many a mile,—
Great is the passage and small is the while.
So great is the profit, as to me doth seem,
That no man's wisdom the wealth can esteem.
And since the wind is conveyer of all
Who but the wind should have thanks above
      all?   [here to grow,
    Water-miller. Admit in this place a tree
And thereat the wind in great rage to blow;
When it hath all blown, this is a clear case,
The tree removeth no hair-breadth from his
      place.   [could.
No more would the ships, blow the best it
Although it would blow down both mast and
Except the ship flete upon the water [shroud,
The wind can right nought do,—a plain matter.
Yet may ye on water, without any wind,

Row forth your vessel where men will have her
Nothing more rejoiceth the mariner,   [synde.
Than mean cooles of wind and plenty of water.
For, commonly, the cause of every wreck
Is excess of wind, where water doth lack.
In rage of these storms the peril is such
That better were no wind than so far too much.
   Wind-miller. Well, if my reason in this
     may not stand,
I will forsake the sea and leap to land.
In every church where God's service is,
The organs bear brunt of half the quere, i-wys.
Which causeth the sound, of water or wind?
Moreover for wind this thing I find
For the most part all manner minstrelsy,
By wind they deliver their sound chiefly,
Fill me a bagpipe of your water full,
As sweetly shall it sound as it we stuffed with
     wool.   [be at the full,
   Water-miller. On my faith I think the moon
For frantic fancies be then most plentiful.
Which are at the pride of their spring in your
     head—   [fled.
[*Aside.*] So far from our matter he is now
As for the wind in any instrument,
It is no parcel of our argument,
We spake of wind that cometh naturally
And that is wind forced artificially,
Which is not to purpose. But, if it were,
And water, indeed, right nought could do
     there,
Yet I think organs no such commodity,
Whereby the water should banished be,
And as for your bagpipes, I take them as
     nyfuls,
Your matter is all in fancies and trifles.

                             I

Wind-miller. By God, but ye shall not trifle
   me off so !
If these things serve not, I will rehearse mo.
And now to mind there is one old proverb
      come,   [ransom,
One bushel of March dust is worth a king's
What is a hundred thousand bushels worth
      then?   [self, to no man.
   Water-miller. Not one mite, for the thing
   Wind-miller. Why shall wind everywhere
      thus be object?
Nay, in the highways he shall take effect,
Where as the rain doth never good but hurt,
For wind maketh but dust and water maketh
      dirt.
Powder or syrup, sirs, which like ye best?
Who liketh not the tone may lick up the rest.
But, sure, whosoever hath assayed such sips,
Had liever have dusty eyes than dirty lips.
And it is said, since afore we were born,
That drought doth never make dearth of corn.
And well it is known, to the most fool here,
How rain hath priced corn within this seven
      year.   [little season.
   Water-miller. Sir, I pray thee, spare me a
And I shall briefly conclude thee with reason.
Put case one summer's day without wind to be,
And rageous wind in winter days two or three,
Much more shall dry that one calm day in
      summer,
Than shall those three windy days in winter.
Whom shall we thank for this, when all is
      done?   [sun.
The thank to wind? Nay ! Thank chiefly the
And so for drought, if corn thereby increase,
The sun doth comfort and ripe all doubtless,

And oft the wind so layeth the corn, God wot,
That never after can it ripe, but rot.
If drought took place, as ye say, yet may ye
    see,
Little helpeth the wind in this commodity.
But, now, sir, I deny your principal.
If drought ever were, it were impossible
To have any grain, for, ere it can grow,
Ye must plow your land, harrow and sow,
Which will not be, except ye may have rain
To temper the ground, and after again
For springing and plumping all manner corn
Yet must ye have water, or all is forlorn.
If ye take water for no commodity
Yet must ye take it for thing of necessity,
For washing, for scouring, all filth cleansing,
Where water lacketh what beastly being!
In brewing, in baking, in dressing of meat,
If ye lack water, what could ye drink or eat?
Without water could live neither man nor
    beast,
For water preserveth both most and least.
For water could I say a thousand things mo,
Saving as now the time will not serve so;
And as for that wind that you do sue for,
Is good for your windmill and for no more.
Sir, sith all this in experience is tried,
I say this matter standeth clear on my side.
    Wind-miller. Well, since this will not
        serve, I will allege the rest.
Sir, for our mills I say mine is the best.
My windmill shall grind more corn in one hour
Than thy water-mill shall in three or four,
Yea more than thine should in a whole year,
If thou mightest have as thou hast wished here.
For thou desirest to have excess of rain,

Which thing to thee were the worst thou
   couldst obtain.
For, if thou didst, it were a plain induction
To make thine own desire thine own destruc-
For in excess of rain at any flood   [tion.
Your mills must stand still; they can do no
   good.
And when the wind doth blow the uttermost
Our windmills walk amaine in every coast.
For, as we see the wind in his estate,
We moder our sails after the same rate.
Since our mills grind so far faster than yours,
And also they may grind all times and hours,
I say we need no water-mills at all,
For windmills be sufficient to serve all.
   Water-miller. Thou speakest of all and con-
      siderest not half!
In boast of thy grist thou art wise as a calf!
For, though above us your mills grind far
   faster,   [farther?
What help to those from whom ye be much
And, of two sorts, if the tone should be con-
   served,
I think it meet the most number be served.
In vales and wealds, where most commodity is,
There is most people: ye must grant me this.
On hills and downs, which part are most
   barren,
There must be few; it can no mo sustain.
I dare well say, if it were tried even now,
That there is ten of us to one of you.
And where should chiefly all necessaries be,
But there as people are most in plenty?
More reason that you come seven mile to mill
Than all we of the vale should climb the hill.
If rain came reasonable, as I require it,

We should of your windmills have need no
    whit.   [*Entereth Merry Report.*
  Merry Report. Stop, foolish knaves, for
    your reasoning is such,
That ye have reasoned even enough and too
    much.
I heard all the words that ye both have had,
So help me God, the knaves be more than mad !
Neither of them both that hath wit nor grace,
To perceive that both mills may serve in place.
Between water and wind there is no such let,
But each mill may have time to use his fet.
Which thing I can tell by experience;
For I have, of mine own, not far from hence,
In a corner together a couple of mills,
Standing in a marres between two hills,
Not of inheritance, but by my wife;
She is feofed in the tail for term of her life,
The one for wind, the other for water.
And of them both, I thank God, there standeth
For, in a good hour be it spoken,   [nother;
The water-gate is no sooner open,
But clap, saith the windmill, even straight be-
    hind !   [grind !
There is good speed, the devil and all they
But whether that the hopper be dusty,
Or that the millstones be somewhat rusty,
By the mass, the meal is mischievous musty !
And if ye think my tale be not trusty,
I make ye true promise : come, when ye list,
We shall find mean ye shall taste of the grist.
  Water-miller. The corn at receipt haply is
    not good.   [the sweet rood !
  Merry Report. There can be no sweeter, by
Another thing yet, which shall not be cloaked,
My water-mill many times is choked.

Water-miller. So will she be, though ye
    should burst your bones,
Except ye be perfect in setting your stones.
Fear not the lydger, beware your runner.
Yet this for the lydger, or ye have won her,
Perchance your lydger doth lack good pecking.
    Merry Report. So saith my wife, and that
    maketh all our checking.
She would have the mill pecked, pecked,
    pecked, every day!   [may!
But, by God, millers must peck when they
So oft have we pecked that our stones wax
    right thin,
And all our other gear not worth a pin,
For with pecking and pecking I have so
    wrought,   [nought,
That I have pecked a good pecking-iron to
Howbeit, if I stick no better till her,
My wife saith she will have a new miller.
But let it pass! and now to our matter!
I say my mills lack nother wind nor water;
No more do yours, as far as need doth require.
But, since ye cannot agree, I will desire
Jupiter to set you both in such rest
As to your wealth and his honour may stand
    best.
    Water-miller. I pray you heartily remember
    me.   [beseech ye.
    Wind-miller. Let not me be forgotten, I
        [*Both Millers go forth.*
    Merry Report. If I remember you not both
    alike
I would ye were over the ears in the dike.
Now be we rid of two knaves at one chance.
By Saint Thomas, it is a knavish riddance.
        [*The Gentlewoman entereth.*

Gentlewoman.   Now, good god, what a folly
    is this?
What should I do where so much people is?
I know not how to pass into the god now.
    Merry Report.   No, but ye know how he
        may pass into you.   [back side.
Gentlewoman.   I pray you let me in at the
Merry Report.   Yea, shall I so, and your
    fore side so wide?
Nay not yet; but since ye love to be alone,
We twain will into a corner anon.
But first, I pray you, come your way hither,
And let us twain chat a while together.
    Gentlewoman.   Sir, as to you I have little
My coming is to speak with Jupiter.   [matter.
    Merry Report.   Stand ye still a while, and I
        will go prove
Whether that the god will be brought in love.
My lord, how now! look up lustily!
Here is a darling come, by Saint Antony.
And if it be your pleasure to marry,
Speak quickly; for she may not tarry.
In faith, I think ye may win her anon;
For she would speak with your lordship alone.
    Jupiter.   Son, that is not the thing at this
        time meant.   [resort,
If her suit concern no cause of our hither
Send her out of place; but if she be bent
To that purpose, hear her and make us report.
    Merry Report.   I count women lost, if we
        love them not well,
For ye see God loveth them never a deal.
Mistress ye cannot speak with the god.
    Gentlewoman.   No! why?   [is right busy.
    Merry Report.   By my faith, for his lordship
With a piece of work that needs must be done;

Even now is he making of a new moon.
He saith your old moons be so far tasted,
That all the goodness of them is wasted,
Which of the great wet hath been most matter
For old moons be leak; they can hold no water.
But for this new moon, I durst lay my gown,
Except a few drops at her going down,
Ye get no rain till her arising,
Without it need, and then no man's devising
Could wish the fashion of rain to be so good;
Not gushing out like gutters of Noah's flood,
But small drops sprinkling softly on the
    ground;   [no sound.
Though they fell on a sponge they would give
This new moon shall make a thing spring more
    in this while   [mile.
Than an old moon shall while a man may go a
By that time the god hath all made an end,
Ye shall see how the weather will amend.
By Saint Anne, he goeth to work even boldly.
I think him wise enough; for he looketh oldly!
Wherefore, mistress, be ye now of good cheer;
For though in his presence ye cannot appear,
Tell me your matter and let me alone.
Mayhap I will think on you when you be gone.
    Gentlewoman. Forsooth, the cause of my
        coming is this:
I am a woman right fair, as ye see;
In no creature more beauty than in me is;
And, since I am fair, fair would I keep me,
But the sun in summer so sore doth burn me,
In winter the wind on every side me.
No part of the year wot I where to turn me,
But even in my house am I fain to hide me.
And so do all other that beauty have;
In whose name at this time, this suit I make,

Beseeching Jupiter to grant that I crave;
Which is this, that it may please him, for our
To send us weather close and temperate, [sake,
No sunshine, no frost, nor no wind to blow.
Then would we jet the streets trim as a parrot.
Ye should see how we would set ourself to
     show.
   Merry Report. Jet where ye will, I swear
     by Saint Quintin,
Ye pass them all, both in your own conceit and
     mine.   [at our pleasure,
   Gentlewoman. If we had weather to walk
Our lives would be merry out of measure.
One part of the day for our apparelling
Another part for eating and drinking,
And all the rest in streets to be walking,
Or in the house to pass time with talking.
   Merry Report. When serve ye God?
   Gentlewoman. Who boasteth in virtue are
     but daws.   [since there is no cause.
   Merry Report. Ye do the better, namely
How spend ye the night?
   Gentlewoman. In dancing and singing
Till midnight, and then fall to sleeping.
   Merry Report. Why, sweetheart, by your
     false faith, can ye sing?   [all thing.
   Gentlewoman. Nay, nay, but I love it above
   Merry Report. Now, by my troth, for the
     love that I owe you,
You shall hear what pleasure I can show you.
One song have I for you, such as it is,
And if it were better ye should have it, by Gys.
   Gentlewoman. Marry, sir, I thank you even
     heartily.   [us sing lust[i]ly.
   Merry Report. Come on, sirs; but now let
                              [*Here they sing.*

Gentlewoman. Sir, this is well done; I
    heartily thank you.
Ye have done me pleasure, I make God avow.
Once in a night I long for such a fit;
For long time have I been brought up in it.
    Merry Report. Oft-time it is seen, both in
        court and town,   [brought down.
Long be women a bringing up and soon
So fet it is, so neat it is, so nice it is,
So trick it is, so quick it is, so wise it is.
I fear myself, except I may entreat her,
I am so far in love I shall forget her.   [ye—
Now, good mistress, I pray you, let me kiss
    Gentlewoman. Kiss me, quoth a! Why,
        nay, sir, I wis ye.
    Merry Report. What! yes, hardly! Kiss
        me once and no more.
I never desired to kiss you before.
            [*Here the Launder cometh in.*
    Launder. Why! have ye alway kissed her
        behind?
In faith, good enough, if it be your mind.
And if your appetite serve you so to do,
By'r lady, I would ye had kissed mine arse too!
    Merry Report. To whom dost thou speak,
        foul whore? canst thou tell?   [very well!
    Launder. Nay, by my troth! I, sir, not
But by conjecture this guess I have,
That I do speak to an old baudy knave.
I saw you dally with your simper de cocket.
I rede you beware she pick not your pocket.
Such idle housewives do now and then
Think all well won that they pick from a man.
Yet such of some men shall have more favour,
Than we, that for them daily toil and labour.
But I trust the god will be so indifferent

That she shall fail some part of her intent.

   Merry Report. No doubt he will deal so
      graciously
That all folk shall be served indifferently.
Howbeit, I tell the truth, my office is such
That I must report each suit, little or much.
Wherefore, with the god since thou canst not
      speak,   [break.
Trust me with thy suit, I will not fail it to
   Launder. Then leave not too much to
      yonder giglet.
For her desire contrary to mine is set.
I heard by her tale she would banish the sun,
And then were we poor launders all undone.
Except the sun shine that our clothes may dry,
We can do right nought in our laundry.
Another manner loss, if we should miss,
Than of such nycebyceters as she is.

   Gentlewoman. I think it better that thou
      envy me,
Than I should stand at reward of thy pity.
It is the guise of such gross queans as thou art
With such as I am evermore to thwart.
By cause that no beauty ye can obtain
Therefore ye have us that be fair in disdain.

   Launder. When I was as young as thou
I was within little as fair as thou,   [art now,
And so might have kept me, if I had would,
And as dearly my youth I might have sold
As the trickest and fairest of you all.
But I feared perils that after might fall,
Wherefore some business I did me provide,
Lest vice might enter on every side,   [reign.
Which hath free entry where idleness doth
It is not thy beauty that I disdain,
But thine idle life that thou hast rehearsed,

Which any good woman's heart would have
For I perceive in dancing and singing, [pierced.
In eating and drinking and thine apparelling,
Is all the joy, wherein thy heart is set.   [get;
But nought of all this doth thine own labour
For, hadst thou nothing but of thine own
        travail,
Thou mightest go as naked as my nail.
Methink thou shouldst abhor such idleness
And pass thy time in some honest business;
Better to lose some part of thy beauty,
Than so oft to jeopard all thine honesty.
But I think, rather than thou wouldst so do,
Thou hadst liever have us live idly too.   [have
And so, no doubt, we should, if thou mightest
The clear sun banished, as thou dost crave:
Then were we launders marred and unto thee
Thine own request were small commodity.   &
For of these twain I think it far better
Thy face were sun-burned, and thy clothes the
        sweeter,   [smitten,
Than that the sun from shining should be
To keep thy face fair and thy smock beshitten.
Sir, how like ye my reason in her case?
    Merry Report.   Such a railing whore, by the
        holy mass,
I never heard, in all my life, till now.
Indeed I love right well the tone of you,
But, ere I would keep you both, by God's
        mother,
The devil shall have the tone to fet the tother.
    Launder.   Promise me to speak that the sun
        may shine bright,
And I will be gone quickly for all night.
    Merry Report.   Get you both hence, I pray
        you heartily;

Your suits I perceive and will report them truly
Unto Jupiter, at the next leisure,
And in the same desire, to know his pleasure;
Which knowledge had, even as he doth show it,
Fear ye not, time enough, ye shall know it.
    Gentlewoman. Sir, if ye meddle, remember
      me first.   .   [shall be the worst.
    Launder. Then in this meddling my part
    Merry Report. Now, I beseech our lord, the
      devil thee burst.
Who meddleth with many I hold him accurst,
Thou whore, can I meddle with you both at
    once.
        [*Here the Gentlewoman goeth forth.*
    Launder. By the mass, knave, I would I
      had both thy stones
In my purse, if thou meddle not indifferently,
That both our matters in issue may be likely.
    Merry Report. Many words, little matter,
      and to no purpose,
Such is the effect that thou dost disclose,
The more ye bib the more ye babble,
The more ye babble the more ye fable,
The more ye fable the more unstable,
The more unstable the more unable,
In any manner thing to do any good.   [rood!
No hurt though ye were hanged, by the holy
    Launder. The less your silence, the less
      your credence,
The less your credence the less your honesty,
The less your honesty the less your assistance,
The less your assistance the less ability [save,
In you to do ought. Wherefore, so God me
No hurt in hanging such a railing knave.
    Merry Report. What monster is this? I
      never heard none such.

For look how much more I have made her too
    much,
And so far, at least, she hath made me too
    little.
Where be ye Launder? I think in some spital.
Ye shall wash me no gear, for fear of fretting
I love no launders that shrink my gear in
    wetting,
I pray thee go hence, and let me be in rest.
I will do thine errand as I think best.
    Launder. Now would I take my leave, if I
        wist how.
The longer I live the more knave you.
    Merry Report. The longer thou livest the
        pity the greater,
The sooner thou be rid the tidings the better!
Is not this a sweet office that I have,
When every drab shall prove me a knave?
Every man knoweth not what God's service is,
Nor I myself knew it not before this.
I think God's servants may live holily,
But the devil's servants live more merrily.
I know not what God giveth in standing fees,
But the devil's servants have casualties
A hundred times mo than God's servants have.
For, though ye be never so stark a knave,
If ye lack money the devil will do no worse
But bring you straight to another man's purse.
Then will the devil promote you here in this
    world,
As unto such rich it doth most accord.
First *pater noster que es in celis,*   [heels.
And then ye shall sense the sheriff with your
The greatest friend ye have in field or town,
Standing a-tiptoe, shall not reach your crown.
    [*The Boy cometh in, the least that can play.*

Boy. This same is even he, by all likeli-
Sir, I pray you, be not you master God? [hood,
   Merry Report. No, in good faith, son. But
      I may say to thee
I am such a man that God may not miss me.
Wherefore with the god if thou wouldst have
      ought done
Tell me thy mind, and I shall show it soon.
   Boy. Forsooth, sir, my mind is this, at few
      words.
All my pleasure is in catching of birds, [same;
And making of snow-balls and throwing the
For the which purpose to have set in frame,
With my godfather God I would fain have
      spoken,
Desiring him to have sent me by some token
Where I might have had great frost for my
      pitfalls,
And plenty of snow to make my snow-balls.
This once had, boys' lives be such as no man
      leads.   [heads,
O, to see my snow-balls light on my fellows'
And to hear the birds how they flicker their
      wings
In the pitfall! I say it passeth all things.
Sir, if ye be God's servant, or his kinsman,
I pray you help me in this if ye can.
   Merry Report. Alas, poor boy, who sent
      thee hither?
   Boy. A hundred boys that stood together,
Where they heard one say in a cry
That my godfather, God Almighty,
Was come from heaven, by his own accord,
This night to sup here with my lord,
And farther he said, come whos[o] will,
They shall sure have their bellies full

Of all weathers who list to crave,
Each sort such weather as they list to have.
And when my fellows thought this would be
And saw me so pretty a prattling lad,   [had,
Upon agreement, with a great noise,
" Send little Dick," cried all the boys.
By whose assent I am purveyed
To sue for the weather aforesaid.
Wherein I pray you to be good, as thus,
To help that God may give it us.
    Merry Report.   Give boys weather, quoth a !
    nonny, nonny !
    Boy.   If God of his weather will give nonny,
I pray you, will he sell any?
Or lend us a bushel of snow, or twain,
And point us a day to pay him again?   [light,
    Merry Report.   I cannot tell, for, by this
I chept not, nor borrowed, none of him this
But by such shift as I will make   [night.
Thou shalt see soon what way he will take.
    Boy.   Sir, I thank you.   Then I may de-
    part.   [*The Boy goeth forth.*
    Merry Report.   Yea, farewell, good son,
    with all my heart,
Now such another sort as here hath been
In all the days of my life I have not seen.
No suitors now but women, knaves, and boys,
And all their suits are in fancies and toys.
If that there come no wiser after this cry
I will to the god and make an end quickly.
Oyez, if that any knave here
Be willing to appear,
For weather foul or clear,
Come in before this flock
And be he whole or sickly,
Come, show his mind quickly,

And if his tale be not likely
Ye shall lick my tail in the nock.
All this time I perceive is spent in waste,
To wait for mo suitors I see none make haste.
Wherefore I will show the god all this process
And be delivered of my simple office.
Now, lord, according to your commandment,
Attending suitors I have been diligent,
And, at beginning as your will was I should,
I come now at end to show what each man
        would.
The first suitor before yourself did appear,
A gentleman desiring weather clear,
Cloudy nor misty, nor no wind to blow,
For hurt in his hunting; and then, as ye know,
The merchant sued, for all of that kind,
For weather clear and measurable wind
As they may best bear their sails to make
        speed.   [deed,
And straight after this there came to me, in-
Another man who named himself a ranger,
And said all of his craft be far brought in
        danger,
For lack of living, which chiefly is windfall.
But he plainly saith there bloweth no wind at
        all,   [fleeces,
Wherefore he desireth, for increase of their
Extreme rage of wind, trees to tear in pieces.
Then came a water-miller and he cried out
For water and said the wind was so stout
The rain could not fall, wherefore he made re-
        quest
For plenty of rain, to set the wind at rest.
And then, sir, there came a wind-miller in,
Who said for the rain he could no wind win,
The water he wished to be banished all,

                                    K

Beseeching your grace of wind continual.
Then came there another that would banish all
A goodly dame, an idle thing i-wys.   [this
Wind, rain, nor frost, nor sunshine, would she
     have,
But fair close weather, her beauty to save.
Then came there another that liveth by laundry,
Who must have weather hot and clear her
     clothes to dry.   [tinual,
Then came there a boy for frost and snow con-
Snow to make snow-balls and frost for his pit-
     fall,
For which, God wot, he sueth full greedily.
Your first man would have weather clear and
     not windy;   [meanly;
The second the same, save cooles to blow
The third desired storms and wind most ex-
     tremely;   [wind;
The fourth all in water and would have no
The fifth no water, but all wind to grind;
The sixth would have none of all these, nor no
     bright sun;   [won;
The seventh extremely the hot sun would have
The eighth, and the last, for frost and snow he
     prayed.
By'r lady, we shall take shame, I am afraid!
Who marketh in what manner this sort is led
May think it impossible all to be sped.   [ten,
This number is small, there lacketh twain of
And yet, by the mass, among ten thousand men
No one thing could stand more wide from the
     tother;
Not one of their suits agreeth with another.
I promise you, here is a shrewd piece of work.
This gear will try whether ye be a clerk.
If ye trust to me, it is a great folly;

For it passeth my brains, by God's body!
　Jupiter.　Son, thou hast been diligent and
　　done so well,
That thy labour is right much thank-worthy.
But be thou sure we need no whit thy counsel,
For in ourself we have foreseen remedy,
Which thou shalt see.　But, first, depart hence
　　quickly
To the gentleman and all other suitors here
And command them all before us to appear.
　Merry Report.　That shall be no longer in
Than I am in coming and going.　　　　[doing
　　　　　[Merry Report goeth out.
　Jupiter.　Such debate as from above ye have
　　heard,
Such debate beneath among yourselves ye see;
As long as heads from temperance be deferred,
So long the bodies in distemperance be,
This perceive ye all, but none can help save we.
But as we there have made peace concordantly,
So will we here now give you remedy.
　[Merry Report and all the suitors entereth.
　Merry Report.　If I had caught them
Or ever I raught them,
I would have taught them
To be near me;　　　　　　　　　ᵠ
Full dear have I bought them,
Lord, so I sought them,
Yet have I brought them,
Such as they be.　　　　　　　　[so it is,
　Gentleman.　Pleaseth it your majesty, lord,
We, as your subjects and humble suitors all,
According as we hear your pleasure is,
Are pressed to your presence, being principal
Head and governor of all in every place,
Who joyeth not in your sight, no joy can have.
　　　　　　　　　　　　K 2

Wherefore we all commit us to your grace
As lord of lords us to perish or save.
  Jupiter. As long as discretion so well doth
Obediently to use your duty,   [you guide
Doubt ye not we shall your safety provide,
Your griefs we have heard, wherefore we sent
      for ye
To receive answer, each man in his degree,
And first to content most reason it is,   [this,
The first man that sued, wherefore mark ye
Oft shall ye have the weather clear and still
To hunt in for recompense of your pain.
Also you merchants shall have much your will.
For oft-times, when no wind on land doth re-
      main,
Yet on the sea pleasant cooles you shall obtain.
And since your hunting may rest in the night,
Oft shall the wind then rise, and before day-
      light
It shall rattle down the wood, in such case
That all ye rangers the better live may;
And ye water-millers shall obtain this grace
Many times the rain to fall in the valley,
When at the self times on hills we shall purvey
Fair weather for your windmills, with such
      cooles of wind
As in one instant both kinds of mills may grind.
And for ye fair women, that close weather
      would have,
We shall provide that ye may sufficiently
Have time to walk in, and your beauty save;
And yet shall ye have, that liveth by laundry,
The hot sun oft enough your clothes to dry.
Also ye, pretty child, shall have both frost and
      snow,   [arow.
Now mark this conclusion, we charge you

Much better have we now devised for ye all
Than ye all can perceive, or could desire.
Each of you sued to have continual
Such weather as his craft only doth require,
All weathers in all places if men all times might
          hire,   [gence
Who could live by other? what is this negli-
Us to attempt in such inconvenience.
Now, on the tother side, if we had granted
The full of some one suit and no mo,
And from all the rest the weather had forbid,
Yet who so had obtained had won his own woe,
There is no one craft can preserve man so,
But by other crafts, of necessity,
He must have much part of his commodity.
All to serve at once and one destroy another,
Or else to serve one and destroy all the rest,
Neither will we do the tone nor the tother
But serve as many, or as few, as we think best;
And where, or what time, to serve most or
          least,
The direction of that doubtless shall stand
Perpetually in the power of our hand.
Wherefore we will the whole world to attend
Each sort on such weather as for them doth
          fall,
Now one, now other, as liketh us to send.
Who that hath it, ply it, and sure we shall
So guide the weather in course to you all,
That each with other ye shall whole remain
In pleasure and plentiful wealth, certain.
     Gentleman.   Blessed was the time wherein
          we were born,   [presence.
First for the blissful chance of your godly
Next for our suit was there never man beforne
That ever heard so excellent a sentence

As your grace hath given to us all arow,
Wherein your highness hath so bountifully
Distributed my part that your grace shall
    know,   [chivalry.
Your self sooll possessed of hearts of all
  Merchant. Likewise we merchants shall
    yield us wholly,
Only to laud the name of Jupiter
As god of all gods, you to serve solely;
For of everything, I see, you are nourisher.
  Ranger. No doubt it is so, for so we now
    find;
Wherein your grace us rangers so doth bind,
That we shall give you our hearts with one
    accord,
For knowledge to know you as our only lord.
  Water-miller. Well, I can no more, but
    " for our water
We shall give your lordship our lady's psalter."
  Wind-miller. Much have ye bound us; for,
    as I be saved,
We have all obtained better than we craved.
  Gentlewoman. That is true, wherefore your
    grace shall truly
The hearts of such as I am have surely.
  Launder. And such as I am, who be as
    good as you,
His highness shall be sure on, I make a vow.
  Boy. Godfather god, I will do somewhat for
    you again.
By Christ, ye may hap to have a bird or twain,
And I promise you, if any snow come,
When I make my snow-balls ye shall have
    some.
  Merry Report. God thank your lordship.
Lo, how this is brought to pass!

Sir, now shall ye have the weather even as it
    was.   [farther to boast,
  Jupiter. We need no whit ourself any
For our deeds declare us apparently.
Not only here on earth, in every coast,
But also above in the heavenly company,
Our prudence hath made peace universally,
Which thing we say, recordeth us as principal
God and governor of heaven, earth, and all.
Now unto that heaven we will make return,
When we be glorified most triumphantly,
Also we will all ye that on earth sojourn,
Since cause giveth cause to know as your lord
And now here to sing most joyfully,   [only,
Rejoicing in us, and in meantime we shall
Ascend into our throne celestial.

                 FINIS.

         Printed by W. Rastell.
             1533.
         Cum Privilegio.

THE PLAY OF LOVE

A New Interlude

By JOHN HEYWOOD

(137)

The Players' Names

THE LOVER LOVED

THE LOVER NOT LOVED

NEITHER LOVER NOR LOVED

THE WOMAN BELOVED NOT LOVING

THE PLAY OF LOVE

Lover not Loved. Lo Sir, whoso that
    looketh here for courtesy
And seeth me seem as one pretending none,
But as unthought upon thus suddenly
Approach the midst among you everyone,
And of you all saith nought to anyone,
May think me rude perceiving of what sort
Ye seem to be, and of what stately port.
But I beseech you in most humble wise
To omit displeasure and pardon me.
My manner is to muse and devise
So that some time myself may carry me,
Myself knoweth not where; and I assure ye
So hath myself done now; for, our lord wot,
Where I am, or what ye be, I know not;
Or whence I came, or whither I shall—
All this in manner as unknown to me.
But, even as fortune guideth my foot to fall
So wander I, yet wheresoever I be,
And whom, or how many soever I see,
As one person to me is everyone
So every place to me but as one.
And, for that one person every place seek I,
Which one, once found, I find of all the rest
Not one missing; and, in the contrary,

[T]hat one absent, though that there were here
    pressed
[A]ll the creatures living, most and least,
[Y]et lacking her I should, and ever shall,
Be as alone since she to me is all.
And alone is she without comparison
Concerning the gifts given by nature;
In favour fairness and port as of person
No life beareth the like of that creature,
Nor no tongue can attain to put in ure
Her to describe, for how can words express
That thing the full whereof no thought can
And, as it is a thing inestimable   [guess?
To make report of her beautifully,
So is my love toward her unable
To be reported, as who saith rightly;
For my whole service and love to that lady
Is given under such abundant fashion   [tion.
That no tongue thereof can make right rela-
Wherein I suppose this well supposed
' Unto you all; that since she perceiving ·
As much of my love as can be disclosed,
Even of very right in recompensing
She ought for my love again to be loving.
For what more right to grant, when love love
    requireth,   [sireth?
Than love for love, when love nought else de-
But even as far worse as otherwise, then so
Stand I in case in manner desperate.
No time can time my suit to ease my woe;
Before none too early, and all times else too
    late,
Thus time out of time mistimeth my rate;
For time to bring time to hope of any grace
That time timeth no time in any time or place.
Whereby, till time have time so far extinct

That death may determine my life thus deadly,
No time can I rest. Alas ! I am so linked
To griefs, both so great and also many,
That by the same I say, and will verify,
Of all pains the most incomparable pain
Is to be a lover not loved again.
   [*The Woman Beloved not Loving entereth.*
   Loved not Loving. Sir, as touching those
     words of comparison
Which ye have said and would seem to verify,
If it may please you to stand thereupon,
Hearing and answering me patiently,
I doubt not by the same incontinently
Yourself to see, by words that shall ensue,
The contrary of your words verified for true.
   Lover not Loved. Fair lady, pleaseth it you
     to repair near,
And in this cause to show cause reasonable
Whereby cause of reformation may appear—
Of reason I must and will be reformable.
   Loved not Loving. Well, since ye pretend
     to be conformable
To reason in avoiding circumstance,
Briefly by reason I shall the truth avance.
Ye be a lover no whit loved again,
And I am loved of whom I love nothing,
Then standeth our question between these twain
Of loving not loved, or loved not loving—
Which is the case most painful in suffering?
Whereto I say that the most pain doth move
To those beloved of whom they cannot love.
   Lover not Loved. Those words approved
     too, might make a change
Of mine opinion, but verily
The case as ye put it I think more strange
Than true, for though the beloved party

Cannot love again, yet possibly
Can I not think, nor I think never shall,
That to be loved can be any pain at all.
    Loved not Loving. That reason, perceived,
      and received for truth,   [me :
From proper comparison should clear confound
Between pain and no pain, no such comparison
    groweth.
Then, or I can on comparison ground me, [me;
To prove my case painful ye have first bound
To which, since ye drive me by your denial,
Mark what ensueth before farther trial.
I say I am loved of a certain man
Whom for no suit I can favour again;
And that have I told him since his suit began
A thousand times, but every time in vain.
For, never ceaseth his tongue to complain,
And ever one tale which I never can flee;
For ever, in manner, where I am is he.
Now, if you to hear one thing everywhere,
Contrary to your appetite, should be led, [ear,
Were it but a mouse, lo! should peep in your
Or alway to harp on a crust of bread—
How could you like such harping at your head?
    Lover not Loved. Somewhat displeasant it
      were, I not deny.
    Loved not Loving. Then somewhat painful,
      as well said, say I.
Displeasure and pain be things jointly annexed;
For, as it is displeasant in pain to be,
So it is painful in displeasure to be vexed.
Thus, by displeasure in pain, ye confess me;
Whereby, since ye part of my pain do see,
In my further pain I shall now declare
That pain by which with your pain I compare.
Small were the quantity of my painful smart

If his jangling pierced no further than mine
    ears.
But, through mine ears directly to mine heart
Pierceth his words, even like as many spears;
By which I have spent so many and such tears
That, where they all red as they be all white,
The blood of my heart had be gone or this
    quite.
And, almost in case as though it were gone
Am I, except his suit take end shortly;
For it doth like me even like as one
Should offer me service most humbly
With an axe in his hand, continually
Beseeching me gently that this might be sped
To grant him my good will to strike off my
    head.
I allege for general this one similitude,
Avoiding rehearsal of pains particular
To abbreviate the time, and to exclude
Surplusage of words in this our matter;
By which ensample, if ye consider
Rightly my case, at leastwise ye may see
My pain as painful as your pain can be.   [pain
And yet, for shorter end, put case that your
Were oft-times more sharp and sore in degree
Than mine is at any time, yet will I prove plain
My pain, at length, sufficient to match ye:
Which proof to be true yourself shall agree
If your affection in that I shall recite
May suffer your reason to understand right.
You stand in pleasure having your love in
    sight;
And, in her absence, hope of sight again
Keepeth most times possession of some delight.
Thus have you oft-times some way ease of pain,
And I never no way; for when I do remain

In his presence, in deadly pain I sojourn;
And absent, half dead in fear of his return.
Since presence nor absence absenteth my pain,
But alway the same to me is present,   [again
And that by presence and hope of presence
There doth appear much of your time spent,
Out of pain methinketh this consequent—
That my pain may well, by mean of the length,
Compare with your shorter pain of more
          strength.   [pain be no stronger
    Lover not Loved.   Mistress, if your long
Than is your long reason against my short pain,
Ye lack no likelihood to live much longer
Than he that would strike off your head so fain;
Yet, lest ye would note me your words to dis-
I am content to agree for a season   [dain,
To grant and enlarge your latter reason.
Admit, by her presence, half my time pleasant,
And all your time as painful as in case can be,
Yet your pain to be most reason will not grant.
And, for ensample, I put case that ye
Stood in cold water all a day to the knee,
And I half the same day to mid leg in the fire,
Would ye change places with me for the dryer?
    Loved not Loving.   Nay! that would I not,
      be ye assured.   [above yours is as ill
    Lover not Loved.   Forsooth! and my pain
As fire above water, thus to be endured.
Came my pain but at times, and yours continue
      still,
Yet should mine many ways to whom can skill
Show yours, in comparison between the twain
Scantly able for a shadow to my pain.
Felt ye but one pang such as I feel many,
One pang of despair, or one pang of desire,
One pang of one displeasant look of her eye,

One pang of one word of her mouth as in ire,
Or in restraint of her love which I require—
One pang of all these, felt once in all your life,
Should quaile your opinion and quench all our
					strife.
Which pangs, I say, admitted short at ye list,
And all my time beside pleasant as ye please,
Yet could not the shortness the sharpness to
					resist.					[these,
The piercing of my heart is the least of all
But much it overmatcheth all your disease;
For no whit in effect is your case displeasant
But to deny a thing which ye list not to grant.
Or, to hear a suitor by daily petition,
In humble manner as wit can devise,
Require a thing, so standing in condition
As no portion of all his enterprise
Without your consent can speed in any wise—
This suit thus attempted never so long [strong.
Doubt ye no death till your pain be more
Now, since in this matter between us disputed,
Mine admittance of your words notwithstand-
I have thus fully your part confuted,		[ing,
What can ye say now I come to denying
Your principle, granted in my foresaying?
Which was this, by the presence of my lady
I granted you half my time spent pleasantly.
Although mine affection leadeth me to consent
That her selde presence is my relief only,
Yet, as in reason appeareth, all my torment
Bred by her presence—and mark this cause
Before I saw her I felt no malady;		[why !—
And since I saw her I never was free
From twain the greatest pain that in love be.
Desire is the first upon my first sight,
And despair the next upon my first suit;

					L

For, upon her first answer hope was put to
  flight
And never came since in place to dispute—
How bringeth then her presence to me any
  fruit?
For hopeless and helpless, in flames of desire
And drops of despair, I smoulder in fire.
These twain being endless since they began,
And both by the presence of her wholly
Began and continued, I wonder if ye can
Speak any word more, but yield immediately;
For had I no mo pains but these, yet clearly
A thousand times more is my grief in these
  twain   [plain.
Than yours in all the case by which ye com-
    Loved not Loving.   That is as ye say, but
    not as I suppose,
Nor as the truth is, which yourself might see
By reasons that I could and would disclose
Saving that I see such partiality
On your part, that we shall never agree
Unless ye will admit some man indifferent,
Indifferently to hear us, and so give judgment.
    Lover not Loved.   Agreed! for though the
    knowledge of all my pain
Ease my pain no whit, yet shall it declare
Great cause of abashment in you, to complain
In counterfeit pains with my pain to compare—
But here is no judge meet, we must seek else-
    where.   [same to condescend—
    Loved not Loving.   I hold me content the
Please it you to set forth and I shall attend.
    [*Here they go both out and the Lover Be-
    loved entereth with a song.*   [can deny
    Lover Loved.   By common experience who
Impossibility for man to show

His inward intent, but by signs outwardly—
As writing, speech, or countenance—whereby
     doth grow
Outward perceiving inwardly to know,
Of every secrecy in man's breast wrought,
From man unto man the effect of each thought.
These things well weighed in many things show
     need
In our outward signs to show us so that plain,
According to our thoughts, words and signs
          proceed;   [feign
For, in outward signs where men are seen to
What credence in man to man may remain?
Man's inward mind, with outward signs to
     fable,
May soon be more common than commendable.
Much are we lovers then to be commended,
For love his appearance dissembleth in no wise,
But as the heart feeleth like signs alway pre-
     tended—   [enemies :
Who feign in appearance are love's mortal
As, in despair of speed, who that can mirth de-
          vise,   [mourners—
Or, having grant of grace can show them as
Such be no lovers but even very shorners.
The true lover's heart that cannot obtain
Is so tormented, that all the body
Is evermore so compelled to complain,
That sooner may the suffrant hide the fury
Of a fervent fever, than, of that malady,
By any power human, he possible may
Hide the least pain of a thousand, I daresay.
And he who in loving hath loth to such luck
That love for love of his love be found
Shall be of power, even as easily to pluck
The moon in a moment with a finger to ground,
                                             L 2

As of his joy to enclose the rebound,
But that the reflection thereof from his heart
To his beholders shall shine in each part.
Thus, be a lover in joy or in care,
Although will and wit his estate would hide,
Yet shall his semblance as a dial declare
How the clock goeth; which may be well ap-
        plied
In abridgment of circumstance for a guide
To lead you in few words, by my behaviour,
To know me in grace of my lady's favour.
For being a lover, as I am indeed,
And thereto disposed thus pleasantly,
Is a plain appearance of my such speed
As I in love could wish, and undoubtedly
My love is requited so lovingly
That in everything that may delight in mind
My wit cannot wish it so well as I find.
Which thing, at full considered, I suppose
That all the whole world must agree, in one
I being beloved, as I now disclose,   [voice,
Of one being chief of all the whole choice
Must have incomparable cause to rejoice;
For the highest pleasure that man may obtain
Is to be a lover beloved again.
            [*Neither Lover nor Loved entereth.*
    Neither Lover nor Loved.   Now God you
        good even, Master Woodcock!
    Lover Loved.   Cometh of rudeness or lewd-
        ness that mock?
    Neither Lover nor Loved.   Come whereof it
        shall ye come of such stock
That God you good even, Master Woodcock!
    Lover Loved.   This losel by like hath lost
        his wit!   [Woodcock, not a whit!
    Neither Lover nor Loved.   Nay, nay, Master

I have known you for a woodcock or this;
Or else like a woodcock I take you amiss.
But, though for a woodcock ye deny the same,
Yet shall your wit witness you meet for that
   Lover Loved. How so?   [name.
   Neither Lover nor Loved. Thus, lo!
I do perceive, by your former process,
That ye be a lover whereto ye confess
Yourself beloved in as loving wise
As by wit and will ye can wish to devise:
Concluding therein, determinately
That, of all pleasures pleasant to the body,
The highest pleasure that man may obtain
Is to be a lover beloved again.
In which conclusion, before all this flock,
I shall prove you plain as wise as a woodcock.
   Lover Loved. And methink this woodcock
      is turned on thy side
Contrary to courtesy and reason to use
Thus rudely to rail or any word be tried
In proof of thy part, whereby I do refuse
To answer the same; thou canst not excuse
Thy folly in this; but, if thou wilt say ought,
Assay to say better for this saying is nought.
   Neither Lover nor Loved. Well, since it is
      so that ye be discontent
To be called fool or further matter be spent,
Will ye give me leave to call ye fool anon
When yourself perceiveth that I have proved
      you one?
   Lover Loved. Yea, by my soul, and will
      take it in good worth!
   Neither Lover [nor] Loved. Now, by my
      father's soul! then will we even forth
That part rehearse of your saying or this
Of all our debate the only cause is;

For, where ye afore have fastly affirmed
That such as be lovers again beloved
Stand in most pleasure that to man may move,
That tale to be false truth shall truly prove.

    Lover Loved. What folk above those live
      more pleasantly?

    Neither Lover nor Loved. What folk?
      marry! even such folk as am I.

    Lover Loved. Being no lover what man
      may ye be?

    Neither Lover nor Loved. No lover! no, by
      God, I warrant ye!

I am no lover in no manner meant,
As doth appear in this purpose present,
For, as touching women, go where I shall
I am at one point with women all—
The smotest, the smirkest, the smallest,
The truest, the trimmest, the tallest,
The wisest, the wiliest, the wildest,
The merriest, the mannerliest, the mildest,
The strangest, the straightest, the strongest,
The lustiest, the least, or the longest,
The rashest, the ruddyest, the roundest,
The sagest, the sallowest, the soundest,
The coyest, the curstest, the coldest,
The busiest, the brightest, the boldest,
The thankfullest, the thinnest, the thickest,
The saintliest, the sourest, the sickest—
Take these with all the rest, and of everyone,
So God be my help I love never one!

    Lover Loved. Then I beseech thee this one
      thing tell me—

How many women thinkest thou dost love thee?

    Neither Lover nor Loved. Sir, as I be
      saved, by ought I can prove,

I am beloved even like as I love.

Lover Loved.   Then, as appeareth by those
   words rehearsed,
Thou art nother lover nor beloved.
   Neither Lover nor Loved.   Nother lover nor
   beloved, that is even true !
Lover Loved.   Since that is true I marvel
   what can ensue   [avaunt,
For proof of thy part, in that thou madest
Of both our estates, to prove thine most
   pleasant.   [pleasant may soon be guessed
Neither Lover nor Loved.   My part for most
By my continual quieted rest.   [quiet be?
   Lover Loved.   Being no lover, who may
   Neither Lover nor Loved.   Nay, being a
   lover, what man is he
That is quiet?
   Lover Loved.   Marry, I !
   Neither Lover nor Loved.   Marry, ye lie !
   Lover Loved.   What ! patience my friend, ye
   are too hasty !
If ye will patiently mark what I shall say
Yourself shall perceive me in quiet alway.
   Neither Lover nor Loved.   Say what thou
   will, and I therein protest
To believe no word thou sayest, most nor lest.
   Lover Loved.   Then we twain shall talk both
   in vain, I see,
Except our matter awarded may be
By judgment of some indifferent hearer.
   Neither Lover nor Loved.   Marry ! go thou
   and be an inquirer;
And, if thou canst bring one anything lyckly,
He shall be admitted for my part quickly.
   Lover Loved.   Now, by the good God, I
   grant to agree;
For, be thou assured it scorneth me

That thou shouldst compare in pleasure to be
Like me; and surely, I promise thee,
One way or other, I will find redress.
    Neither Lover nor Loved. Find the best and
      next way thy wit can guess;
And, except your nobs for malice do need ye,
Make brief return, a fellowship speed ye!
              [*The Lover Loved goeth out.*
    Neither Lover nor Loved. My marvel is no
      more than my care is small
What knave this fool shall bring, being not
      partial;
And yet, be he false and a foolish knave too,
So that it be not much ado,
To bring a daw to hear and speak right
I foresee for no man the worth of a mite.
And since my doubt is so small in good speed
What should my study be more than my need?
Till time I perceive this woodcock coming
My part hereof should pass even in mumming.
Saving for pastime, since I consider,
He being a lover and all his matter
To depend on love, and contrary, I
No lover, by which all such standing by
As favour my part, may fear me too weak
Against the loving of this lover to speak
I shall, for your comfort, declare such a story
As shall perfectly plant in your memory
That I have knowledge in lovers' laws
As deep as some dozen of those doting daws.
Which told, all ye whose fancies stick near me,
Shall know it causeless in this case to fear me.
For though, as I show, I am no lover now,
Nor never have been, yet shall I show you
How that I once chanced to take in hand
To feign myself a lover, ye shall understand,

Toward such a sweeting, as by sweet scent
    savour,
I know not the like in fashion and favour.
And to begin   So fair, so ruddy,
At setting in: It axeth study
First was her skin   The whole to tell,
White, smooth and   It did excel;
And every vein [thin;   It was so made
So blue seen plain;   That even the shade
Her golden hair;   At every glade
To see her wear   Would hearts invade;
Her wearing gear,   The paps so small,
Alas! I fear,   And round withal;
To tell all to you   The waist not mickle,
I shall undo you;   But it was tickle;
Her eye so rolling   The thigh, the knee
Each heart control-   As they should be;
   ling;   But such a leg
Her nose not long,   A lover would beg
Nor stood not wrong;   To set eye on
Her finger tips   But it is gone;
So clean she clips;   Then sight of the
Her rosy lips—   foot   [root;
Her cheeks gossips—   Rift hearts to the
And last of all, Saint Katherine's wheel
Was never so round as was her heel.
Assault her heart and who could win it;
As for her heel do hold in it;
Let over that her beauty was so much;
In pleasant qualities her graces were such
For dalliant pastaunce, pass where she should,
No greater difference between lead and gold
Than between the rest and her; and such a wit
That no wight I ween might match her in it;
If she had not wit to set wise men to school
Then shall my tale prove me a stark fool.

But, in this matter to make you meet to guess,
Ye shall understand that I with this mistress
Fell late acquainted; and for love no whit,
But, for my pleasure, to approve my wit,
How I could love to this tricker dissemble
Who, in dissimilling, was perfect and nimble.
For, where or when she list to give a mock
She could, and would, do it beyond the nock.
Wherein I thought that if I teased her
I should thereby like my wit the better;
And, if she chanced to trip or trise me,
It should to learn wit a good lesson be.
Thus, for my pastime, I did determine
To mock, or be mocked, of this mocking
          vermin.
For which her presence I did first obtain,
And that obtained, forthwith fell we twain
In great acquaintance, and made as good cheer
As we had been acquainted twenty year.
And I, through fair flattering behaviour,
Seemed anon so deep in her favour
That though the time then so far passed was,
That time required us asunder to pass,
Yet could I no passport get of my sweeting
Till I was full wooed for the next day's meet-
For surance whereof I must, as she bade, [ing;
Give her in gage best jewel I there had.
And, after much mirth as our wits could devise,
We parted; and I the next morn did arise,
In time, not too timely, such time as I could:
I allow no love where sleep is not allowed.
I was, or I entered this journey vowed,
Decked very cleanly, but not very proud;
But trim must I be, for slovenly lobers
Have, ye wot well, no place among lovers.
But I thus decked at all points point device,

At door where this trull was I was as a trice.
Whereat I knocked, her presence to win;
Wherewith it was opened, and I was let in;
And, at my first coming my minion seemeth
Very merry, but anon she misdeemed
That I was not merrily disposed.
And so might she think, for I disclosed
No word nor look, but such as showed as sadly
As I indeed inwardly thought madly:
And so must I show, for lovers be in rate
Sometimes merry, but most times passionate.
In giving thanks to her of over night
We set us down an heavy couple in sight;
And therewithal I set a sigh, such one
As made the form shake which we both sat on.
Whereupon she, without more words spoken,
Fell in weeping as her heart should have
And I, in secret, laughing so heartily   [broken;
That from mine eyes came water plenteously.
Anon I turned, with look sadly, that she
My weeping as watery as hers might see;
Which done, these words anon to me she
        spake.   [take
" Alas! dear heart, what wight might under-
To show one so sad as you this morning,
Being so merry as you last evening;
I so far then the merrier for you,
And without desert thus far the sadder now."
" The self thing," quoth I, " which made me
        then glad,
The selfsame is thing that maketh me now sad;
The love that I owe you is original,
Ground of my late joy and present pain all.
And, by this mean, love is evermore lad
Between two angels, one good and one bad—
Hope and Dread—which two be alway at strife,

Which one of them both with love shall rule
    most rife.   [night
And Hope, that good angel, first part of last
Drew Dread, that bad angel, out of place quite.
Hope sware I should straight have your love
    at once;   [bones !
And Dread, this bad angel, sware, Blood and
That if I won your love all in one hour
I should lose it all again in three or four
Wherein this good angel hath lost the mastery,
And I, by this bad angel, won this agony.
And be ye sure I stand now in such case
That, if I lack your continued grace,
In heaven, hell, or earth, there is not that he
Save only God that knoweth what shall come
I love not in rate all the common flock, [on me.
I am no feigner, nor I cannot mock;
Wherefore I beseech you that your reward
May witness that ye do my truth regard.''
'' Sir, as touching mocking,'' quoth she, '' I
    am sure
Ye be too wise to put that here in ure.
For nother give I cause why ye so should do,
Nor nought could ye win that way worth an old
    shoe.
For, whoso that mocketh shall surely stir
This old proverb, *Mockum moccabitur.*
But, as for you, I think myself assured
That very love hath you hither allured.
For which,'' quoth she, '' let Hope hop up
    again,
And vanquish Dread so that it be in vain
To Dread or to doubt, but I in everything,
As cause giveth cause, will be your own
    darling.''   [smarts
'' Sweetheart,'' quoth I, '' after stormy cold

Warm words in warm lovers bring lovers warm
    hearts.   [now
And so have your words warmed my heart even
That, dreadless and doubtless now must I love
    you."
Anon there was " I love you," and " I love
    you "—
Lovely we lovers love each other.
" I love you," and " I, for love, love you—
My lovely loving loved brother."
" Love me," " love thee," " love we," " love
    he," " love she."
Deeper love apparent in no twain can be;
Quite over the ears in love, and felt no
    ground—   [drowned.
Had not swimming holpe in love I had been
But I swam by the shore, the vantage to keep
To mock her in love seeming to swim more
Thus continued we, day by day,   [deep.
Till time that a month was passed away,
In all the which time such a wayt she took
That, by no mean I might once set one look
Upon any woman in company
But straightway she set the finger in the eye.
And, by that same aptness in jealousy,
I thought sure she loved me perfectly;
And I, to show myself in like loving,
Dissimilled like cheer in all her like looking.
By this, and other like things then in hand,
I gave her mocks, methought, above a
    thousand.
Whereby I thought her own tale like a burr
Stuck to her own back—*Mockum moccabitur!*
And upon this I fell in devising
To bring to end this idle disguising.
Whereupon, suddenly, I stole away;

And, when I had been absent half a day [me !—
My heart misgave me—by God that bought
That if she missed me where I thought she
    sought me   [me.
She sure would be mad by love that she ought
Wherein, not love, but pity so wrought me
That to return anon I bethought me;
And so returned till chance had brought me
To her chamber door, and hard I knocked.
"Knock soft," quoth one who the same un-
    locked—
An ancient wise woman who was never
From this said sweeting, but about her ever.
"Mother," quoth I, "how doth my dear
    darling?"   [absenting."
"Dead, wretch," cried she, "even by thine
And without mo words the door to her she shyt,
I, standing without, half out of my wit
In that this woman should die in my fault.
But since I could in there by none assault,
To her chamber window I gat about
To see, at the last way, the corse laid out;
And there, looking in, by God's blessed
I saw her naked abed with another; [mother !
And with her bedfellow laughed me to scorn
As merrily as ever she laughed beforne.
The which, when I saw, and then remembered
The terrible words that mother brendered,
And also bethought me of everything
Showed in this woman true love betokening,
Myself to see served thus prately
To myself I laughed even heartily,
With myself considering to have had like speed
If myself had been a lover indeed.
But now to make some matter whereby
I may take my leave of my love honestly—

" Sweetheart," quoth I, " ye take too much
      upon ye."   [quoth she,
" No more than becomes me, know thou well,"
" But thou hast taken too much upon thee
In taking that thou took in hand to mock me.
Wherein, from beginning, I have seen thee jet
Like as a fool might have jetted in a net,
Believing himself, save of himself only,
To be perceived of no living body.
But well saw I thine intent and beginning
Was to bestow a mock on me at ending. [heart,
When thou laughedst, dissimilling a weeping
Then I, with weeping eyes, played even the like
      part,
Wherewith I brought in, *Moccum moccabitur.*
And yet thou, being a long snouted cur,
Could no whit smell that all my meaning was
To give mock for mock, as now is come to
      pass.   [some,
Which now, thus passed, if thy wit be hand-
May defend thee from mocks in time to come
By clapping fast to thy snout every day,
Moccum moccabitur, for a nosegay."   [to ;
Wherewith she start up and shut her window
Which done, I had no more to say nor do
But think myself, or any man else, a fool
In mocks or wiles to set women to school.
But now to purpose wherefore I began :
Although I were made a fool by this woman
Concerning mocking, yet doth this tale approve
That I am well seen in the art of love.
For I, intending no love, but to mock,
Yet could no lover of all the whole flock
Circumstance of love disclose more nor better
Than did I, the substance being no greater.
And, by this tale afore, ye all may see

Although a lover as well loved be
As love can devise him for pleasant speed,
Yet two displeasures—jealousy and dread—
Is mixed with love; whereby love is a drink
    meet   [sweet.
To give babes for worms, for it drinketh bitter
And, as for this babe, our lover, in whose head
By a frantic worm his opinion is bred,
After one draught of this medicine ministered
Into his brain by my brain appointed,
Reason shall so temper his opinion
That he shall see it not worth an onion.
And if he have any other thing to lay
I have to convince him every way.
And since my part now doth thus well appear,
Be ye, my partners, now all of good cheer—
But, silence, every man, upon a pain,
For Master Woodcock is now come again.
                        [*The Lover Loved entereth.*

  Lover Loved. The old saying saith, he that
    seeketh shall find;
Which, after long seeking, true have I found.
But, for such a finding myself to bind,
To such a seeking as I was now bound,
I would rather seek to lose twenty pound.
Howbeit I have sought so far to my pain
That at the last I have found and brought
    twain.
[*The Lover not Loved, and Loved not Loving
    entereth.*

  Neither Lover nor Loved. Come they a-
    horseback?

  Lover Loved. Nay, they come a-foot, [mist.
Which thou might see here, but for this great

  Neither Lover nor Loved. By Jys! and yet
    see I, thou blind bald coot!

That one of those twain might ride if he list.
    Lover Loved. How?
    Neither Lover nor Loved. Marry! for he
    leadeth a nag on his fist—
Mistress, ye are welcome, and welcome ye be!
    Loved not Loving. Nay, welcome be ye, for
    we were here before ye!
    Neither Lover nor Loved. Ye have been
    here before me before now,
And now I am here before you,
And now I am here behind ye,
And now ye be here behind me,
And now we be here even both together,
And now be we welcome even both hither.
Since now ye find me here, with courtesy I may
Bid you welcome hither, as I may say.
But, setting this aside, let us set a-broach
The matter wherefore ye hither approach;
Wherein I have hope that ye both will be
Good unto me, and especially ye;
For I have a mind that every good face
Hath ever some pity of a poor man's case,
Being as mine is a matter so right
That a fool may judge it right at first sight.
    Lover not Loved. Sir, ye may well doubt
    how my wit will serve,
    But my will from right shall never swerve.
    Loved not Loving. Nor mine, and as ye sue
    for help to me,
Like suit have I to sue for help to ye,
For as much need have I of help as you.
    Neither Lover nor Loved. I think well that,
    dear heart, but tell me how!
    Loved not Loving. The case in this: ye
    twain seem in pleasure,
And we twain in pain; which pain doth procure,
                              M

By comparison between him and me,
As great a conflict which of us twain be
In greatest pain, as is between ye twain [main.
Which of you twain in most pleasure doth re-
Wherein we somewhat have here debated,
And both, to tell truth, so greedily grated
Upon affection, each to our own side
That, in conclusion, we must needs provide
Some such as would and could be indifferent,
And we both to stand unto that judgment.
Whereupon, for lack of a judge in this place,
We sought many places; and yet, in this case,
No man could we meet that meddle will or can,
Till time that we met with this gentleman
Whom, in like errand, for like lack of aid,
Was driven to desire our judgment, he said.
  Lover Loved.   Forsooth! it is so, I promis-
      ing plain,   [plain,
They twain between us twain giving judgment
We twain between them twain should judge
      right again.   [perform I did not disdain;
  Neither Lover nor Loved.   That promise to
For, touching right, as I am a righteous man
I will give you as much right as I can.
  Loved not Loving.   Nothing but right de-
      sire I you among,
I willingly will nother give nor take wrong.
  Neither Lover nor Loved.   Nay, in my
      conscience I think, by this book! [a-crook.
Your conscience will take nothing that cometh
For, as in conscience, whatever ye do,
Ye nothing do but as ye would be done to,
O hope of good end! O Mary mother!
Mistress! one of us may now help another.
But, sir, I pray you some matter declare
Whereby I may know in what grief ye are.

Lover not Loved.   I am a lover not loved,
  which plain
Is daily not doleful but my deadly pain.
  Neither Lover nor Loved.   A lover not loved
    —have ye knit that knot?
  Lover not Loved.   Yea, forsooth.
  Neither Lover nor Loved.   Forsooth! ye be
    the more sot.
Now, mistress, I heartily beseech ye
Tell me what manner case your case may be.
  Loved not Loving.   I am beloved not loving,
    whereby
I am not in pain but in tormentry.
  Neither Lover nor Loved.   Is this your
    torment?   God turn him to good!
  Loved not Loving.   Nay! there is another
    man, one me [h]as woed
As this man on an nother woman is.
  Neither Lover nor Loved.   Ye think them
    both mad, and do I, by Jys!
So mote I thrive, but who that list to mark
Shall perceive here a pretty piece of wark.
Let us fall somewhat in these parts to
  scanning—
Loving not loved, loved not loving,
Loved and loving, not loving nor loved—
Will ye see these four parts well joined?
Loving not loved, and loved not loving—
Those parts can join in no manner reckoning;
Loving and loved, loved nor lover—
These parts in joining in like wise differ.
But, in that ye love ye twain joined be;
  [*Here Neither Loved nor Loved points to his
    co-disputants as the case may be.*
And, being not loved ye join with me;
And being no lover with me joineth she;
                                    M 2

And being beloved with her join ye.
Had I a joiner with me joined jointly,
We joiners should join joint to joint quickly;
For, first I would part these parts in sleses,
And once departed these parted pieces,   [part,
Part and part with part I would so part like
That each part should part with quiet heart.
   Lover not Loved.   Sir, since passeth your
      power that part to play
Let pass, and let us partly now essay
To bring some part of that purpose to end
For which all parties yet in vain attend.
   Loved not Loving.   I do desire the same,
      and that we twain
May first be heard that I may know my pain.
   Lover Loved.   I grant for my part, by faith
      of my body!—
Why, where the devil is this whoreson noddy?
   Neither Lover nor Loved.   I never in justice
      but evermore
I use to be shriven a little before;
And now, since that my confession is done,
I will depart and come take penance soon.
When conscience pricketh, conscience must be
      searched by God   [bod;
In discharging of conscience, or else God for-
Which maketh me mets, when conscience must
      come in place,
To be a judge in every common case;
But who may like me, his avancement avaunt,
Now am I a judge and never was servant,
Which ye regard not much, by ought that I
By any reference that ye do to me.   [see,
Nay, yet I praise women; when great men go
      by   [they lie:
They crouch to the ground—look here how

They shall have a beck by Saint Antony.
But, alas! good mistress, I cry you mercy
That you are unanswered; but ye may see
Though two tales at once by two ears heard
    may be,
Yet cannot one mouth two tales at once answer.
Which maketh you tarry; but, in your matter,
Since ye, by haste, in having furthest home
Would first be sped of that for which ye come,
I grant, as he granted your will to fulfil, [will.
You twain to be heard first—begin when you
    Lover not Loved. As these twain us twain
      now grant first to breke
Since twain to be heard at once cannot speak,
I now desire your grant that I may open
First tale, which now is at point to be spoken;
Which I crave no whit my part to avance,
But with the pith to avoid circumstance.
    Loved not Loving. Speak what and when-
      soever it please you;
Till reason will me, I will not disease you.
    Lover not Loved. Sirs, either here is a very
      weak brain,
Or she hath, if any, a very weak pain;
For, I put case that my love I her gave,
And that, for my love, her love I did crave;
For which, though I daily sue day by day,
What loss or pain to her if she say " Nay " ?
    Neither Lover nor Loved. Yes, by Saint
      Mary! so the case may stand;
That some woman had liever take in hand
To ride on your errand one hundredth mile
Than to say " Nay " one Paternoster while.
    Lover not Loved. If ye, on her part, any
      pain define—
Which is the more painful, her pain or mine?

Neither Lover nor Loved. Your pain is
     most if she say " Nay " and take it;
But, if that she say " Nay," and forsake it—
Then is her pain a great way the greater.
     Loved not Loving. Sir, ye allege this nay
     in this matter
As though my denial my suitor to love [move;
Were all or the most pain that to me doth
Wherein the truth is a-contrary plain. [pain,
For, though too oft speaking one thing be a
Yet is that one word the full of my hoping
To bring his hoping to despair at ending.
Thus is this nay, which ye take my most grief,
Though it be painful yet my most relief.
But my most pain is all another thing,   [ing,
Which, though ye forget or hide by dissimul-
I partly showed you, but all I could nor can.
But, masters! to you, with pain of this man
That pain that I compare is partly this—
I am loved of one whom, the truth is,
I cannot love; and, so it is with me
That, from him, in manner, I never can flee;
And every one word in suit of his part [heart;
Nips through mine ears, and runs through my
His ghastful look, so pale that unneth I
Dare for mine ears cast toward him an eye;
And when I do, that eye my thought presenteth
Straight to my heart, and thus my pain aug-
     menteth.
One tale so oft, alas! and so importune!
His exclamations, sometime on fortune,
Sometime on himself, sometime upon me;
And for that thing that, if my death should be
Brought straight in place except I were content
To grant the same, yet could I not assent;
And he, seeing this, yet ceaseth not to crave—

What death could be worse than this life that
    I have?   [porteth no more
  Lover not Loved. This tale to purpose pur-
But sight and hearing; complaint of his sore
Is only the grief that ye do sustain.
Alas! tender heart, since ye die in pain
This pain to perceive by sight and hearing,
How could you live to know our pain by feel-
    ing?   [can—
Mark well this question, and answer as ye
A man that is hanged or that man's hangman
Which man of those twain suffereth most pain?
  Loved not Loving. He that is hanged.
  Neither Lover nor Loved. By the mass, it
    is so, plain.   [am the sufferer,
  Lover not Loved. Well said for me; for I
And ye the hangman understand, as it were;
These cases vary in no manner a thing
Saving this serves in: this man's hanging
Commonly is done against the hangman's will,
And ye, of delightful will, your lover kill.
  Loved not Loving. Of delightful will! nay,
    that is not so;
As ye shall perfectly perceive ere we go! [by
But of those at whose hanging have hangman
How many have ye known hang willingly?
  Neither Lover nor Loved. Nay, never one
    in his life, by'r lady!
  Loved not Loving. In this, lo! your case
    from our case doth vary;
For ye that love, where love will take no place,
Your own will is your own leader—a plain
    case;
And, not only uncompelled, without allure,
But sore against her will your suit ye endure.
Now, since your will to love did you procure,

And with that will ye put that will in ure;
And now that will by wit seeth love such pain
As witty will would will love to refrain;
And ye, by will that love in each condition
To extinct, may be your own physician.
Except ye be a fool, or would make me one,
What saying could set a good ground to sit on
To make any man think your pain thus strong
Making your own salve your own sore thus
        long?   [this process purposed
   Lover not Loved. Mistress, much part of
Is matter of truth truly disclosed.
My will, without her will, brought me in love;
Which will, without her will, doth make me
        hove
Upon her grace, to see what grace will prove.
But, where ye say my will may me remove,
As well from her love as will brought me to it,
That is false : my will cannot will to do it.
My will as far therein outweighed my power
As a sow of lead outweigheth a saffron flower.
   Loved not Loving. Your will outweigheth
        your power, then where is your wit?
I marvel that ever ye will speak it.
   Lover Loved. Nay, marvel ye mistress
        thereat no whit !
For, as far as this point may stretch in verdict,
I am clearly of this man's opinion.
   Neither Lover nor Loved. And I, contrary,
        with this minion.
   Lover Loved. Then be we come to a de-
        murrer in law.
   Neither Lover nor Loved. Then be ye come
        from a woodcock to a daw;
And, by God ! it is no small cunning, brother,
For me to turn one wild fool to another.

Lover not Loved. Nay, masters, I heartily
  pray you both
Banish contention till ye see how this goeth.
I will repeat and answer her tale forthwith,
The pith for your part whereof pretendeth
A proof for your pain to be more than mine
In that my will not only did me incline   [will,
To the same; but, in the same, by the same
I willingly will to continue still.   [bay,
And, as will brought me, and keepeth in this
When I will, ye say, will will bring me away.
Concluding thereby that, if my pain were
As great as yours, that I should surely bear
As great and good will to flee my love thus
  ment.
As do ye your suitor's presence to absent.
  Loved not Loving. This tale showeth my
    tale perceived every dell.   [it as well,
  Lover not Loved. Then, for entry to answer
Answer this put case: ye as deeply now
Did love your lover as he doth love you,
Should not that loving, suppose ye, redress
That pain which lack of loving doth possess.
  Loved not Loving. Yes.
  Lover not Loved. Since love given to him
    giveth yourself ease, than,
Except ye love pain why love ye not this man?
  Loved not Loving. Love him? nay, as I
    said, must I straight choose
To love him, or else my head here to lose?
I know well I could not, my life to save,
With loving will grant him my love to have.
  Lover not Loved. I think ye speak truly,
    for will will not be
Forced in love, wherefore the same to ye.
Since this is to you such difficulty,

Why not a thing as difficult to me   [set,
To will the let of love, where will my love hath
As you to will to set love where will is your let?
    Loved not Loving. Well said and put,
      cause it as hard now be
For you to will to love her, as for me
To love him; yet have ye, above me, a mean
To learn you, at length, to will to leave love
    clean;   [brought
Which mean many thousands of lovers hath
From right fervent loving to love right nought;
Which long and oft approved mean is absence,
Whereto when ye will ye may have license,
Which I crave, and wish, and cannot obtain,
For he will never my presence refrain.
    Lover not Loved. This is a medicine like
      as ye, would will me—   [me—
For thing to cure me the thing that would kill
For presence of her, though I selde when may
    have,
Is solely the medicine that my life doth save.
Her absence can I with as ill will will
As I can will to leave to love her still.
Thus is this will brought in incidently
No aid in your purpose worth tail of a fly.
And, as concerning our principal matter,
All that ye lay may be laid even a water.
I wonder that shame suffereth you to compare
With my pain, since ye are driven to declare
That all your pain is but sight and hearing
Of him that, as I do, dieth in pain feeling.
O pain upon pain, what pains I sustain!
No craft of the devil can express all my pain;
In this body no limb, joint, sinew, nor vein
But martyreth each other; and this brain,
Chief enemy of all, by the inventing

Mine unsavoury suit to her discontenting;
My speaking, my hearing, my looking, my
    thinking,
In sitting, in standing, in waking, or winking,
Whatever I do, or wherever I go,
My brain and mishap in all these do me woe.
As for my senses, each one of all five
Wondereth as it can to feel itself alive.
And then hath love gotten all in one bed,
Himself and his servants to lodge in this
    head—
Vain hope, despair, dread, and audacity,
Haste, waste, lust, without liking or liberty,
Diligence, humility, trust, and jealousy,
Desire, patient sufferance, and constancy,
These, with other in this head, like swarms of
Sting in debating their contrarities;   [bees,
The venom whereof from this head distilleth
Down to this breast, and this heart it killeth.
All times in all places of this body
By this distemperance thus distempered am I;
Shivering in cold, and yet in heat I die,
Drowned in moisture parched parchment dry.
    Neither Lover nor Loved.   Cold, hot, moist,
        dry, all in all places at once—
Marry! sir, this is an ague for the nonce;
But, or we give judgment I must search to view
Whether this evidence be false or true.
Nay, stand still! your part shall prove never
    the worse.
Lo, by saint Saviour! here is a wet arse,
Let me feel your nose; nay, fear not, man! be
    bold!   [cold,
Well, though this arse be warm, and this nose
Yet these twain, by attorney brought in one
    place

Are, as he saith, cold and wet, both in like
    case.
O, what pain drought is! see how his dry lips
Smack for more moisture of his warm moist
    hips!   [is quicker,
Breathe out, these eyes are dull, but this nose
Here is most moisture, your breath smelleth
    of liquor!   [opened, in this tale telling
    Loved not Loving. Well, since ye have
The full of your pain, for speed to ending
I shall, in few words, such one question dis-
As if your answer give cause to suppose [close
The whole of the same to be answered at full;
We need no judgment for yield myself I will.
Put case: this man loved a woman; such one
Who were in his liking the thing alone,
And that his love to her were not so mickle,
But her fancy toward him were as little;
And that she hid herself so, day and night,
That selde time when he might come in her
    sight.   [bear,
And then put case: that one to you love did
A woman that other so ugly were [Gyb's feast;
That each kiss of her mouth called you to
Or, that your fancy abhorred her so at least
That her presence were a[s] sweet to suppose
As one should present.   [nose!
    Neither Lover nor Loved. A turd to his
    Loved not Loving. Yea, in good faith!
    whereto the case is this,
That her spiteful presence absent never is.
Of these two cases if chance should drive you
To choose one, which would ye choose? tell
What ye study!   [truth now
    Neither Lover nor Loved. Tarry! ye be too
Men be not like women alway ready. [greedy;

Lover not Loved. In good sooth, to tell
   truth, of these cases twain
Which case is the worst is to me uncertain.
   Loved not Loving. First case of these
   twain I put for your part,   [smart;
And by the last case appeareth mine own
If they proceed with this first case of ours
Then is our matter undoubtedly yours;   [fine,
And if judgment pass with this last case, in
Then is the matter assuredly mine;
Since by these cases our parts so do seem
That which is most painful yourself cannot
If ye now will all circumstance eschew, [deem.
Make this question in these cases our issue;
And, the pain of these men to abbreviate,
Set all our other matter as frustrate.
   Lover not Loved. Agreed!
   Loved not Loving. Then, further, to
   abridge your pain
Since this our issue appeareth thus plain,
As folk not doubting your conscience nor cun-
   ning,
We shall, in the same let, pass all reasoning,
Yielding to your judgment the whole of my
   part.   [with will and good heart.
   Lover not Loved. And I, likewise, mine
   Neither Lover nor Loved. So lo! make you
   low curtsey to me now,   [you.
And straight I will make as low curtsey to
Nay, stand ye near the upper end, I pray ye,
For the nether end is good enough for me;
Your cases which include your grief each whit
Shall dwell in this head.
   Lover Loved. And in mine, but yet,
Or that we herein our judgment publish,
I shall desire you that we twain may finish

As far in our matter toward judgment
As ye have done in yours; to the intent
That we our parts, brought together thither,
May come to judgment fro thence together.
    Neither Lover nor Loved. By'r lady, sir,
        and I desire the same !
    Loved not Loving. I would ye began.
    Lover not Loved. Begin then, in God's
    Lover Loved. Shall I begin?   [name !
    Neither Lover nor Loved. Since I look but
        for winning
Give me the end and take you the beginning.
    Lover Loved. Who shall win the end, the
        end at end shall try;
For my part, whereof now thus begin I,
I am, as I said, a beloved lover;
And he no lover nor beloved nother;
In which two cases he maketh his avaunt
Of both our parts to prove his most pleasant;
But, be ye assured, by ought I yet see,
In his estate no manner pleasure can be.
    Neither Lover nor Loved. Yes ! two manner
        pleasures ye must needs confess—
First I have the pleasure of quietness,
And the second is I am contented.
    Lover Loved. That second pleasure, now
        secondly invented,
To compare with pleasure by contentation
Is a very second imagination.
    Neither Lover nor Loved. Then show your
        wit for proof of this in hand—
How may pleasure without contentation stand?
    Lover Loved. Pleasure without contentation
        cannot be;
But contentation without pleasure we see
In things innumerable every day;

Of all which, mark these which I shall now lay.
Put case that I, for pleasure of, some friend,
Or something which I longed to see at end,
Would be content to ride three score mile this
    night,
And never would bait nor never alight—
I might be right well content to do this,
And yet, in this doing, no pleasure there is.
Moreover, ye by patient sufferance
May be contented with any mischance,
The loss of your child, friend, or anything
That in this world to you can belonging
Wherein ye, contented never so well,
Yet is your contentation pleasure no dell.
    Neither Lover nor Loved.   These two exam-
        ples, by aught that I see,
Be nothing the things that anything touch me.
With death of my child my being contented,
Or pain with my friend willingly assented,
Is not contentation voluntary:
For that contentation cometh forcibly;
But my contentation standeth in such thing
As I would first wish if it went by wishing.
    Lover Loved.   Sir, be ye contented even as
Yet your contentation can nother excel, [ye tell,
Nor be compared equal to mine estate;
For, touching contentation, I am in rate
As highly contented to love as ye see,
As ye to forbear love can wish to be.
Had I no more to say in this argument
But that I am, as well as you, content,
Yet hath my part now good approbation
To match with yours even by contentation.
But contentation is not all the thing
That I, for my love, have in recompensing.
Above contentation pleasures feeling

Have I so many, that no wight living
Can by any wit or tongue the same report.
O, the pleasant pleasures in our resort!
After my being from her any wither
What pleasures have we in coming together!
Each tap on the ground toward me with her
Doth bath in delight my very heart root; [foot
Every twink of her alluring eye
Reviveth my spirits even throughoutly;
Each word of her mouth, not a preparative,
But the right medicine of preservative;
We be so jocund and joyfully joined,
Her love for my love so currently coined,
That all pleasures earthly, the truth to declare,
Are pleasures not able with ours to compare.
This mouth, in manner, receiveth no food;
Love is the feeding that doth this body good;
And this head despiseth all these eyes winking
Longer than love doth keep this heart thinking
To dream on my sweetheart; love is my feeder,
Love is my lord, and love is my leader!
Of all mine affairs in thought, word, and deed,
Love is the Christ cross that must be my speed!
    Neither Lover nor Loved.   By this, I per-
        ceive well, ye make reckoning
That love is a goodly and a good thing.
    Lover Loved.   Love good! what ill in love
        canst thou make appear?
    Neither Lover nor Loved.   Yes, I shall
        prove this love, at this time meant here,
In this man's case, as ill as is the devil;
And, in your case, I shall prove love more evil.
What tormentry could all the devils in hell
Devise to his pain that he doth not tell?
What pain bringeth that body these devils in
        that head

Which ministers alway by love are led?
He freezeth in fire, he drowneth in drought;
Each part of his body love hath brought about,
Where each to help other should be diligent,
They martyr each other the man to torment;
That no fiend may torment man in hell more!
Without stint of rage his pains be so sore
And, as in your case, to prove that love is
Worse than the devil, my meaning is this:
Love distempereth him by torment in pain,
And love distempereth you as far in joy plain.
Your own confession declareth that ye
Eat, drink, or sleep even as little as he;
And he that lacketh any one of those three,
Be it by joy, or by pain, clear ye see
Death must be sequel however it be.
And thus are ye both brought by love's induc-
     tion,
By pain or by joy, to like point of destruction;
Which point approveth love, in this case past,
Beyond the devil in tormentry to have a cast;
For I trow ye find not that the devil can find
To torment man in hell by any pleasant mind:
Whereby, as I said, I say of love still—
Of the devil and love, love is the more ill.
And, at beginning, I may say to you,
If God had seen as much as I say now
Love had been Lucifer; and doubt ye no whit
But experience now hath taught God such wit
That, if aught come at Lucifer other than good
To whip souls on the breech, love shall be the
     blood.
And sure he is one that cannot live long,
For aged folk ye wot well cannot be strong;
And another thing his physician doth guess
That he is infect with the black jaundice.

N

Lover Loved.   No further than ye be infect
 with folly !
For, in all these words no word can I espie
Such as, for your part, any proof avoucheth.
 Neither Lover nor Loved.   For proof of my
 part? no ! but it toucheth
The disproof of yours; for where you alleged
Your part above mine to be compared   [such
By pleasures in which your displeasures are
That ye eat, drink, nor sleep, or at most not
 much,
In lack whereof my tale proveth plainly
Each part of your pleasure a tormentry;
Whereby your good love I have proved so evil
That love is apparently worse than the devil.
And, as touching my part, there can arise
No manner displeasures nor tormentries
In that I love not, nor am not loved;
I move no displeasures nor none to me moved,
But all displeasures of love fro me absent,
By absence whereof I quietly content.
 Lover Loved.   Sir, where ye said, and think
 ye have said well,
That my joy by love shall bring death in sequel,
In that by the same, in manner, I disdain
Food and sleep, this proverb answereth you
 plain,   [man ''—
'' Look not on the meat, but look on the
Now look ye on me and say what ye can.
 Neither Lover nor Loved.   Nay, for a time
 love may puff up a thing,
But lacking food and sleep death is the ending.
 Lover Loved.   Well, sir, till such time as
 death approve it
This part of your tale may sleep every whit,
And where ye by absent displeasure would

Match with my present pleasure ye seem more
    bold
Than wise, for those twain be far different sure.
    Neither Lover nor Loved. Is not absence of
      displeasure a pleasure?   [pleased;
    Lover Loved. Yes! in like rate as a post is
Which, as by no mean it can be diseased
By displeasure present, so it is true
That no pleasure present in it can ensue,
Pleasures or displeasures feeling sensibly.
A post, ye know well, cannot feel possibly;
And, as a post, in this case, I take you,
Concerning the effect of pleasure in hand now
For any feeling ye in pleasure endure
More than ye say ye feel in displeasure.
    Neither Lover nor Loved. Sir, though the
      effect of your pleasure present
Be more pleasant than displeasure absent,
Yet how compare ye with mine absent pain
By present displeasures in which ye remain?
    Lover Loved. My present displeasures? I
      know none such.
    Neither Lover nor Loved. Know ye no pain
      by love, little nor much?
    Lover Loved. No.
    Neither Lover nor Loved. Then shall I
      show such a thing in this purse
As shortly shall show herein your part the
      worse [*looks in purse*].
Now, I pray God, the devil in hell blind me!
By the mass! I have left my book behind me.
I beseech our lord, I never go hence
If I would not rather have spent forty pence!
But since it is thus I must go fetch it,
I will not tarry, a, sir! the devil stretch it!
    Lover Loved. Farewell, dawcock!

Neither Lover nor Loved.   Farewell, wood-
Lover Loved.   He is gone.   [cock !
Loved not Loving.   Gone, yea ! but he will
   come again anon.   [more disease you ;
   Lover Loved.   Nay, this night he will no
Give judgment heartily even when it please
   you ;   [shall
Which done, sith he is gone, myself straight
Righteously between you give judgment final.
But lord ! what a face this fool hath set here
Till shame defaced his folly so clear ;
That shame hath shamefully, in sight of you all,
With shame driven hence to his shameful fall.
Wherein, although I nought gain by winning
That aught may augment my pleasure in lov-
Yet shall I win thereby a pleasure to see [ing,
That ye shall see the matter pass with me :
What though the profit may lightly be loaden
It grieveth a man to be overtrodden.
Nay, when I saw that his winning must grow
By pain pretending in my part to show,
Then wist I well the noddy must come
To do as he did, or stand and play mum.
No man, no woman, no child in this place
But I durst for judgment trust in this case ;
All doubt of my pain by his proof by any mean
His running away hath now scraped out clean.
Wherefore, give judgment, and I shall return
In place hereby where my dear heart doth so-
And, after salutation between us had, [journ ;
Such as is meet to make lovers' hearts glad,
I shall to rejoice her in merry tidings
Declare the whole rabble of this fool's lesynges.
   [*Here the Vice cometh in running suddenly
      about the place among the audience with
      a high* [*opper tank*] *on his head full of*

squibs fired crying, water! water! fire!
fire! fire! water! water! fire! till the
fire in the squibs be spent.
Lover Loved. Water and fire!
Neither Lover nor Loved. Nay, water for
  fire, I mean.   [out now clean!
Lover Loved. Well, thanked be God, it is
How came it there?   [going
Neither Lover nor Loved. Sir, as I was
To fetch my book, for which was my departing,
There chanced in my way a house hereby
To fire, which is burned piteously;
But marvellously the people do moan
For a woman, they say a goodly one,
A sojourner, whom in this house burned is;
And shouting of the people for help in this
Made me run thither to have done some good;
And, at a window thereof, as I stood
I thrust in my head, and even at a flush
Fire flashed in my face and so took my bush.
Lover Loved. What house?
Neither Lover nor Loved. A house paintëd
  with red ochre,
The owner whereof they say is a broker.
Lover Loved. Then, break heart! alas,
  why live I this day?
My dear heart is destroyed, life and wealth
  away!
Neither Lover nor Loved. What, man! sit
  down and be of good cheer!
God's body! Master Woodcock is gone clear.
O Master Woodcock! fair mot befal ye; [ye.
Of right, Master Woodcock, I must now call
Masters! stand you here afore and rub him,
And I will stand here behind and dub him;
Nay, the child is asleep, ye need not rock—

Master   Woodcock,   Master   Wood-Wood-
    Woodcock!
Where folk be far within a man must knock;
Is not this a pang, trow ye, beyond the nock?
Speak Master Woodcock! speak parrot, I
    pray ye!
My leman, your lady, aye will ye see;
My lady, your leman, one undertakes
To be safe from fire by slipping through a
    jakes.
    Lover Loved.   That word I heard but yet I
    see her not.
    Neither Lover nor Loved.   No more do I,
        Master Woodcock, our lord wot. [see her
    Lover Loved.   Unto that house where I did
I will seek to see her, and if she be past
So that to appear there I cannot make her,
Then will I burn after and overtake her.
                    [*The Lover Loved goeth out.*
    Neither Lover nor Loved.   Well, ye may
        burn together for all this,
And do well enough for aught that is yet amiss.
For God's sake! one run after and baste him,
It were great pity the fire should waste him;
For, being fat, your knowledge must record
A woodcock well roast is a dish for a lord;
And, for a woodcock ye all must now know him
By matter of record that so doth show him.
And briefly to bring you all out of doubt,
All this have I feigned to bring about,
Himself to convince himself even by act
As he hath done here in doing this fact. [now
He taketh more thought for this one woman
Than could I for all in the world, I make avow;
Which hath so shamefully defaced his part
That to return nother hath he face nor heart;

Which seen, whilst he and she lose time in
    kissing,
Give ye with me judgment a God's blessing.
              [*The Lover Loved returneth.*
  Lover Loved. The proof of my saying at
    my first entry   [lied
That wretch bringeth now in place in that I
Dissembling man's mind by appearance to be
Thing inconvenient, which thing, as I said
Is proved now true, how was I dismayed
By his false facing the death of my darling
Whom, I thank God! is in health and aileth
    nothing.
  Neither Lover nor Loved. Sir, I beseech
    you, of all your dismaying,
What other cause can ye lay than your loving?
  Lover Loved. My loving! nay, all the cause
    was your lying. [done if ye had not loved.
  Neither Lover nor Loved. What had my lie
  Lover Loved. What did my love till your lie
    was moved.
  Neither Lover nor Loved. By these two
    questions it seemeth we may make
Your love and my lie to part evenly the stake.
Loving and lying have we brought now hither
Lovers and liars to lay both together
But put case my lie of her death were true—
What excuse for your love could then ensue?
  Lover Loved. If fortune, God save her!
    did bring her to it
The fault were in fortune and in love no whit.
  Neither Lover nor Loved. The whole fault
    in fortune? by my sheth well ye!
God send your fortune better than your wit!
  Lover Loved. Well, sir, at extremity I can
The fault in fortune as much as in love. [prove

Neither Lover nor Loved.   Then fortune in
   like case with love now join you,
As I with loving joined lying even now;
And well they may join all, by aught that I see,
For each of all three I 'take like vanity.
But, sirs, ye confess that your part of such pain
Cometh half by love, and that it is certain
That certain pains to loved lovers do move,
In which the fault in nothing save only love;
As dread and jealousy each of which, with mo,
To your estate of love is a daily foe;
And I clear out of love declaring such show
As in my case no pain to me can grow—
I say this considered hath pith sufficient
In proof of my part to drive you to judgment.
   Lover Loved.   Nay, first a few words, sir,
      though I confess   [painless,
That love bringeth some pain, and your case
By mean of your contented quietness,
Yet th'actual pleasures that I possess
Are as far above the case that ye profess
As is my pain in your imagination
Under the pleasures of contentation.
Thus weighed how ye will, one way or other,
If ye win one way ye shall lose another;
But if ye intend for end to be brief
Join with me herein for indifferent prefe.
A tree, ye know well, is a thing that hath life
And such a thing as never feeleth pain nor
But ever quiet and alway contented;   [strife,
And, as there can no way be invented
To bring a tree displeasure by feeling pain,
So no feeling pleasure in it can remain.
A horse is a thing that hath life also,   [woe,
And he, by feeling, feeleth both wealth and
By driving or drawing all day in the mire,

Many painful journeys hath he in hire,
But after all those he hath alway at night
These pleasures following to his great delight—
First fair washed at a river or a weir;   [fair;
And straight brought to a stable, warm and
Dry rubbed, and chafed from head to heel,
And curried till he be slick as an eel;
Then is he littered in manner nose high,
And hay as much as will in his belly;   [bread,
Then provender hath he, either peas, beans or
Which feeding in feeling as pleasant to his
As to a covetous man to behold,   [head
Of his own, Westminster Hall full of gold;
After which feeding, he sleepeth in quiet rest
During such time as his meat may digest—
All this considered, a horse or a tree
If ye must choose the one which would ye be?
        Neither Lover nor Loved.   When the horse
            must to labour, by our lady!
I had liever be a tree than a horse I!
        Lover Loved.   But how when he resteth and
            filleth his gorge?
        Neither Lover nor Loved.   Then would I be
            a horse and no tree, by Saint George!
        Lover Loved.   But what if ye must needs
            stick to the one?
        Neither Lover nor Loved.   Which were
            then best, by the mass! I can name none.
        Lover Loved.   The first case is yours, and
            the next is for me:
In case like a tree I may liken ye;
For, as a tree hath life without feeling
Whereby it feeleth pleasing nor displeasing,
And cannot be but contented quietly,
Even the like case is yours now presently.
And, as the horse feeleth pain and not the tree,

Likewise I have pain and no pain have ye.
And, as a horse above a tree feeleth pleasure,
So feel I pleasure above you in rate sure;
And, as the tree feeleth nother, and the horse
          both,   [goeth.
Even so pleasure and pain between us twain
Since these two cases so indifferently fall
That yourself can judge, nother for partial,
For indifferent end I think this way best :
Of all our reasoning to debar the rest
And in these two cases this one question
To be the issue that we shall join on.

    Neither Lover nor Loved.   Be it so !
    Lover Loved.   Now are these issues chosed
          so nigh
That both sides, I trust, shall take end shortly.
    Lover not Loved.   I hope and desire the
          same, and since we
Were first heard, we both humbly beseech ye,
That we in like wise may have judgment first.
    Lover Loved.   I grant.
    Neither Lover nor Loved.   By the mass !
          and I come best or worst.
    Lover Loved.   Though nature force man
          stiffly to incline
To his own part in each particular thing, [mine
Yet reason, would man, when man shall deter-
Other men's parts by indifferent awarding,
Indifferent to be in all his reasoning ;
Wherefore, in this part cut we off affection,
So that indifferency be our direction.
    Neither Lover nor Loved.   Contented with
          that, and by ought I espy
We may, in this matter, take end quickly.
Scan we their cases as she did apply them
That we may perceive what is meant by them.

He loveth unloved a goodly one—
She is loved, not loving, of an ugly one;
Or, in his eye his lover seemeth goodly,
And in her eye her lober seemeth as ugly;
Her most desired angel's face he cannot see,
His most lotely hell-hound's face she cannot
    flee;
He loveth, she abhorreth; whereby presence is
His life, her death; whereby I say even this,
Be his feelings pains in every degree,
As great and as many, as he saith they be,
Yet in my judgment by these cases hath she
As great and as many feeling pains as he.
    Lover Loved. When matter at full is in-
      differently laid
As ye in this judgment have laid this now,
What reason the time by me should be delayed?
Ye have spoken my thought; wherefore, to
    you,
In peasing your pains my conscience doth allow
A just counterpoise, and thus your pains be
A-judged by us twain one pain in degree.
    Lover not Loved. Well, since your con-
      science driveth you thus to judge, [grudge.
I receive this judgment without grief or
    Loved not Loving. And I, in like rate,
      yielding unto you twain.
Hearty thanks for this your undeserved pain.
    Lover nor Loved. Now, mistress, may it
      please you to declare,
As touching their parts, of what mind ye are.
    Loved not Loving. With right good will,
      sir, and sure I suppose   [well.
Their parts in few words may come to point
The two examples, which he did disclose,
All errors or doubts do clearly expel.

The estate of a tree his estate doth tell;
And, of the horse, his tale well understand
Declareth as well his case now in hand.
For, as nothing can please or displease a tree,
By any pleasure or displeasure feeling,
Nor never bring a tree discontent to be,
So like case to him not loved nor loving
Love can no way bring pleasing or displeasing :
Live women, die women, sink women, or
      swim—
In all the content, for all is one to him.
And, as a horse hath many painful journeys,
A lover best loved hath pains in likewise;
As here hath appeared by sundry ways;
Which showeth his case in worst part to arise.
But then, as the horse feeleth pleasure in sise,
At night, in the stable above the tree,
So feeleth he some pleasure as far above ye.
In some case he feeleth much more pleasure
      than ye;   [less;
And, in some case, he feeleth even as much
Between the more and the less it seemeth to me
That, between their pleasures no choice is to
      guess :
Wherefore, I give judgment in short process—
Set the one pleasure even to the other.
      Neither Lover nor Loved. Womanly spoken,
      mistress, by the rood's mother !
      Lover not Loved. Who heareth this tale
      with indifferent mind,
And seeth, of these twain, each one so full bent
To his own part, that nother in heart can find
To change pleasures with other, must needs
      assent   [ment :
That she in these words hath given right judg-
In affirmance whereof I judge and award

Both these pleasures of yours as one in regard.
    Lover Loved. Well, since I think ye both
    without corruption,
I shall move no matter of interruption.
    Neither Lover nor Loved. Nor I ! but mis-
    tress, though I say naught in this
May I not think my pleasure more than his?
    Loved not Loving. Affection unbridled may
    make us all think
That each of us hath done other wrong;
But, where reason taketh place it cannot sink,
Since cause to be partial here is none us among.
That one head that would think his one wit so
    strong
That on his judges he might judgment devise,
What judge in so judging could judge him
    wise?   [contenteth me.
    Lover Loved. Well, mine estate right well
    Neither Lover nor Loved. And I, with mine
    as well content as ye. [wise be contented
    Lover not Loved. So should ye both like-
Each other to see content in such degree
As, on our parts, our judgment hath awarded;
Your neighbour in pleasure like yourself to be;
Gladly to wish Christ's precept both bind ye :
Thus contentation should alway prefer
One man to joy the pleasure of another.
    Lover Loved. True ! and contentation may
    be in like case
Although no health yet help and great relief
In both your pains; for, ye having such grace
To be contented in sufferance of grief
Shall, by contentation, avoid much mischief,
Such as the contrary shall surely bring you
Pain to pain as painful as your pain is now.
Thus, not we four, but all the world beside

Knowing themself or other in joy or pain,
Hath need of contentation for a guide;
Having joy or pain content let us remain
In joy or pain of other, flee me disdain!
Be we content, wealth or woe, and each for
Rejoice in the one and pity the other. [other
   Lover not Loved. Since such contentation
     may hardly accord
In such kind of love as here hath been meant,
Let us seek the love of that loving Lord
Who, to suffer passion for love was content;
Whereby His lovers, that love for love assent,
Shall have in fine above contentation
The feeling pleasure of eternal salvation.
Which Lord of Lords, whose joyful and blessed
Is now remembered by time presenting— [birth
This accustomed time of honest mirth—
That Lord we beseech in most humble meaning
That it may please Him, by merciful hearing,
The state of this audience long to endure
In mirth, health, and wealth, to grant His
   pleasure.
AMEN.

Printed at London in Farster Laen
by Johan Waley.
Cum priuilegio ad imprimendum solum.

A DIALOGUE CONCERNING
WITTY AND WITLESS

(191)

Interlocutors:

JOHN   JAMES
        JEROME

A DIALOGUE CONCERNING
WITTY AND WITLESS

[The introduction is lost : little, however, can be missing]

John. A marvellous matter, merciful lord,
If reason with this conclusion accord,
Better to be a fool, than a wise man.
   James. Better or worse, I say as I began,
Better is for man that may be witless
Than witty.
   John. Ye show some witty wittiness. [true,
   James. Experience shall witness my tale
And for temporal wealth let us first view :
And that experience may show the truer,
Accept we reason to be our viewer,
In which reason by experience we know
That folk most witty, to whom there doth grow
By friends dead before, nought left them be-
Nor by living friends no living assign,   [hind,
Except they will starve, their finding must they
    find
By much pain of body or more pain of mind.
And as for the witless, as who saith the sot,
The natural fool call'd or th'idiot :   [strain,
From all kinds of labour that doth pain con-
As far as sufficiency needeth obtain,
In surety of living the sot doth remain.   [pain,
   John. In surety of living, but not without
For admit all sots in case as be many

(193)   o

That live without labour, yet where is any
But for that one pleasure, he hath more pain
Than the witty worker in all doth sustain.
What wretch so feareth pain having any wit
Like the witless wretch?—none! if ye mark
Who cometh by the sot who cometh he by [hit;
That vexeth him not some way usually.
Some beat him, some bob him,
Some joll him, some job him,
Some tug him by the arse,
Some lug him by the ears,
Some spit at him, some spurn him,
Some toss him, some turn him,
Some snap him, some scratch him,
Some cramp him, some cratch him,
Some cuff, some clout him,
Some lash him, some lout him,
Some whisse him, some whip him,
With sharp nails some nip him,   [fool,
Not even Master Somer, the king's grace's
But tasteth some time some nips of new school.
And beside this kind of frettling p'suming,
Another kind of torment in consuming
The witty to the witless oft Invent,
After Invention of yer full intent.
The fool of flattery to torment is brought,
So far overjoy'd, and his brain so wide
        wrought,
That by joy of a jewel scant worth a mite
The sot oft sleepeth no wink in a whole night;
And for ensample with a Walsingham ring,
This distemperance to the sot ye may bring,
And make him joy therein as it were a thing
Of price to pay the ransom of a king.
In joying whereof, if any man got way,
To get it from him as every child may,

Then man and child seeth the sot in such case
That nought but painful sorrow taketh any
    place.
By these small proofs a small wit may guess
That wide were the witty to wish them witless.
    James. Th'effect of this your matter as ye
        speak it,
Standeth much in two points as I take it,
Of which twain the tone is, that the sot hath
By jolling and jobbing and other like scath,
Extreme pain with extremity of yer;
Th'other is after fretting furious fire,
That the fool with each fruitless trifling toy
Is so distempered with distemperate joy,
That as much pain bringeth his pleasant
    passion,   [fashion:
As doth the pinching of his most painful
These two points considered, the sot as ye say,
Hath some pain sometime, but most times I
    say nay.   [witless are brought.
    John. Then from no pain to some pain the
    James. Yea, but witty and witless wittily
        wrought
By some pain to such pain that witty feel most,
Then witty and witless each part his part boast;
Take, of witty the degrees, and number all,
And of that number I think the number small
But that each one of them is of need assigned
To labour sore, in body or else in mind;
And few to all that fortune so doth favour
But in body and mind both they do labour,
And of body these labours the most painfullest
Is the labour of mind, I have heard guessed.
And lest both pains or most of twain be too
    tough   [enough;
For you to match with, and the least pain

To the first most pain of the witless noddy,
Join we the wittiest least pain, pain of body;
Who seeth what pain labour bodily bringeth,
Shall   easily   see   thereby,   how   the   body
        wringeth;   [ing,
Husbandmen's ploughing, or earing and sow-
Hedging and ditching, with reaping and mow-
        ing;
In carting such lifting, such burdens bearing,
That pain of the body bringeth these to staring;
And much of this done in time of such het
That in cold cave covered the carcase must
        sweat.   .   [small,
Some other use crafts in which work is so
That in summer pleasantly they live all, [wark,
Who in winter when husbandmen warm with
In that they may not stir, for cold are even
        stark,
Some in winter freeze, some in summer fry,
And the witless doth neither, for commonly
Other with worshipful or honourable,
He temperately standeth in house at the table;
And of all his labours reckon the whole rabble,
Bigger burden beareth he none than his babble;
So that from these pains, or the like received,
The witless hath warrant to be acquitted.
And sure the sot's pleasure in this last acquittal
Countervaileth his pain, in your first recital,
For unto the sot's nipping and beating,
Join the witty labourer's nips and fretting,
And whether ye count by year, month, or week,
Ye shall find these of the witty to seek,
As far as of the witless; and of both sorts
This is the difference; that to me imports [self.
Sots are coiled of other, the witty coileth him-
What choice thus alleged?

John.   Small, ah whoreson elf !
Somewhat he toucheth me now in very deed !
Howbeit to this am not I yet full agreed ;
The witty who beat themselves by business,
May oft in beating favour themselves I guess ;
Such opportunity by wit is oft espied,
That labour by wit is oft qualified,
In taking time or place as best may stand,
Most easily to dispatch things coming in hand.
Wit hath provision alway for relief.
To provide some remedy against mischief ;
Witty take business as witty will make it,
And as witty beat witless, witless must take it.
    James.   Take it how ye list, ye can make it
        no less,
But witty have such pain as my words witness ;
For though wit for time sometime may pain
        prevent,
Yet in most times their foresaid pain is present,
Which pain in the witty wittily weighed,
May match pain of the witless by ye first laid ;
And to the second point for distemperate joys,
By having or hoping of fancies or toys,
In witless or witty both take I as one,   [on,
For though the things that witty have or hope
Are in some kind of account ; things much
        greater   [better,
Than things of the sot's joyings, yet no whit
Nor less pain bringeth that passion, but indif-
        ferent
To both, except witty have the worse torment.
Think you aright, good witty having clearly
A thousand pound suddenly given him yearly,
Who before that hour might dispend no penny,
Nor till that hour never looked for any,
Might not joy as much that sudden receiving,

As joyeth the sot receipt of his Walsingham
      ring?
And thereby be kept from quiet sleep a week,
As well as the ring maketh the sot sleep to
And in a sudden losing that gift again, [seek;
Might not the witty be pressed with pain
As deep as the witless, his ring stolen or lost?
And though this ensample chance seeld when
      at most,
Yet sometime it happeth, and daily we see
That folk far from witless passioned be,
By joyful hope of things to them like to hap,
Or having of things pleasant late light in the
      lap,
As much to their unrest; for distemperancy
As ye showed the witless restless formerly,
And oft-time, for cause considered and weighed
As light as your Walsingham ring aforesaid.
Wit in witty hath seeled such perfection,
To bring disposition full in abjection;
And the difference of disposition is such,
Some wits hope too little, some wits hope too
      much.
By which overmuch I say, and say must ye,
That witty and witless one in this case be.
And thus in both cases, reasoning cause
      showeth,
Cause to conclude, that to the witty groweth
As much pain, as to the witless; whereby,
As good be witless, as witty, say I!
      John.   That conclusion is concluded wisely!
Your prime proposition did put precisely
Better to be witless than witty, and now
As good to be witless as witty say you!
But that wit which puts case in degree com-
      parative,

And concludeth case in degree positive,
Shall not in that case claim degree superlative!
   James. Ye pass in this taunt your preroga-
      tive;   [ning,
But that wit which boasteth the full of his win-
As though he knew th' end of thing at begin-
      ning,
That wit shall show witless impediment,
To be taken witty with wits excellent; [midst,
I conclude here not for th' end, but for the
Which, if ye will hear to end, as reason bids,
Ye shall perceive; and also condescend
To grant me thanks then in that I intend.
Your fall by fierce handling to be the more fair,
To set ye down featly, stair after stair;
And so by a fair figure of induction,   •
To bring your part soft and fair to destruction;
For where ye grant fully, for aught your words
      make,
That as much pain witty as witless do take,—
So from this midst to the end I shall prove,
That most pain of twain to the witless doth
For as I load equally pains of body   [move:
To witty and witless, likewise will I
Overload the witty with pain of mind,
In matter as plain as can be assigned—
Which pain of mind in meet measure to weigh,
Is more painful than pain of body I say.
    John. Ye say so; and said so, but so said
      not I!
Nor say it not yet, but that saying deny;
And till saying prove your saying more plainly,
I will assay to say the contrary!
I think pains of body counted in each kind,
May compare with all kinds of pains of mind.
    James. If ye assuredly think as ye say now,

I think ye think as few men think but you!
Howbeit, that being but an incident,
To principal purpose presently meant;
Yet that exception took you wittily,
For had ye granted that, as ye shall shortly,
Then forthwith should our principal process,
Have concluded in the part that I profess:
For a mean, whereunto as measure may
Meet unmeasurable things, as who say
Join in like proportion, as may be meant,
The mean labourer to the mean student;
And ye shall anon find the student's pain,
More painful than the labourer's labour plain.
    John.   The student's pain is oft pleasantly
      mixed,
In feeling what fruit by his study is fixed.
    James.   The labourer's labour quitteth that
      at a whip,
In feeling the fruit (of) his workmanship;
As much delight carters oft have in carts neat
    trimmed,
As do students in books with gold neat limned:
And as much envy who may drive his cart best,
As among students who may seem learned
    highest.
Whereby inward delight to toll forth each part,
Seemeth me indifferent to art, or to cart!
And further, mean labour in most common
    wise,   [cise,
Is most part handsome, and wholesome exer-
That purgeth humours to man's life and quick-
    ness,
Which study breedeth to man's death or sick-
    ness.
Also, most kinds of labour, most commonly
Strene most gross outward parts of the body;

Where study, sparing shoulders, fingers, and
    toes,
To the head and heart directly study goes.
Pervert is your judgment if ye judge not plain,
That less is the peril, and less is the pain,
The knocking of knuckles which fingers doth
    strain,   [brain?
Than digging in the heart, or drying of the
    John. For common mean kinds in both parts
    now laid,
I see not but reason saith as ye have said.
    James. The labour of body and mind thus
    compare,
In what degrees ye can; devise to declare
Between both, being not knit in such degree
But that th'one from th'other separate may
    be;—
And that both labours in joining ye arecte
As like in degree as wit may conject,—
And both ones searched, search shall make
    warantyse,
In labour of mind the worst pain doth arise.
    John. Methinketh I could make it otherwise
    appear,
Save I lack time to dilate matter here:
For time of reasoning would be long therein,
And time of reasoning must be short herein:
Which weighed with that, this standeth but in-
To our present purpose principally: [cidently
I grant to agree, as ye have defined,
Of labour of body and labour of mind,
That labour or pain of mind is the greater:
And this now granted, what be ye the better?
    James. So much the better, and you so much
    the worse,   [purse,
That ye may now put your tongue in your

For any word in defence your tongue shall tell!
After these my next words, give ear and mark
    well.
This labour of mind, which we now agree
Above labour of body we must decree,
To join sole to the witty; for possibly
Cannot the witless take part of that pain.
    John. Why?   [tion
    James. How can he have pain by imagina-
That lacketh all kinds of consideration?
And in all sense is so insufficient   [be meant
That nought can he think, in ought that may
By any mean to devise any self thing,
Nor device in thing, past present or coming.
No more hath he in mind, either pain or care,
Than hath other Cock-my-horse, or Gyll-my-
    mare!   [penses;
This cause, with witless, pain of mind dis-
But the witty, having all vital senses,
Hath thereby an inward clock, which mark
    who will,   [still.
May oft-times go false, but it never standeth
The plummets of that clock come never to
    ground,
Imagination is watch, and goeth so round,
To which consideration giveth so quick ear,
That in the witty mind the restless rest is there.
A small wit may guess, no one wit can deem
How many, or how much are their pains ex-
    treme,   [breast.
Nor how many contrary kinds in some one
If ye perceive this tale, ye see it witnessed
Three things; of which the first is, that the
    witless
Off labour or pain of mind have release;
The second is, that the witty have in dure

All pains of mind, and that wit doth that pro-
    cure;
Thirdly I glanced at pain of mind, alluding
That pain to be most pain. As in for conclud-
Perceive ye this?   [ing,
    John. Yea! and grant it true, too!
    James. Then must ye grant witty to have
    most pain.
    John. So I do!
    James. If witty have most pain of twain,
    ye must say
Better to be witless than witty.
    John. Nay!
    James. I say, yes!
    John. I say, nay!—and will so inveigh,
That I will hold ye wag another way.
As I grant witty of twain most pain endure,
So will I prove witty to have most pleasure:
Which pleasure shall both drown the wittiest
    pain,
And the pleasure in which the witless remain.
    James. This promise will hardly bring good
    payment;
For it is a strange kind of argument,
To prove him in most pleasure who hath most
    pain,   [sustain.
Or him in least pain who least pleasure doth
    John. Let us reason all pleasure on both
    sides,   [vides.
And then let that side have best that best pro-
    James. All pleasures on both sides! that
    were a thing
To make us make end to-morrow morning!
    John. As now the best part of my part
    cometh on,   [gone!
Ye make marvellous haste, ye would fain be

James.   Right now yourself could weigh in
   right witty sort,   [short.
That reasoning here now, of reason must be
John.   It shall be short enough if ye take
   away
All that part, that for my part, effect doth lay.
   James.   I will nother take away all, nor take
      all;   [shall
But for a mean between both, myself straight
Allege not pleasures all I say, but such one
As overweigheth other pleasures everyone:
Which pleasure where it is fine doth not re-
   main,   .
All pleasures in all parts are pleasures but vain,
Of which one pleasure the witless are sure ever,
And of that pleasure, witty are sure never!
   John.   What pleasure is that?
   James.   Pleasure of salvation!
I think yourself will affirm affirmation
That from our forefathers sin original,
Baptism sealeth us all acquittance general;
And faith of infants, while they infants abide,
In faith of parents for the church is supplied:
Whereby till wit take root of discerning,
And between good and ill give perfect warning,
Wherever innocents, innocency dispute,
For thoughts, words, or deeds, God doth none
   ill impute.
Where God giveth no discerning, God taketh
   none account;
In which case of account, the sot doth amount;
For no more discerneth the sot, at years three
   score,   [before.
Than th'innocent born within years three
This short saying, if ye in mind revolve,
Then shall this long debate forthwith dissolve.

    John. Sir, I grant sots shall be saved as ye
      tell,
And safe shall witty be too; if they do well.
    James. If they do well! that *if* altereth
Th'effect of my sentence to witless! [much, lo,
    John. How so?   [a doubt,
    James. That if laid for the witty purporteth
But all doubts in the witless are scraped clean
    out :
Sans doubt the witless is sure of salvation;
Whereby to conclude this communication,
Make witty sure of all pleasures can be laid,
Doubting lack of none, but this one pleasure
    last said,
And of all pleasures witless to have none,
Saving he standeth in surety of this one,—
Is not the surety of this one much better,
Than of the rest, though the number be greater.
    John. Yes!   [hys,
    James. Like as a goose can say nothing but
So hath he now nothing to say but *yes!*
And in affirming my saying, he saith this,
In which he granteth his part not partly amiss,
But all amiss! as who saith in all places,
The sum whereof in both parts standeth in
    three cases :   [thus—
Off which three th'argument of the first was
In laborious pain of body to discuss
Who suffereth more, the witty or the sot :
In which, by both assents, we knit this knot,—
That as much pain of body in effect hath the
    one,
As th'other, concluding thus far thereupon,—
As good to be witless, as witty; and then
We argued labour or pain of mind in men :
Wherein I driving him to grant pain of mind

More than pain or labour bodily defined;
In the second case, I pain of mind proving
To witty, and not to witless to be moving;—
Drave him to grant further, that by that pain
Better without wit, than with wit to remain.
Now in this third case, where ye made a brag,
By pleasures in the witty to hold me wag;
And pleasures of the witless to overwhelm,
I staming in with him, stack so to the helm,
That his part finally to shipwreck is brought!
The surety of all pleasures in this world
    wrought
Match not the surety of pleasure eternal!
And the state of sots have none account so
    carnal
That God imputeth any ill to them I say.
And the wittiest account augmenteth every day,
And th'auditors wit who shall take th'account
    so clear,
He forgeth not one word in a thousand year!
What need mo words, I think the least wit
    here,
Seeth these three cases on my side appear
That in the two first cases temporally,
And in this third and last case spiritually,
Is seen fully I may conclude finally,
Better to be witless than to be witty.   [lady!
    John. So say I now too, by our blessed
I give up my part, and your part plainly
Of witty and witless I wish now rather,
That my child may have a fool to his father!
The pith of your conclusions be all so pure,
That better be a fool than a wise man sure!
    Jerome. Not so! although your fancy do
        so surmise;
Not better for man to be witless than wise;

Nor so good to be witless as witty nother,
Thus is your wit deceived in other.
   John. Why, what difference between wise
     and witty?   [wisdom and folly.
   Jerome. As much sometime as between
   John. Man can in no wise be wise without
     wit.   [and wisdom nought!
   Jerome. No! and man may have great wit
Wit is the worker of all perceiving,
And indifferent to good or ill working;
And as much wit may be in things of most ill,
As in the best things wit can aspire until;
In virtue or vice I mean: wit hath receipt
Off none ill; where wit upon wisdom doth wait,
Wisdom governeth wit alway, virtue to use,
And all kinds of vice alway to refuse.
Thus is wisdom in good part taken always,
And guideth wit in all things being things of
     praise;   [ground,
Thus, though ye must (as ye need not) grant his
Which is: better witless than witty to be
     found,
Yet as much as wisdom above wit showeth,
So much granted ye him, more than of need
     groweth.   [fresh commoner,
   James. This is some young schoolman, a
Heard ye the principal that planted this jar?
   Jerome. I heard all!
   James. And doth not all on my side fall?
   Jerome. No, if ye had reasoned as I shall.
   James. If ye, as ye say, have heard all he
     said,
And that is that saying have so widely weighed,
To weigh my part worst herein in conclusion,
Then are ye witless, that we two talked on.
But babble your will, this will I bid upon;

Better be sot Somer than sage Solomon!
   Jerome. Give ye sentence, or ye hear what
     I can say, ·
Lo! how will carrieth him and his wit away.
   John. Sir, if ye heard all, in my part how
     say ye,
What did I grant him to far, show I pray ye.
   Jerome. All that ye granted willingly.
   John. Nay, I trow.
   Jerome. Ye shall when we have done, not
     trow, but know
For entry whereto, I pray ye answer me
A question or twain, or mo' if need be.
And first unto this answer as ye can,
Whether would ye be a reasonable man,
Or an unreasonable beast?
   John. Buy and sell!   [and hell,
I would be the simplest man between heaven
Rather than the best beast that ever was bred!
Then if ye of one of the twain must be sped,
Ye would be a maltman, ye a miller,
Rather than a mill-horse?
   John. Be ye my well willer?
   Jerome. Yea!   [man! fye!
   John. Speak no more of this then, what
I would not be a beast, for all this world, I!
Were it for nought else but for this life present.
   Jerome. The time of this life indeed I mean
     and meant.
But tell me why, by your faith, even plainly,
Ye will not change estate with the mill-horse?
   John. Why, there be whys and wherefores
     I think a thousand
In count of two kinds of things coming in hand,
Sensible pleasure, and sensible pain; ·
And, first for pain, sustained in these twain,

Begin with the mill-horse whom ye put for
    prefe,
Or any like beast sustaining the like grief,
An or I would take the pain the poor beasts
    take,   [stake !
I would each day be twigged and tied to a
Carrying fro the mill, carrying to the mill,
Drawing in the mill, poor jade he jetteth still !
Amble he, trot he, go he a foot pace,
Wallop he, gallop he, rack he in trace,
If his pace please not, be it soft or faster,
The spurs or whip shall be his paymaster !
Were not a man, trow ye, in pleasant case,
With a beast in this case to change case or
    place?
No man, except some few so unfortunate
That they be out of tha'count of man's estate,
That would agree to leave to change pains I
    trow,
With beasts' pain, being such as all men know.
Now to speak of pleasure in these twain as-
    signed,
The beasts' to compare is too far behind,
Pleasure discussable in these thus doth fall,—
The beast in effect hath none,—the man hath
The reasonable man's imagination   [all :
Joined with reasonable consideration,
Bringeth man much pleasure in considering
The pleasant property of each pleasant thing,
Possessed to man's behoof at commanding,
Beasts have things of need, but no further
    pleasing.
Since man hath relief for all necessity,
As well as beast, and above beast commodity.
Of pleasures planted for man's recreation,
In the highest kind to man's contentation,

Whereby pleasure in effect between these twain
Showeth thus,—man hath all,—beast hath
   none,—and more pain
Hath beast than reasonable man, by these both
Exchange fro man to beast who will, I would
   be loth.   [defined,
   Jerome. Ye have in my mind this right well
And for cause keep it well awhile in your mind;
Set we aside man and beasts similitude,
And full disposition in both see we viewed,
What thing disposeth most the variety
Between man and beast?
   John. Reason in man, perde.
   Jerome. That man who of reason is as
   destitute
As a beast is, what difference shall we dispute?
   John. Small in this case, except it be this
   one;—   [none.
The sot hath a reasonable soul, beasts have
   Jerome. What helpeth wit of the soul in
   the sot,
Since the body is such it useth it not;
Where impotency planteth such impediments,
That use of senses are void to all intents,
For use of reason; so that for use of wit
They are as beasts witless, using wit nought;
In man thus witless, and the unreasonable
   beast,
I see small difference for this life at least.
   John. I grant the witless and the beast thus
   as one.   [man, and mill-horse, draw on,
   Jerome. Then shall these beasts, witless
Both in one yoke; for think you the number
Standeth as Somer doth, all day in slumber.
Nay! Somer is a sot! fool for a king!
But sots in many other men's housing

Bear water, bear wood, and do in drudgery;
In kitchen, coal-house, and in the nursery:
And daily for faults which they cannot refrain,
Even like the mill-horse, they be whipped
    amain.   [ceits,
Other fools that labour not, have other con-
Upon th'idle fool the flak evermore waits;
They toss him, they turn him, he is job'd and
    jol'd,
With fretting and fuming, as ye afore told:
Except Master Somer, of sots not the best,
But the mill-horse may compare with him for
    rest!
Therefore pleasure conceiving or receiving,
The witless and mill-horse are both as one
    thing!
Your last tale and this tale together conferred,
By matter of both let your answer be heard.
Whether ye would be a man reasonable,
Or unreasonable; and except ye fable
This answer shall show plain and undoubtedly,
Whether ye would be witless or witty.   [full
    John. In good faith I take this conclusion so
That I may give over, and even so I will,
For this life.
    Jerome. Well then for the life to come,
Few words where reason is, may knit up the
    sum.
Concerning pleasure after this life present,
By which he and you dissolved argument;
Both parts by both parties were so ended,
That your part full faintly ye defended;
Though the more merit of our redemption
Stand in Christ's passion, yet in execution
Thereof, shall we stand, by God's justice, ex-
    cept

Having time and wit, his commandments be
    kept;
And who in which doth most diligently
Plant imps of good works, given by God chiefly,
Most highly of God shall he have reward.
    John. How prove ye that?
    Jerome. By Scripture,—have in regard
Christ in the gospel of John doth this declare,—
In the house of my Father, saith Christ, there
    are
Divers and many mansions,—that is to say,
As th'exposition of Saint Awstyne doth
    weigh,—
There are in heaven divers degrees of glory,
To be received of men accordingly;
Each man as he useth God's gifts of grace,
So shall he have in heaven his degree or place.
But, mark this chief ground, the sum of Scrip-
    ture saith   [faith;
We must walk with these gifts in the path of
In which walk who worketh most in God's com-
    mandment,   [like intent:
He shall have most, and Saint Powle showeth
As one star differeth from another in shining,
So the resurrection of the dead; which like
Appeareth in other places of Scripture. [thing
    John. I grant this, and what then?
    Jerome. That what cometh straight in ure,
Since he that useth God's gifts best shall have
    best;   [rest;
And he next, who doeth next, and so for the
And that the witty do daily work or may,
And the witless nought worketh by no way,
So that his reward may compare in degree,
If witty have this advantage, thinketh me,
The wise wittiest place wish I discernfully,

Rather than place of witless.
　　John.　So do I,
If wish would win it ! but where the sot is sure,
The witty standeth in hazardous adventure,
To lose all ; and so in fine fair and well　　[hell.
Instead of way to heaven, to take the way to
In works commanded who in faith walketh not
By God's justice he hath damnation in lot ;
And what other folks feel I cannot tell,
But such frail falls feel I in myself to dwell,
And by them to lose heaven I am so adread,
The sot's surety of least joy there, would God
　　I had !　　　　　　　　　　　　　[good,
An old proverb maketh with this, which I take
Better one bird in hand than ten in the wood !
　　Jerome.　What if of the ten birds in the
　　wood, each one
Were as good as that one in your hand alone,
And that ye might catch them all ten if ye
　　would,　　　　　　　　　　　　　[told !
Would ye not leave one bird, for the ten now
　　John.　Yes !　　　　　　[reasonable pain
　　Jerome.　Would ye not having help, take
For the chance of ten birds for one in gain ?
　　John.　Yes !　　　　　　　[flee this one,
　　Jerome.　Then in God's name fear not ! let
Ye shall, I trust, catch these ten birds every
　　one !
Your fleshly frail falls are such that ye drede
As much as hope, in having heavenly mede ;
By which dread surety of joys there the most
　　small,　　　　　　　　　　　　　[all ;
Wish ye rather than bid venture to have joys
And the sooner by this ye choose this I deem,
The least joy there is more than man can
　　esteem.

But now to remove this block your great drede
We have a lever that removeth dread with
    speed;   [sin,
God suffereth but not willeth he any man to
Nor God willeth no sinner's death, but he be in
Such endless males that his final estate
In lack of penitence make himself reprobate,
In time of this life at each penitent call
Our merciful Maker remitteth sins all,
From the perpetual pain infernal,
Whatever they be, from least to most carnal.
By which goodness of God we are set in hope's
    chair   .   [spair;
Not to breed presumption, but to banish de-
The grace of God alway to grace allureth man,
And when man will call for grace, of grace as-
    sureth man.
To assist man God's commandments to fulfil,
At all times if man cast out ill willing will.
Now since the Christian, that worketh most in
    faith,   [saith,
Shall have most in reward, as the Scripture
And that God's grace by grace called for, will
    assist   [list,—
Man's will to work well, alway when man
And at instant of due ordered penitence,
Man hath God's mercy of all former offence;
Which showeth for mercy man is not mor'
    greedy
To ax, than God to grant mercy is ready.
This seen, what show you to maintain the fear
Which ye toward desperation were in while
    here?
    John.   What show I? nay, the show of that
        fear is extinct,
Even by this pretty tale thus pithily linked!

Since God to the most faithful worker giveth
    most,   [post,
And to make man work much God hasteth as in
And when man hath not wrought at contrition,
God granteth man of damnation remission.
Making man sure of fruit of Christ's passion,
Except man's wilful will mar all good fashion;
By this I dread God, as standeth with love and
    hope,   [grope.
But no desperate dread doth my heart now
    Jerome.   Ten birds in the wood, or one in
Which choose ye now?   [hand alone,
    John.   I will not change ten for one!
Since the birder will help me to take them all,
As sure to mine use as the one bird could fall!
    Jerome.   Well, for conclusion, since ye
    soundly see
That witty have pleasure here in more degree,
Than witless, and also witty wise see ye,
In heaven by Scripture in higher joys be
Than the witless; you seeing this clearly,—
Whether would ye now, be witless or witty?
    John.   Witty! and the more witty am I for
Of which heartily I thank you; and now [you,
Where my mate, my lords, said that is gone,
Better be sot Somer than sage Solomon,
In forsaking that I would now rather be
Sage Solomon than sot Somer I assure ye!
    Jerome.   As ye show wit in change of
    former mind,
Being now from witless to witty inclined,
So aptly your wit in what wit shall devise,
As in good use of wit by grace ye may rise,
To be both witty and wittily wise.
In governance of God's gifts in such size [fall
As wisdom alway guideth, whereby this shall

God's gifts to God's glory both ye may use and
    shall.
These words of counsel in which I now waded
    To him whom I told them, I only assign;
I am by all circumstance full persuaded.
    This sort being sorted in sort thus fine,
    Need none exhortation, or at least not mine;
This sort have not only by nature his wit,
But also by grace like wisdom joined to it.

[*These three stave next following in the
King's absence, are void.*]

And as in them thereby God's gifts shine most
    may,   [shall,
    So stand their affairs whereby they so shine
If the gloss of God's shine not bright each way,
    In them who having a realm in governal,
    Set forth their governance to God's glory all,
Charitably aiding subjects in each kind, [find?
The shining of God's gifts where shall we then

And of this high sort, the high head most ex-
    cellent,   [sovereign,
    Is our most loved and dread supreme
The shining of whose most excellent talent
    Employed to God's glory, above all the train,
    Thus wit wanteth her recital to retain;
And that all his faithful feel, the fruit of his
    fame.

Of course I pray pardon in passing the same.
Praying that prince, whom our prince his great
    grace gave,   [estate,
    To grant him long length of increase in
At full fine whereof his most high gifts to have;
    By his most faithful use, reward in such rate,
    As is promised in Scripture, alleged late;

The joys not all only inestimable,
But more the degree of joys incomparable.

Continuance whereof with fruitful increase,
  I heartily wish for increase of reward;
As Scripture alleged late doth witness,
  The witty wise worker to be prefarde,
Above th'idle sot, and ye to regard
Each man himself so to apply in this,
As ye all may obtain the high degree of bliss.

(Amen qd. John Heywod.)

A FOREWORD TO NOTE-BOOK AND WORD-LIST

Reference from text to Note-Book is copious, and as complete as may be; so also, conversely, from Note-Book to text. The following pages may, with almost absolute certainty, be consulted on any point that may occur in the course of reading; but more especially as regards

Biographical and other Notes,
Contemporary references to Author and Plays,
Bibliography,
Variorum Readings,
Words and Phrases, now Obsolete or Archaic.

The scheme of reference from Note-Book to text assumes the division, in the mind's eye, of each page into four horizontal sections; which, beginning at the top, are indicated in the Note-Book by the letters a, b, c, d following the page figure. In practice this will be found easy, and an enormous help to the eye over the usual reference to page alone in " fixing " the " catchword." Thus 126a=the first quarter of page 126; 40c=the third quarter of page 40; and so forth.

Abbreviations.

P.F.   The Pardoner and the Friar.
F.P.   The Four P.P.
J.T.   John, Tib and Sir John.
W.   Play of the Weather.
L.   Play of Love.
W.W. Dialogue of Witty and Witless.

NOTE-BOOK AND WORD-LIST
TO THE DRAMATIC WRITINGS OF
JOHN HEYWOOD

ABHOMINABLE, " most *abhominable* " (P.F. 9c), abominable. Shakspeare, as was often his wont in playing
to the gallery, ridiculed the fine speakers of his day in
Love's Lab. Lost, iv. 1.—" This is *abhominable* which
he would call abominable." The word did not always
carry a bad meaning.

A-BROACH, " set *a-broach* the matter " (L. 161b), properly to tap; hence, to diffuse, to advance.

ACCOMPTED, " afore us merchants *accompted* be "
(W. 105b), accounted, reckoned.

ACCUMBER, " as knavishly you *accumber* " (F.P. 59c),
destroy, vanquish, overcome. " And laft his sheep
accombred in the mire "—Chaucer, *Cant. Tales* (1383),
509.

ACE, " I pass you an *ace* " (F.P. 46b), *i.e.* I surpass you
by the value of an ace.

A-CROOK, " take nothing . . . . *a-crook* " (L. 162d),
crookedly. " This gear goeth *a-crook* "—Udal, *Ralph
Roister Doister* (c. 1553), iv. 3.

AFFECTION, " without *affection* " (W. 98a)—" if your
affection . . . . suffer your reason " (L. 143d), sym-
pathy, partiality. " Some men cannot contain their
urine : for *affection* . . . . sways it to the mood of
what it likes or loathes "—Shakspeare, *Merch. of
Venice* (1598), iv. 1.

AFORE, " *afore* us merchants " (W. 105b), before.

ALE, " ye came of late from the *ale* " (F.P. 32d), alehouse—see *Slang and its Analogues*, Vol. I. (revised
ed.).

ALGATES, " thou wilt *algates* rave " (F.P. 25*a*), always, continually.

ALL A DAY, " *all a day* to the knee " (L. 144*c*), all day.

ALL HALLOWS (P.F. 7*d* ; F.P. 43*c*, 43*d*, *et passim*), All Saints.

ALL-TO, " he would *all-to* clout you " (H. 128*b*)—" and some of the knaves I will *all-to* rent " (T. 178*a*), completely, thoroughly. Originally *all* and *to* were distinct words, *to* being added to verbs of force to indicate a complete break-up or destruction : subsequently they were compounded when *all-to* seems to have acquired the value of quite, altogether, wholly, thoroughly.

ALMIGHT, " God *Almight* " (P.F. 22*d*), Almighty.

ALMS-DEED, " their penny or *alms-deed* " (P.F. 9*b*)—" I showed you . . . . of *alms-deed* " (P.F. 13*c*), an act of charity. " It were an *alms-deed* to knock her in the head "—*Thersytes* (E.E.D.S., Anony. Pl., 1st Series). " Full of good works, and *alms-deeds* which she (Dorcas) did "—*Bible*, Author. Vers. (1611), Acts, ix. 36.

AMIAS (F.P. 30*a*), ? Emmaus, near Jerusalem.

AN, AND (*passim*), (a) if ; (b) on. " Beware . . . . *and* they be small . . . . he hath no help at all "—*Everyman* (E.E.D.S., Anony. Pl., 1st Ser.).

ANNE OF BUXTON, SAINT (F.P. 30*a* ; W. 101*a* ; 106*c*). " Within the parish of Bacwell, in Derbyshyre, is *a Chappel* (*somtyme dedicated to St Anne*), in a place called *Bucston*, wheare is a hoate Bathe, of suche like Qualitie as those mentioned in Bathe be. *Hyther they weare wont to run on pilgrimage*, ascribinge to St Anne miraculously, that Thinge which is in that and sondrye other Waters naturrally "—Lambarde, *Dictionarium*, 48. " I can again produce those wondrous wells Of *Bucston*, as I have, that most delicious fount Which men the second Bath of England do account, Which in the primer reigns, when first this well began To have her virtues known, unto the blest St Anne, Was consecrated then "—Drayton, *Poly-Olbion* (1622), xxvi.

ANTONY-PIG, " like an *Antony-pig* " (J.T. 67*c*), close at heel. " The Officers . . . of the Markets [London] did take from the Market people Pigs starved, or otherwise unwholesome for Man's sustenance. One of the Proctors of St Anthonies tyed a Bell about the neck, and let it feed on the Dunghills ; no man would hurt or take it up ; but if anyone gave to them bread, or other feeding, such would they know, watch for and daily follow. . . . Whereupon was raised a Proverbe, Such an one will FOLLOW such an one, and whine AS IT WERE AN ANTHONIE PIG "—Stowe, *Surv. London* (1595), 190.

APE, " to make her husband her *ape* " (J.T. 83*c*), to befool or dupe him.

ARCH, " a noble *arch* dame " (C. 70*d*), chief, pre-eminent : in modern use chiefly in a bad or odious sense. " Thies wysefooles and verye *arch*edoltes "—Robinson, *More's Utopia*, 39 (1551). " Lads that are arch knaves at the nominative case "—Eachard, *Contempt. Clergy* (1670).

A-ROW, " the stations all *a-row* " (F.P. 29*d*)—" each one *a-row* " (W. 65*a*)—" given to us all *a-row* " (W. 134*a*), in order (as in a row), successively.

ARRAYED, " *arrayed* at the skirt " (J.T. 75*b*), soiled, dirtied, bedraggled, disfigured. " Indeed, age hath *arrayed* thee "—*Calisto and Melibæa* (E.E.D.S., Anony. Pl., 1st Ser., which see). " My fingers were *arrayed* with lime " (*Ibid.*).

ARSEFETITA (F.P. 47*b*), asafœtida.

AS, " All this in manner *as* unknown to me " (L. 139*c*), should be *is*.

ASSOILED, " till he be *assoiled* " (P.F. 13*b*), absolved.

AT, " *at* him, Sir John " (J.T. 88*c*), attack, i.e. *be at*.

ATTEMPERING, " each thing *attempering* " (W. 95*b*), regulating, tempering, mollifying.

AUCTORITY, " mine *auctority* now shall ye see " (P.F. 8*c* and 8*d*), authority.

AVANCE, AVANCED, AVANCEMENT, " to heaven *avanced* " (F.P. 51*d*)—" I shall the truth *avance* " (L. 141*c*)—" his *avancement* avaunt " (L. 164*d*), advance, advanced, advancement.

AWSTYNE, SAINT (W.W. 212b), St. Augustine.

AX, AXED, AXETH (passim), ask, asked.

BABBLE, " bigger burden beareth he none than his babble " (W.W. 196c), bauble. A short stick or wand, with a head with asses' ears carved at the end of it : this was carried by fools and jesters. For curious particulars and engravings see Douce's *Illustrations of Shakespeare*.

BACKSIDE, " in at the *backside* " (W. 119a), the back of a building, room or place.

BALD COOT, " thou blind *bald coot* " (L. 160d), a term of contempt : the frontal plate of the coot (*Fulica atra*) is destitute of feathers (Tyndale, *Works*, 1530, ii. 224).

BALDOCK (W. 99d), in Hertfordshire.

BARFOLD (W. 99d), " perhaps one of the numerous Barfords " (Pollard).

BARN-DOORS, " broad as *barn-doors* " (F.P. 54d), as broad as may be : usually of a target too large to be missed.

BAUD, BAWD, BAWDY, " the errantest *bawd* " (J.T. 82a) —" the most *bawdy* hence to Coventry " (J.T. 72a), a procuress, go-between, harlot ; as adj. wanton, lewd, obscene.

BAY, " in this *bay* " (L. 169b), stopped, at a standstill, as by amorous feeling, or by some restraint on motion imposed by others : modern *at bay*.

BECK, *subs.* and *verb,* " did give a *beck* " (F.P. 52b)— " thus he *becked* " (F.P. 54d), a beckoning with the hand, a nod, a salutation. " A serving of *becks*, and jutting out of bums "—Shakspeare, *Timon of Athens* (1609) : cf. (modern) *at beck and call*.

BEEN, " declare what each of them *been* " (P.F. 5c)— " as many as *been* assembled " (P.F. 5c) are : an old indicative plural. " They be desceyved that say thay *ben* not tempted in here body "—Chaucer, *Persones Tale* (1383).

BEFORNE, " never man *beforne* " (W. 133d)—" as ever she laughed *beforne* " (L. 158c), before.

BESHREW, " I *beshrew* your knave's heart " (F.P. 59*b*), a mild imprecation : generally in imperative. " *Beshrew* your heart "=woe to you. " I *beshrew* all shrews "—Shakspeare, *Love's Labour Lost* (1594), v. 2.

BIB, " the more ye *bib* " (W. 125*c*), drink. " This miller has so wisely *bibbed* ale "—Chaucer, *Cant. Tales* (1383), 4160.

BIBLIOGRAPHY, see the Plays by name.

BIOGRAPHICAL NOTES, see Heywood, John.

BLACK AND BLUE, " till she be *black and blue* " (J.T. 69*c*), so beaten that the varied coloring of a bruise is shown.

BLESS, " I come to *bless* the board " (J.T. 82*c*), compare Pernet's " Vous irayje signer la table? Je scay bien le benedicite " : see *John, Tib, and Sir John* infra.

BLIND HEW, " Marry that I would see, quod *blind Hew* " (P.F. 21*d*), a proverb : it does not, however, occur in Heywood's *Effectual Proverbs*.

BOMBARD, " loosed her *bombard* " (F.P. 50*c*), properly a piece of ordnance : a mortar of large bore employed to project stone shot which are said sometimes to have weighed 3cwt. apiece.

BONGRACE, " her *bongrace* which she ware " (P.F. 7*c bis*), " a forehead cloth or covering for the head ; a kind of veil attached to a hood " (Skinner) : afterwards the hood itself.

BONIFACE THE NINTH (P.F. 10*b*), ascended the papal chair in 1389.

BOOT, " shall be her *boot* " (J.T. 69*a*), remedy, cure, help, advantage. " This knight thinketh his *boot* thou may'st be "—*Calisto and Melibæa* (Farmer, E.E.D.S., Anony. Pl., 1st Ser.).

BOSTON, OUR LADY OF (F.P. 30*b*), in Lincolnshire : see Saint Botolph.

BOTOLPH, SAINT (F.P. 30*a*), is said to have been born in Cornwall, and was eminent for working miracles about the time of Lucius. He was buried at Boston, in Lincolnshire. " Delicious Wytham leads to holy *Botolph's town* "—Drayton, *Poly-Olbion* (1622), xxv.

BREAK, BREKE, " not fail it to *break* " (W. 123*a*)—" first to *breke* " (L. 165*b*), communicate : cf. (modern) *to break news*.

BREAST, " is your *breast* anything sweet " (F.P. 38*b*), the breast is here regarded as essential to good singing : hence a musical voice, voice in general. In the next line a distinction is made between the breast and the voice. " In singing the sound is originally produced by the action of the lungs, which are so essential an organ in this respect, that to have a good *breast* was formerly a common periphrasis to denote a good singer. The Italians make use of the terms *Voce di Petto* and *Voce di Testa* to signify two kinds of voice, of which the first is the best. In Shakspeare's *Twelfth Night*, after the clown is asked to sing, Sir Andrew Aguecheek says—' By my troth, the fool hath an excellent *breast*.' And in the statutes of Stoke College, in Suffolk, founded by Parker, Archbishop of Canterbury, is a provision in these words : ' Of which said queristers, after their *breasts* are changed (*i.e.* their voices broke), we will the most apt of wit and capacity be holpen with exhibitions of forty shillings ' "—Hawkins, *Hist. Musick* iii. 466, note. " *Duke.* ' Yea the voice too, sir ? ' *Fab.* ' Ay, and a *sweet brest* too, my lord, I hope, or I have cast away my money wisely ' "—Middleton, *Women Beware Women* (Dyce), iv. 583.

BRENNING, " *brenning* fire " (P.F. 11*b*)—" tapers . . . *brenning* bright " (P.F. 19*c*), burning. " The more thine herte *brenneth* in fier " (*Romaunt of the Rose*).

BRISTOW (W. 100*a*), Bristol.

BULL, " *bulls* under lead " (6*a*), originally the seal appended to the papal edicts, but subsequently applied to a letter, brief, or rescript of the pope sealed with such a seal.

BUSH, " so took my *bush* " (L. 181*c*), properly the metal box in which the axle of a machine works ; here applied to the " copper tank " carried by the Vice.

BUTSBURY (W. 100*a*), ? Butsbury in Essex.

BY AND BY, " thou shalt go to prison *by and by* " (P.F. 25*b*)—" fell sick so suddenly that dead she was even *by and by* " (F.P. 51*c*)—" he cometh *by and by* " (W. 104*d*), immediately, as soon as possible. " I will that thou give me *by and by* in a charger the head of John the Baptist "—*Bible*, Auth. Vers. (1611), Mark vi. 25 :

in the original Greek *ex antes* = at the very point of time.

C., " many a *C.* stroke " (J.T. 67*d*), hundred.

CAN, " I *can* some skill " (F.P. 42*a*), able, know, possess, am skilled in. " Thy wif hath this day spoken with a man that *can* of nigromancy."—*Gesta Romanorum* (Herrtage), 2. " Though he be ignorant and *can* little skill."—*Four Elements* (E.E.D.S., Anonys. Plays, 1st Ser.), 7.

CAP, " have ye nother *cap nor knee* " (W. 99*c*), acknowledgment, salutation; either by removing the cap or bending the knee. " Three great ones of the city, in personal suit to make me his lieutenant, oft *capp'd* to him."—Shakspeare, *Othello*, i. 1.

CARK, " for . . . other thing they will *cark* " (P.F. 18*c*), care, take thought, be concerned about.

CARTERLY, " *carterly* caitiffs " (W. 99*b*), clownish, rude, like a carter. " A *carterly* or churlish trick."—Cotgrave, *Dict.* (1611), s.v., *Charterie*.

CASUALTIES, " the devil's servants have *casualties* " (W. 126*c*), chance perquisites.

CATTERWAULING, " to go a *catterwauling* " (J.T. 70*c*), properly to cry like cats in heat; hence to woo, to make love, to wanton. " The friars and monks *caterwawld* from the abbots and priors to the novices."—Nashe, *Lenten Stuffe* (1599), Wks. v. 284.

CATWADE (F.P. 30*c*), " *Catwade* Bridge is in Samford Hundred, in the county of Suffolk, where there may have been a famous chapel and rood " (Gifford).

CERTES (*passim*), certainly, assuredly. " And *certes*, if it nere to long to heere, I wolde han told yow fully the manere."—Chaucer, *The Knight's Tale* (1383), 877-8.

CHANCE, " for the *chance* of ten birds " (W.W. 213*c*), these words are very indistinct, and the reading given may not be the right one (Fairholt).

CHASES, " purlieus and *chases* " (W. 107*b*), the woods adjacent to a royal forest, chases being unenclosed portions.

CHEAP, *subs.* and *verb*, " as good *cheap* " (F.P. 33*a*)—
" I *chept* not nor borrowed " (W. 128*c*), price, value,
to buy, to bargain for : hence *good cheap* (Fr. *bon
marché*)=great plenty, very cheap : the expression was
common enough. " To gret *chep* is holden at little
price " (Chaucer). " Seeing thou wilt not buy counsel
at the first hande good *cheape*, thou shalt buye repent-
ance at second-hande at such an vnreasonable rate that
thou wilt cursse thy hard penyworth, and ban thy
harde heart."—Lyly, *Euphues* (1579), 8. " He buyes
other men's cunning good *cheap* in London, and sels
it deare in the countrey."—Decker's *Lanthorne and
Candlelight*, H4.

CHECKING, " maketh all our *checking* " (W. 118*a*), scold-
ing, reviling, reproaching.

CHOP, " at the first *chop* " (F.P. 34*d*), attack, onset, beginning. " Believe them at the first *chop*, whatsoever they say."—Tyndale, *Works*, i. 241.

CLAP, " stint thy *clap* " (P.F. 21*b*), chatter, idle talk :
see Chaucer, *Cant. Tales* (1383), 3146.

CLEPED, " *cleped* sweet Jesus " (4*b*), called, named.
" . . . he *clepeth* a calf, cauf ; half, hauf ; neighbour,
vocatur, nebour."—Shakspeare, *Love's Labour Lost*,
v. 1.

COCK, " *Cock's blood, body, bones, lilly nail, lilly
wounds, mother, soul*," &c. (J.T. *passim*), God's blood,
&c. : a euphemistic oath, *cf.* Gog's blood, &c.

COLLATION, " a simple *collation* " (P.F. 5*b*), conference,
discourse. " I and thou and sche have a *collacioun*."
—Chaucer, *Cant. Tales* (1383), 8199.

COMEN, " I am *comen* " (P.F. 5*d*)—" when that he
comen home again was " (J.T. 84*c*), come : A.S.
cuman.

COMMODITY, " the wind in this *commodity* " (W. 115*a*),
advantage, profit, convenience, opportunity.

COMMONER, " some fresh *commoner* " (W.W. 207*c*), a
student : at Oxford a commoner is one who is not
dependent for support on the foundation of any college,
but pays his way independently. Here probably *fresh
commoner* is equivalent to the modern *freshman*.

Conject, " I do *conject* " (J.T. 72*c*), conjecture, surmise. " Now reason I or *conject* with myself."— *Acolastus*, 1540. " Madam, the reason of these vehement tearmes, Cyrus doth neither know, nor can *conjéct*."—*Wars of Cyrus* (1594), 4to E, 1b.

Conning, see Cunning.

Contemporary references, see Heywood, John.

Contention, " pleasure by *contentation* "—" pleasure without *contentation* " (L. 174*d*), content, satisfaction.

Cooles, " mean *cooles* of wind " (W. 113*a*)—" save *cooles* to blow meanly " (W. 130*b*)—" pleasant *cooles* ye shall obtain " (W. 132*b*), cool breezes.

Cornelys, Saint (F.P. 30*b*). " *Saint Cornelys*, according to the *Legenda Aurea*, succeeded Fabyan in the Papacy (A.D. 251 : Fabian was martyred A.D. 250), and was beheaded in the reign of Decius (A.D. 250), for refusing to sacrifice in the Temple of Mars. There was a fraternity in his honour at Westminster " (*Dod.*, i. 336).

Corpus Christi, " in the play of *Corpus Christi* " (F.P. 53*a*), see *Coventry Mysteries,* ed. Halliwell (1841). " Before the suppression of the monasteries, this city (*i.e.* Coventry) was very famous for the pageants that were played therein upon *Corpus Christi* day (this is one of their ancient faires), which occasioning very great confluence of people thither from far and near, was no small benefit thereto ; which pageants being acted with mighty state and reverence by the friers of this house, had theaters for the several scenes very large and high, placed upon wheels, and drawn to all the eminent parts of the city, for the better advantage of spectators, and contained the story of the New Testament, composed in old English rithme, as appeareth by an ancient MS. entitled *Ludus Corporis Christi,* or *Ludus Coventriæ,* in Bibl. Cotton. (sub Effigie Vesp. D. 9) " (Dugdale's *Warwickshire,* p. 116).

Cost, " of the place's *cost* " (P.F. 20*d*), *i.e.* charge.

Costard, " knock thee on the *costard* " (P.F. 21*d*), head : properly a large kind of apple. " I knocke youre *costarde* if ye offer to strike me."—Udall, *Roister Doister* (1534), iii. 5.

Q 2

COVETISE, " fye on *covetise* " (P.F. 9*b*)—" all thy sermon goeth on *covetise* " (P.F. 17*d*), coveteousness (A.N.). " Seven deadly sins . . . as pride, *covetise*, wealth and lechery."—*Everyman* (E.E.D.S., Anony. Pl., 1st Ser.), 94*c*.

CRATCH, " some *cratch* him " (W.W. 194*b*), claw, scratch.

CROME (F.P. 30*c*; J.T. 67*c*),? in Kent, near Greenwich. But, " there are three Croomes in the Manor of Ripple, Worc., and the church of Ripple is dedicated to the Blessed Virgin, but Nash's *Worcestershire* says nothing of our Lady of Crome " (Pollard).

CRY, " according to the *cry* " (W. 109*a*; also W. 127*d*), a public notification by authority : here Jupiter's proclamation.

CUCKOLD, " look how the *cuckold*," &c. (J.T. 83*b*), the husband of an unfaithful wife.

CUNNING, " my doctrine and *cunning* " (P.F. 4*b*)—" ye all be like *conning* " (F.P. 41*d*)—" no small *cunning* " (L. 168*d*)—" not doubting your conscience nor *cunning* " (L. 175*c*), orig. knowledge, skill, learning, no bad sense being implied : as early as the time of Lord Bacon, however, the word was on the down-grade in meaning, influenced, no doubt, by the mundane truth that skill in the hands of the unscrupulous is used to defraud those less gifted. " If I forget thee, O Jerusalem, let my right hand forget her *cunning*."—*Bible*, Auth. Vers. (1611), Psalm cxxxvii. 5. " With all the *cunning* manner of our flight, Determined of."— Shakspeare, *Two Gent.*, ii. 4.

DAGENHAM (F.P. 30*b*), in Essex.

DAVID'S, SAINT (F.P. 30*c*), said to have been bishop 65 years and to have lived 146 (!). " *St. David's* in Pembrokeshire is the ancient Menapia, now a poor decayed place, but once the metropolitan see of Wales, and archiepiscopal. When Christianity was planted in Britain, there were three archbishops' seats appointed, viz. London, York, and Caerleon upon Usk, in Monmouthshire. That at Caerleon being too near the dominions of the Saxons, was removed to Mynyw, and called St. David's, in honour of the archbishop who

removed it, 519. St. Sampson was the last archbishop
of the Welsh ; for he, withdrawing himself on account
of a pestilence to Dôle, in Brittany, carried the pall
with him. In the reign of Henry I. the archbishops
submitted to the see of Canterbury " (*Haydn*).

DAW, " sir *daw* " (P.F. 15*a*), *i.e.* jackdaw ; hence an
empty-headed fellow, a fool. " Men count him but
a *daw*."—*Four Elements* (E.E.D.S., Anony. Pl., 1st
Ser.), 4*d*. " Good faith, I am no wiser than a *daw*."
—Shakspeare, *Henry VI.*, ii. 4.

DEBATE, " the *debate* between you and her " (J.T. 78*c*),
quarrel, point of contention.

DELL, " will help never a *dell* " (P.F. 23*b*)—" no *dell* "
(L. 175*b*)—" every *dell* " (L. 169*c*), bit, part, portion
(A.S.).

DENIS, SAINT (F.P. 30*c*), the patron of France : " dis-
ciple of St Paul, and the first who preached the gospel
to the French. The legend concerning him affirms
that, after he was beheaded near Paris, he walked four
miles with his head in his hands. His body was said
to be entombed very magnificently at the abbey of *St
Denis* (A.D. 636), to which the pilgrims used to resort "
(REED). The abbey, which had been the burial-place
of the French kings from its foundation by Dagobert,
about 630, was destroyed at the Revolution. The
church was restored by Bonaparte, and again became
a royal burial-place.

DEPARTED, " when we *departed* " (W. 97*d*), separated.

DISCOMMEND, " I *discommend* your wit " (F.P. 31*b*),
dispraise.

DISEASE, " much it overmatcheth all your *disease* "
(L. 145*b*)—" I will not *disease* you " (L. 165*c*)—" he
will no more *disease* you " (L. 180*a*), disturb, trouble,
annoy : also as *subs.* : originally, as here, general in
meaning=absence of ease. " We to hem that ben
with child, and nurishen in tho daies, for a great
disese [Gr. ἀνάγκ (*anangke*), Vulg. *pressura magna*,
Auth. Eng. Vers. *distress*] schal be on the erthe, and
wrathe to this peple."—Wycliffe, *Luke* xxi. 23.

DISTAFF, " more tow on my *distaff* than I can well
spin," &c. (P.F. 25*c*), proverbial : I have more in hand
than I can undertake.

DISTEMPERATE, " temperate or *distemperate* " (W. 98*b*), immoderate : " whence *distemperance* " (L. 170*c* ; W.W. 194*d*)=discomfort, disorder, mental disturbance.

DRAB, " stand still, *drab* " (J.T. 88*a*), a wanton : a general term of abuse.

DRIVEL, " whoreson *drivel* " (P.F. 17*c* ;   J.T. 88*b*), drudge, wretch, fool.

DURE, " in *dure* " (W.W. 202*d*), endurance.

DYRYK, SAINT (J.T. 71*c*), unmentioned by the Bolland-ists ; the name may be a contraction for one of the four St. Theodorics (Pollard).

EDMUND'S BURGH, SAINT (F.P. 30*b*), Bury St. Edmund's. " Is named of Kinge Edmunde, whom the comon Chronicles call St Edmund or Edmund the Martyr; for Bury is but to say a Court or Palace. It was first a Colledge of Priests, founded by Athelstane the kinge of Ingland, to the Honour and Memorye of Edmund that was slayne at Hoxton (then called Eylesdund [or Eglesdon], as Leland thinketh), whose Bones he re-moved thyther. The hole hystorie of this matter is so enterlaced with miracles, that Polydor himselfe (who beleaved them better then I) began to delye with it ; sayinge, *that Monkes weare much delighted with them.*"—Lambarde, *Dict.* 35 (Reed).

EKE, " *eke* here see ye may " (P.F. 7*a*)—" he offereth *eke* " (P.F. 7*b*, *et passim*), also, besides, in addition : obsolete save in poetry, a late instance being " A trainband captain *eke* was he, Of famous London town."—Cowper, *John Gilpin.*

ENRAGE, " I almost *enrage* " (J.T. 69*d*), get furious.

ENSAMPLE, " to the *ensample* " (P.F. 24*a*), example, pattern, model (A.N.).

ENTERED, " hath *entered* such matter " (W. 94*c*), placed on record.

EOLUS (W. 94*b*), *i.e.* Æolus, the god of the winds, and king of what are now known as the Lipari Islands, in the caverns of which the winds were supposed to be confined.

ESTEEM, (W. 112*c*), orig. *exteme.*

EUPULUS, "dives *Eupulus* reigning in welfare" (P.F. 10c), Latin, *Eupulor* = to feast; *Epulum* = a feast.

EVERYCHONE, "then be we lords *everychone*" (F.P. 41*b*, *et passim*), everyone.

EXHIBITION, no prebends ne *exhibition*" (P.F. 19*a*), stipend, allowance of meat and drink : still in use at the Universities, where it signifies a benefaction or endowment for the maintenance of scholars. "What maintenance he from his friends receives, Like *exhibition* thou shalt have from me."—Shakspeare, *Two Gentlemen of Verona* (1595), i. 3.

EXTRE (W. 108*d*), axle tree. "The firmament and also every spere, The golden *extre* and the sterres seven." —Lydgate, *M.S. Ashmole* 39, f. 33.

FABLE, "the more ye *fable*" (W. 125*c*), lie, draw the long bow : also as *subs.* "And tell you *fables* dear enough at a fly" (P.F. 18*c*). "Without *fable* or guile."—*Four Elements* (E.E.D.S., Anony. Pl., 1st Ser.).

FACSIMILE TITLE-PAGES, &c. Portrait of John Heywood (facing general title); *The Four P.P.*, facs. title, ed. 1545 (p. 27); *Ibid.*, facs. title, ed. 1569 (p. 28); *John John, Tib, and Sir John*, facs. title (p. 65); *Play of the Weather*, facs. title (p. 91).

FAIN, "your head so *fain*" (L. 144*b*), so in original, but probably it should read either *vain* (*f* and *v* are phonetically allied) or *fair* (careless copying having confounded *r* and *n*).

FALLING SICKNESS, "this wanton had the *falling sickness*" (F.P. 49*d*), properly epilepsy, but a double meaning attaches to the 'pothecary's use of the term : Heywood was not singular amongst the writers of his own and later times in this respect : *cf.* modern *fallen woman*.

FAR-FORTH, "so *far-forth* lacketh grace" (P.F. 9*d*), far, in a certain or great degree. "Now the humid night was *farforth* spent."—Spenser, *Fairy Queen* (1590), III., ix., 53.

FAY, "by my *fay*" (J.T. 75*a*), faith : a mild oath. "I tell you in *fay*."—*Sir Degrevant*, *MS. Lincoln*, F. 132.

FEASTS, THE FIVE SOLEMN (P.F. 19*b*), Christmas Day, the Circumcision, the Epiphany, Candlemas or the Purification, Lady Day or the Annunciation of the Virgin Mary.

FEATHER, " she will make me wear a *feather* " (J.T. 70*a*), will cuckold me. The bull's feather (or horn) (Fr. *plumes de bœuf*) was the insignia of cuckoldry.

FEATLY, " set ye down *featly* " (W.W. 199*b*), neatly, dexterously, nimbly. " Foot it *featly* here and there." —Shakspeare, *Tempest* (1609) i. 2.

FELLOWSHIP, " friends, a *fellowship* " (W. 98*d*)—" a *fellowship* speed ye " (L. 152*a*), out of good fellowship.

FEOFED, " *feofed* in the tail " (W. 117*c*); invested with or in enjoyment of a fief or corporeal hereditament : the *tail* (as opposed to a fee-simple) limited inheritance to the heirs of the holder's body, general or special, male or female.

FET (1), " *fet* ten souls out of purgatory " (F.P. 58*c*)— " the devil shall have the tone to *fet* the tother (W. 124*d*), fetched. " The qwene anon to hym was *fett*, For sche was best worthy."—*MS. Cantab.* Ff. v. 48, f. 54. (2), " so *fet* it is " (W. 122*a*), neat, trim, skilful, deft. " Noe not an howare, althoughe that shee be never soe fine and *feat.—MS. Ashmole* 208. " So *feat*, so nurselike."—Shakspeare, *Cymbeline* (1605), v. 5.

FEUTERED, " *feutered* in fashion abhominable " (F.P. 55*a*), equipped, *featured* (Hazlitt) : *cf.* " *Fewters* of his face " (*Romeo and Juliet*).

FILLETS (F.P. 36*d*), a band of linen, ribbon, &c., worn round the head. " A golden *fillet* binds his awful brows."—Dryden, *Virgil*, Æneid (1694-7), iv. 213.

FIT, " I long for such a *fit* " (W. 122*a*), an air or bar, a part of a song, division of a poem. " Shalle I now syng you a *fytt* with my mynstrelsy."—*Towneley Mysteries*, p. 51. " And I can whistle you a *fit*."— *World and Child* (E.E.D.S., Anony. Pl., 1st Ser.), 166*b*.

FLEECES, " increase of their *fleeces* " (W. 129*c*), plunder : as a verb fleece=to cheat, to shear (as a sheep) was more common. " Tell me (almost) what gentleman

hath been cast away at sea, or disasterly souldiourizd
it by lande, but they (usurers) have enforst him there-
unto by their *fleecing*."—Nashe, *Christ's Teares* (1593),
Wks. iv. 140. "Down with them : *fleece* them ! "—
Shakspeare, 1 *K. Hen. IV.* (1598), ii. 2.

FLETE, " except the ship *flete* " (W. 112d), float.

FORBOD, FORBODE, " or else God *forbod* " (L. 164c)—
" no man may be *forbode* " (P.F. 10c), God forbid,
forbidden.

FORBORNE, " if we be *forborne* " (W. 108c)—" be best
forborne " (W. 111a), dispensed with, missed.

FORGETH, " he *forgeth* not one word " (W.W. 206c),
forgetteth.

FOUR P.P. (THE). This is one of the four undoubted
Heywood plays (the four P's being a Palmer, a
Pardoner, a 'Pothecary, and a Pedlar), the *Text* of
which is given on pp. 26–64. The *Date of Composition* is uncertain : equally problematical is that of its
First Publication. There are three known editions—
(1) One thought to be the first (but undated), printed
by William Myddleton " probably between 1543–7, and
possibly written fifteen years or so earlier " (Collier) :
this copy, however, now in the British Museum, is in
the Catalogue dated 1545.　(2) An undated copy,
printed by Copland, now in the Bodleian.　(3) A copy
dated 1569, also in the Garrick Collection in the
British Museum.　Also (4) *reprinted* in all editions of
Dodsley's " Old Plays."　(5) In " The Ancient British
Drama " and elsewhere.　The *Present Text* is that of
the earliest edition, the following variorum readings,
except where otherwise mentioned, being those of the
edition of 1569. *Facsimile Title-pages* of Nos. 1 and
3 are given on pages 27 and 28.　*Variorum Readings.*
—" My rudeness showeth me *so homely* " (29b), in
eds. 1545 and 1569 the words *no* and *not* respectively
occur before *so homely* : the negative seems inserted
in error (Collier) ; sue *you* (29b), sue *now* ; *ye* see
(29c), *you* see ; *have* spent (29c), *hath* spent, ed. 1545 ;
fair and far country (29c), *far and fair* country ; *have
I* seen (29c), *I have* seen ; *could* come there (29d),
would come there ; King *Henry* (30c), King *Herry* ;
sooner to *obtain* (30d), *obtaye*, ed. 1545 ; I think *surely*
(30d), *assuredly*, 2nd ed. ; *their* frail body (31a), *thy*,

ed. 1545; as far as *ye* can (31*a*), *you*; *ye will come* (31*a*), *yet welcome*, ed. 1540; *nay*, fore God (31*a*), *for*, fore God; also your *pain* (31*b*), *paynes*, 2nd ed.; *ere* we go (31*b*), or ed. 1569; *mine* humble submission (31*c*), *my*; make *yourself* a fool (31*d*), *you*; *no other* thing (31*d*), *nother*; do but *scoff* (32*c*), *scofte*, ed. 1545; *ye speak* of (32*c*), *kepe*, ed. 1545; *the* first part (32*d*), *this*; *ye came of late* (32*d*), *you come late*, ed. 1540; leave *reasoning* (32*d*), *sonyng*, ed. 1545; wherein *you* (32*d*), *ye*, ed. 1545; for *you* (32*d*), *ye*, ed. 1545; for *you* (33*a*), *ye*, ed. 1545; all that *have* (33*a*), *hath*, ed. 1545; where *you* esteem (33*a*), *ye*, ed. 1545; my pardons *are* such (33*a*), *be*, ed. 1545; in the *least* quarter (33*b*), *leste*, ed. 1545, *leash*, ed. 1569, which reading Collier gave, and is here retained; *is* far a side (33*b*), *as*, ed. 1545; these pardons *bring* (33*b*), *bringeth*, ed. 1545; if we *do* (33*c*), *dyd*, ed. 1545; that *I will* (33*c*), *we will*; *ere* we go (33*d*), *or*, ed. 1545; the knaves rob (33*d*), *they* rob; die *honestly* (34*a*), *hostely*, ed. 1545; *if* ye should (34*b*), *that*; *out* of grace (34*c*), *from state*; ye may perceive (34*d*), *you*; *all kinds of* trifles (35*c*), *every* tryfull, ed. 1540; use we *chiefly* (35*c*), *chefe*, ed. 1545; each man *thinketh* (35*d*), *thinks*; is *here* nothing (35*d*), *there*; wherein is right (36*a*), *where*, ed. 1545; laces *knotted* (36*a*), *unknotted*; *laces*, round, &c. (36*a*), *lace*, ed. 1545; needles, thread, *thimble*, *shears, and all such knacks* (36*a*), *thimbles, and such other knacks*; *arising* (36*c*), *uprising*; *yet* is a thing (36*d*), *it*; have it *pricked* in (37*a*), *prycke*, ed. 1545; then *be they* (37*a*), *they be*; and *sweareth* an oath (37*a*), *swere*; at a *full* point (37*b*), *fall*, ed. 1545; some heads be *swimming* (38*a*), *swynking*; where is no *will* (38*c*), *wyt*, ed. 1545; be lacking *wit* (38*c*), *wyll*, ed. 1545; *and not* refuse (38*d*), *not and*, ed. 1545; that *this* indulgence (39*b*), *his*; and *from* all pain (39*c*), *for*; more than heaven he *cannot* get (39*c*), *may not*; *walk* to heaven (39*c*), *wake*, ed. 1545; *it is* necessary (40*a*), *it is very*; for when ye feel . . . to heaven quickly (40*a*), an addition to ed. 1569; and if *ye* list (40*b*), *he*; should *go* pilgrimage (40*d*), *go on*; as *deputy* (40*d*), original has *debite*; *who* could devise (41*a*), *howe*, ed. 1545; *then be we* lords (41*b*), *were we as*; all *things decay* (41*c*), *thinge decayed*, ed. 1545; *wholly* to be (41*d*), *holly*, ed. 1545: *holy*, ed. 1569; ye have *no* cause (42*b*), *not*, ed. 1545; *be bold* (42*b*), *beholde*; *may here lie* (42*c*), *may lie*; but, *sir*, this gear (42*d*), *sirs*; hop *better* (42*d*), *as well* as; to *hop* so (43*a*), *hope*, ed. 1545; ye shall *hop* without it (43*a*), *hope*, ed. 1545; without *it* (43*a*), *it* is omitted in ed. 1545, but "it is necessary for the rhyme" (Collier); *be ruled* indifferently (43*b*), *to be ruled*; *here be* pardons (43*b*), *here are*; *here be* relics (43*c*), *here are*; no man *can* find (43*c*), *may*; *never be vexed with the toothache* (44*a*), *be ryd of the toth ake*, ed. 1545; *either* the Trinity (44*a*), *other*, ed. 1545; my *friends* (44*c*), *friend*; *here is* a slipper (44*c*), *this is*; *these* two years (44*c*), *thys*, ed. 1545; *unto* Turks' teeth (45*a*), *to*, ed. 1545; I have *yet here* (45*b*), *here* omitted in ed. 1569; I *behold* thee (45*d*), *see*; wrought *one* operation (46*b*), *in*, ed. 1545; this *medicine* (46*d*), *ointment*; *shall* make you (47*a*), *will*; these *be* the things (47*b*), these *are*; dogs that *be* mangy (47*c*), *are* mangy; good *to* me (47*d*), *unto* me; *now* say thy worst (48*a*), *and* say, ed. 1545; *ye be* an honest man (48*a*), *you are*; who told *truth* (48*c*), *true*, ed. 1545; *ere* we proceed (48*c*), *or*, ed. 1545; by *your* faith (48*c*), *our*, ed. 1545; that *none* had lied (48*d*), *one*; both *ye* the truth (49*a*), *your*, ed. 1545; *How that I lied . . . may soon agree* (49*a*), *And that we both my lye so witness*, *That twayne of us thre in one agree*, ed. 1545; most *unlikest* (49*c*), *unlike*, ed. 1545; *of* that likeness (49*d*), *from*, ed. 1545; *could* not with ease (50*b*), *should*, ed. 1545; more *pains* about her (50*b*), *payne*, ed. 1540; but I knew *there* it was too heavy (50*b*), "an addition in the second edition" (Reed); *at this castle did light* (50*d*), *on thys castell lyght*, ed. 1545; may *these* words (51*b*), *this*; to *your* purpose (51*b*), *our*, ed. 1545; *done greater cures ghostly* (51*c*), *done more cures ghostely*; *thus* smilingly (53*a*), *thys*, ed. 1545; *on* this day (53*b*), "addition in the 2nd ed." (Reed); thou *may* thy passport (53*c*), *maist*; without *any* jeopardy (53*d*), *his*, ed. 1545; quoth I *amain* (54*a*), *for playne*, ed. 1545; in *ure* (54*a*), *cure*; residue of the *fiends* (54*c*), *frendes*, ed. 1540; *Did laugh . . . like friends* (54*c*), in first ed. this line reads, *Dyd laugh full well together lyke frendes*; *Of*

Lucifer . . . I could (54*d*), first ed. reads, *Then to
Lucyfer low as I coude* ; *delivered* hence (55*b*), *deliver* ; I *shall* deserve it (55*c*), *wil* ; *Ho, ho* (55*d*),
Nowe, ed. 1545 ; thou *whoreson* (55*d*), *horyson*, ed.
1545 ; all *we* devils (56*a*), *the* ; at this *day* (56*b*),
dayes, ed. 1545 ; *wonders* well (57*a*), *wunderous* ; ye
had in hell (57*b*), *found* ; great *peril* (57*b*), *parell*,
ed. 1545 ; much *perilous* (57*b*), *parellous* ; *This*, in
effect (57*c*), *thus* ; told *for* truth (57*c*), *of* ; long time
tarried (57*d*), *maryed*, ed. 1545 : " it will be observed
that there is no rhyme to this line . . . and it is
probable that a line has here dropped out ending
with *maryed*, which is the word in the oldest of the
three editions " (Collier) ; *gentle* knave (59*b*), *gentleman*, ed. 1545 ; by *our* lady (59*b*), *one*, ed. 1545 ; *ye
can* be (59*c*), *you may* ; three of the *lewdest* (59*d*),
" addition in the third edition " (Reed) ; when *ye*
have it (61*a*), *I*, ed. 1545 ; *gentle* brother (61*a*),
" addition in the third edition " (Reed) ; I had *liever*
(61*b*), *rather* ; *made* courtesy (61*c*), *make* ; loth to be
assigned (61*c*), " I believe we should read *affin'd, i.e.*
joined by affinity to each other " : so in *Othello* : " If
partially *affin'd* or leagued in office " (S.) : " it probably means *assigned* to the Palmer to wait on him,
which was part of the agreement, before the contention began " (Collier) ; live the *better* (61*c*), *beste*,
ed. 1545 ; *And likewise . . . I vow* (61*d*), first edition
reads, *And I lykewyse, I make God a vowe* ; Is *chief*
the thing (61*d*), *cheefest* ; procure *thus* (62*a*), *this* ;
To *show* (62*a*), *Shewell* ; to *one* end (62*b*), *on* ; such
like works (62*c*), *other*, ed. 1545 ; most *plentifully*
(62*d*), *plenteously* ; ye *be* not all (63*b*), *are* ; Ye be
not (63*c*), *nother*, ed. 1545 ; To *make* no judgment
(63*d*), *take* ; that hath *scaped* (64*b*), *escapte*. *Argument*.—" The question at issue between the characters
is which shall tell the greatest lie ; and after each has
told some monstrous story, the determination of the
rest that the Palmer's simple assertion, that he never
saw a woman out of patience in his life, is the most
monstrous falsehood of all (which the other three,
taken by surprise, involuntary declare), is an unex-
pected *and very comic turn of the performance "
(Collier). Fairholt holds (*Percy Soc. Publ.*, LXV.,
page lxix.) that " the absurdity of pardoner's relics is

severely handled, the jaw-bone of All-Hallows and
the great toe of the Trinity being brought forward to
ridicule. . . . Heywood's Pardoner is a close copy of
Chaucer's, and the two first relics he descants on—
the sheep's jaw and the mytten—are derived from
Chaucer, and described as nearly as possible in the
same words, as well as the artful assurance, that all
persons but grievous sinners, may publicly offer to
these relics as the test of their innocence ; as deceptive
and effective an imposition as was ever imputed to
this body. The most spirited and humorous part of
this Play (if indeed it be not Heywood's *chef-d'œuvre*)
is the Pardoner's tale of his descent into hell, to
recover the lost soul of a lady friend."

FRAME, " set in *frame* " (W. 127b), make orderly ar-
rangements, commence, attempt, contrive. " Put
your discourse into some *frame*."—Shakspeare,
Hamlet (1596), iii. 2.

FRENCH HOOD (P.F. 7c). It would appear that fashion
was set by France in the sixteenth century as in the
nineteenth and twentieth. A usurer extorts his pound
of flesh " for my mistress his wife's sake. . . . The
better to maintain and support the *French hood*."—
New Custom (E.E.D.S., Anony. Pl., 3rd Ser.).

FRERES, " poor *freres* " (P.F. 4d), friar : spec. in this
case one of the four mendicant orders for men, and
probably a Dominican or Preaching Friar. The orders
were : (*a*) The Franciscans or Friars Minors, popularly called Grey Friars (q.v.) ; (*b*) the Dominicans, or
Preaching Friars, popularly called Black Friars (q.v.) ;
(*c*) the Augustinians ; (*d*) the Carmelites, popularly
known as White Friars.

FRETTING, " for fear of *fretting* " (W. 126a), rubbing,
i.e. wear away by rubbing.

FRETTLING, " this kind of *frettling* " (W.W. 194c), vexa-
tion, irritation, torment.

FRO, " *fro* damnation " (P.F. 19c, *et passim*), from.

FRONTLET (F.P. 36d). " *Frontal*, Fr., a *frontlet*, or
forehead band.—Cotgrave, *Dict.* (1611). " Hoods,
frontlets, wires, cauls, curling-irons, periwigs, bodkins,
fillets, hair laces, ribbons, rolls, knotstrings, glasses."
—Lyly, *Midas* (1592).

GAYER, "never have I seen a *gayer*" (F.P. 49*d*). This would seem, in view of the general sense of the passage, an early instance of gay=wanton, loose.

GEAR, "let that *gear* pass" (W. 111*a*), a word-of-all-work—moveable property, subject, matter, habits, customs, business, anything in general.

GEORGE IN SOUTHWARK, SAINT (F.P. 30*a*), formerly belonging to the priory of Bermondsey : see Stow's *Survey* (Reed).

GEORGE, SAINT, "*Saint George* to borrow" (J.T. 88*c*), St. George for my backer.

GIGLET, "yonder *giglet*" (W. 123*b*), wanton, loose wench. "What is the matter, foolish *giglotte?* What meanest thou? Whereat laughest thou?"—Udall, *Fluores*, &c. (1533), fo. 101. "Let him speak no more : away with those *giglots* too, and with the other confederate companion."—Shakspeare, *Meas. for Meas.* (1603), v. 1.

GLASTONBURY (W. 100*a*), in Somerset, said to have been the residence of Joseph of Arimathea, and the site of the first Christian church in Britain, about 60. A church was built here by Ina about 708. The town and abbey were burnt, 1184. An earthquake did great damage in 1276. Richard Whiting, the last abbot, who had 100 monks and 400 domestics, was hanged on Tor-hill in his pontificals, with the abbots of Reading and Colchester, for refusing to take the oath of supremacy to Henry VIII., 14 Nov., 1539.

GLISTER, "go to heaven without a *glister*" (F.P. 34*b*)—"give mine old tail a *glister*" (W. 103*d*), a clyster, a purge.

GOD'S SHINE, "gloss of *God's shine*" (216*b*), gloss of God's *gifts* shine.

GOG, "*God's* soul" (P.F. 22*a*)—"*Gog's* blood" (J.T. 67*c*)—"*Gog's* body" (J.T. 69 *b* and *c*), God's soul, &c.

GOOD EVEN, "God you *good even*" (L. 148*c*), God give you good evening—good evening.

GOSSIP, GOSSIPRY, "he is her *gossip*"—"where the devil hath our *gossipry* begone" (J.T. 70*a*), the relation of a child's sponsors at baptism to the parents (Gayley).

GOWN, "Abide a while, let me put off my *gown* " (J.T. 74*d*), in the orig. this line is given to John, the next "cue " being " But yet he shall not have it, by my fay," also to John; " Lo, now . . . as he can " (75*b*), here restored to John is in the orig. given to Tyb : the next three lines, which are clearly Tyb's, are to John in orig. : the next line but one (" But see," &c.) is to Tyb.

GRAVELYN (W. 100*a*), " possibly Gravelye, near Baldock " (Pollard).

GRIST, " *grist* of a bushel " (W. 108*d*), the result of grinding less the toll of a custom-mill : here two pounds of wheat for grinding sixty-four.

GUARDON, " their souls for to *guardon* " (P.F. 9*b*), guerdon, recompense.

GYB'S FEAST (L. 172*c*), *cf.* gib-face=heavy-jowled, ugly-mug.

GYNGIANG, see Jayberd.

GYS, " by *Gys* " (W. 121*d*), see Jis.

HAD, " no *had* " (J.T. 87*a*), elliptical : *cf.* no shall (J.T. 68*a*).

HALES (F.P. 30*b*), the abbey of Hales, in Gloucestershire, founded by Richard, King of the Romans, brother to Henry III. This precious relic, which was commonly called the *blood of Hailes*, was brought out of Germany by Richard's son, Edmund, who bestowed a third part of it on his father's abbey of Hales, and some time after gave the other two parts to an abbey of his own foundation at Ashridge, near Berkamstead. It was given out, and believed to have this property, that if a man was in mortal sin, and not absolved, he could not see it; otherwise he might see it very well : therefore every man that came to see this miracle, this most precious blood, confessed himself first to one of the priests there; and then offering something at the altar, was directed to a chapel, where the miracle was shewn; the priest who confessed him, in the meantime, retiring to the back part of the said chapel, and putting forth a little cabinet or vessel of crystal, which being thick on the one side that nothing could be seen through it, but on the other side thin and transparent, they used diversely, as their interests required. On the dissolution of the abbey, it was discovered to be nothing more than honey clarified and coloured with saffron (REED).

HALIDOM, "so help me God and *halidom*" (F.P. 46*c*), anything sacred or holy—the kingdom of saints, salvation, holiness, a sanctuary, &c.: see Holydam.

HANGER, "lend me his *hanger*" (P.F. 22*b*), properly the girdle or sword-belt in which the sword or dagger was suspended, but also the weapon itself.

HAP, "with an evil *hap*" (P.F. 21*b*), chance, fortune. "He sendyth yowrys bothe *hap* and hele, and for yow dyed my dere sone dere."—*MS. Cantab.* Ff. ii. 38, f. 48.

HARBOROW, "both *harborough* and food" (P.F. 20*a*), lodging, protection. "Leave me those hilles where *harbrough* nis to see."—Spenser, *Shepheards Calender: June.* "Therfor he ledde them ynne and resseyuyde in *herbore*."—Wycliffe, *Dedis* x.

HARDLY, "speak on *hardly*" (P.F. 18*a bis*)—"I shall reward her *hardly*" (J.T. 67*d*), assuredly, confidently.

HATH, "gods and goddesses . . . *hath* late assembled" (W. 94*a*), for another example of the use, as a pl. of the 3rd pers. sing. pres. indicative, see "right humbly *beseecheth* your merchantmen" (W. 104*d*).

HEAL, "your soul's *heal*" (P.F. 3*c*)—"if he love his *heal*" (P.F. 12*a*), health, hence spiritual welfare, salvation: also *hele* (A.S.).

HENRY, KING (F.P. 30*c*), see *Variorum Readings.*

HEYWOOD, JOHN. See Terminal Essay (E.E.D.S., Heywood's *Complete Works*, Vol. III.).

HIP, "a holy Jew's *hip*" (P.F. 6*b*), see *Variorum Readings.*

HIRE, "*hire* me" (F.P. 45*d*), reward: more frequently met with as a *subs.* (=*recompense*) than as a *verb.*

HOLD, "I *hold* a noble" (J.T. 69*d*), I wager or bet 6s. 8d.: see noble and *cf.* "I *hold* a groat."—Udall, *R. Roister Doister*, I, iii. 27.

HOLPE, " and *holpe* you mass to sing " (J.T. 86a)—
" had not swimming *holpe* in love " (L. 157b), helped.

HOLYDOM, " by my *holydom* " (J.T. 82a)—" so help me
God and *holydam* " (W. 109d), see Halidom.

HONESTY, " it will not be for your *honesty* " (P.F. 24d)
—" jeopard all thine *honesty* " (W. 124b), in the
second example *honesty* takes the meaning of chastity,
an old usage now obsolete save in the phrase, to
make an *honest* woman of one who has been seduced.
In the first example *honesty* = honour, credit (A.N.).

HOPPER (W. 108d), the feeder of a mill.

HORNER, HORNS, " who maketh all these *horns?* "
(W. 101a)—" Master *Horner* " (W. 101c)—" I am no
horner, knave " (W. 101d), a play on *horn* = to cuckold,
a word of ancient usage. From an early example of
its use (*infra*) it would seem to have been imported
into English from the Italian ; *Becco* (= he-goat) and
cornuto (= a horned thing) are good Italian for a
cuckold. Also it seems to have begun to be literary
about the middle of the sixteenth century when the
Italian influence was at its height. For the rest it
passed into triumph into written English, was used in
every possible combination, had a run at least two
centuries long, and is still intelligible, though not in
common service.   *Horner* = cuckold maker.   " To
speke plaine Englishe made him cokolde. Alas I was
not auised wel before Vnkonnyngly to speake such
language : I should haue sayde how that he had an
horne. . . . And in some land *Cornodo* men do them
call, and some affirme that such folk have no gall."—
Lydgate, *Falle of Prynces*, ii., leaf 50. " My mother
was a lady of the stews, blood born, And (Knight of
the Halter) my father wore an *horne.*"—*Hickscorner*
(*c.* 1520), E.E.D.S., Anonymous Pl., 1st Ser.   " I
shall have some music yet At my making free o' th'
company of *horners.*"—Beaumont and Fletcher, *Elder
Brother* (1637), iv. 4.   " If I but catch her in a corner,
Humph I 'tis your servant, Colonel *Horner.*"—Somer-
ville, *Occasional Poems* (d. 1742) (Chalmers, *English
Poets*, 1810, xi. 238).

R

HOVE, " doth make me *hove* " (L. 168*b*), hover, wait
upon. " And there he *houed*, and abode To wit what
she wolde mene."—Gower, *Confessio Amantis* (1393), i.

I, " *I* per se *I* " (W. 96*c*), I sounded by itself : in re-
peating the alphabet.

IF, " *if* they do well " (W.W. 205*a*), this play upon the
word *if* appears to have been suggested by the anec-
dote told by Sir Thomas More in his *Life of Richard
the Third*, of Hastings' answer to the accusation
against Shore's wife,—" Certainly, my lord, *if* they
have so done, they be worthy of heinous punishment.
What! (qd. the protector), thou servest me I ween
with *if* and with *and*. I tell thee they have done it,
and that I will make good upon thy body, traitor ! "
An incident powerfully worked out by Shakspeare;
who also has made Touchstone fully aware that
" there is much virtue in *if*."—Fairholt.

ILK, " th' *ilk* peace " (P.F. 4*c*), the same : still good
Scots.

ILLUSTRATIONS, see Facsimile Title-pages, &c.

IMP, " plant *imps* of good works " (W.W. 212*a*), properly a shoot, a graft, but often used metaphorically.
" The king preferred there eighty noble *imps* (=scions
of noble houses) to the order of knighthood."—Stow,
Annals (1592), 385.

INDIFFERENT, INDIFFERENTLY, INDIFFERENCY (F.P. 47*d* ;
W. 98*a* and *b*; L. 146*c* ; *et passim*), impartial, un-
biassed. " No judge *indifferent*."—Shakspeare, *Henry
VIII.* (1601), ii. 4.

INFECT, " he is *infect* " (L. 177*d*), infected. " Whom
assoone as Ioues deare wife saw *infect*, With such a
plage."—Surrey, *Virgile, Æneis* iv.

INNOCENT, POPE (P.F. 10*b*), there were eight occupants
of the papal chair of this name prior to the publication
of *The Pardoner and the Friar*, the last, Pope Innocent VIII., beginning to reign in 1484.

INTREAT, " *intreat* me not " (P.F. 24*d*), treat, use, serve,
deal with. " He shall gather the lambes together

with his arme, and carye them in hys bosome, and shall kyndlye *intreate* those that beare yonge."— *Esaye*, xl. (1551).

I'SH, " *I'sh* lug thee by the ears " (P.F. 21*c*), I shall; *mod. I will, I'll pull thee*, &c.

I-WIS, I-WYS (*passim*), certainly, indeed, truly : often, with weakened sense, as a metrical tag. The writing with capital I, and separation of the two elements, have led later authors to understand and use it erroneously as=*I wot, I know*, as if a present of *I wist* (O.E.D.).

JAMES IN GALES, SAINT (F.P. 30*b*), there were two apostles of this name, but here St James the Greater, chosen as the Patron Saint of Spain, whose shrine at Compostella was a famous centre of pilgrimage. " The Italians, yea, those that dwell neare Rome, will mocke and scoffe at our English (and other) pilgrims that go to Rome to see the Pope's holinesse and St Peter's chaire, and yet they themselves will runne *to see the reliques of Saint Iames of Compostella in the Kingdom of Galicia*, in Spaine, which is above twelve hundred English miles."—Weever, *Funeral Monuments*, 172.

JAPE, " it is a pretty *jape* " (J.T. 83*c*), jest, game : often with an indelicate meaning.

JAYBERD, " Ynge Gyngiang *Jayberd* " (W. 100*a*), " defies explanation " (Pollard) : see, however, a note attached to the Terminal Essay (E.E.D.S., Heywood's *Complete Works*, Vol. III.).

JET, JETTETH, JETTED, JETTER (F.P. 39*c*, and 61*b*; W. 121*a*; L. 159*a*; W.W. 209*a*; *et passim*), strut, swagger; *jetter*=one who assumes a pompous gait or swagger. " Wantonly to goe in and out with the legs."—Cotgrave, *Dict.* (1611).

JIS, GYS, " by *Jis* " (P.F. 21*c*), by Jesus.

JOB, " some *job* him " (W.W. 194*a*), to thrust, poke, stab. " Jenkin Jacon, that *jobbed* jolly Joan."— *Thersites* (E.E.D.S., Anonymous Pl., 1st Ser.), 217*d*.

JOHN, see Sir John.

JOHN JOHN, TYB, AND SIR JOHN. The evidence (mainly
inferential) for Heywood's authorship of this " Merry
Play " is strong, though not absolutely conclusive.
In the " advertisement " to the Chiswick Press reprint of what was then thought to be the unique Ashmolean copy, it is justly stated to be " exclusive of
its antiquity and rarity, . . . valuable as affording
a specimen of the earliest and rudest form of our
comedy . . . and of the liberty with which even the
R. C. authors of that age felt themselves authorised
to treat the established priesthood." It deals with
a favourite theme of the old Middle English satirists—
of intrigue between wife and cleric. *Date of Composition*, unknown. *Previous Editions*—(1) 1533,
copies of this edition are in the Bodleian (Ashmolean) and Magdalen College, Cambridge (Pepys
Collection) Libraries. (2) Reprinted *c* 1819 [?] at the
Chiswick Press by C[harles] Whittingham " from
an unique copy in the Ashmolean Museum, Oxford ";
(3) included in Prof. Brandl's *Quellen des Weltlichen
Dramas in England vor Shakspeare*, the Ashmolean
text being employed; and (4) in Prof. Gayley's
Representative English Comedies, the text there given
being the Ashmolean collated with the Magdalen
copy : the present text follows the last named.
A few variations in orthography and errors in print-
ing which appear in the Chiswick text have been
here incorporated on the authority of Mr. A. W.
Pollard (*Representative English Comedies*). See also
Gown and Shortly.

JOLL, " some *joll* him " (W.W. 194*a*), bump, blow,
knock, or stroke. " There was *jolling*, ther was
rennyng for the sovereynte."—*Pol. Poems* (1470), ii.
276.

JULIUS, POPE (P.F. 10*b*), there were three popes of this
name, the first being St Julius, of great piety and
learning, and who maintained the cause of St Athan-
asius. Pope Julius II. (1503) was of martial character, and he it was who began St Peter's : probably
this pontiff is the one alluded to : see next article.

JULIUS THE SIXTH (P.F. 10*a*), there never was a Julius
the Sixth, the third of the name being the last : pos-

sibly the whole list is an intentional jumble, part of
Heywood's satire.

JYS, " by *Jys* " (L. 163c), by Jesus.

KNACKS, " all such *knacks* " (F.P. 36a), trick, device,
joke, trifle. " She ne used no suche *knakkes* smale."
—Chaucer, *Dethe Blaunche* (c. 1369), 1033.

KNEE, " nother cap nor *knee* " (W. 99c), see Cap.

LAD, " evermore *lad* " (L. 155d), led.

LAUNDER (W. Dram. Pers. 92 and 123b), a washer,
laundress. " A woman that his *lander* was."—*St.
Brice* (c. 1350), 156.

LEAK, " old moons be *leak* " (W. 120a), leaky : a very
early instance of this form in O.E.

LEAST, " the *least* quarter " (F.P. 33b), see *Variorum
Readings*.

LEMAN, " farewell *leman* " (J.T. 86c), a lover, gallant,
or mistress. " With my gud will I wyll no *lemman*
be To no man born."—Henry, *Wallace* (c. 1470), v.
693.

LENGER, " no *lenger* " (P.F. 22a ; F.P. 50c), longer.

LENT, " ten thousand . . . *Lents* of pardon " (P.F. 9b),
i.e. ten thousand periods of pardon of forty days each.
" There is seven year and seven *lents* of pardon."—
Caxton, *Golden Legend* (1483), 158 b. 2.

LEO THE TENTH (P.F. 9a), 1513–1522 : this pope's grant
of indulgences for crime led to the Reformation ; he
was nevertheless a great patron of learning and art.
It has been thought, by some commentators, that this
mention of a reigning pope fixes approximately the
date of writing of *The Pardoner and Frere* as not
later than 1522.

LESE, " *lese* part of his eyesight " (F.P. 45a), lose.

LESYNGS, " this fool's *lesyngs* " (L. 180d), lie, falsehood.
" The treueth is fled farre awaye and *lesynge* is hard
at hande."—Coverdale (1535), 2 *Esdras*, xiv. 18.

LEST, " most nor *lest* " (L. 151c), least.

LET (*a*), " should me disturb or *let* " (P.F. 12*a*)—" *let*
the word of God " (P.F. 17*c*)—" women have many
lets " . . . " by these *lets* and nets, the *let* is such "
(F.P. 36*d*)—" to will the *let* of love " (L. 170*a*), hindrance, obstruction : now archaic save in phrase, *let
or hindrance*. (*b*) " Shall I *let* " (J.T. 68*c*), leave undone, cease, forbear : *i.e.* hinder myself.

LET OVER, " *let over* that her beauty was so much "
(L. 153*d*), admit.

LICK, " fetched of him a *lick* " (J.T. 71*a*), a wheeze of
a kind is here intended. The original spelling shows
the play on the words—" Powder or sirop, syrs,
which *lycke* ye best? Who *lycketh* not the tone maye
lycke up the rest."

LIEVER, LIEF, " I had *liever* thou wert hanged . . .
than I " (P.F. 15*a*)—" as *lief* ye kist mine arse "
(W. 101*d*)—" had *liever* have " (W. 114*c*), rather.

LIMITATION, " we friars . . . go on *limitation* " (P.F.
14*c*), a friar-limiter (or limiter) was licensed to beg
within certain limits. " A limitoure of the graye
fryers, in the time of his *limitation* preached manye
tymes, and had but one sermon."—Latimer, *Sermons*
(1562), 94.

LOBERS, " slovenly *lobers* " (L. 154*d*)—" her *lober*
seemeth as ugly " (L. 187*a*), a clumsy, stupid fellow,
an idle lout : in the second example a play on the
word *lover*.

LORD, " with my *lord* " (W. 127*d*). " Cardinal Wolsey
suggests himself as the person most likely to be thus
referred to, but if the reference of l. 636 is to the
excessive rain of 1527–28, Wolsey's disgrace followed
it rather too closely for the phrase ' within this seven
vere ' ". (Pollard).

LORE, " but *lore* against her will " (L. 167*d*), ? sore.

LOSEL, " this *losel* . . . hath lost his wit " (L. 148*d*),
profligate, rake, scoundrel ; and in weaker sense,
ne'er-do-well. " *Losels* ye ar and thefys."—*Towneley
Mysteries* (*c.* 1400), xvi. 154.

LOTELY, " *lotely* hell-hound's face " (L. 187*a*), loathly,
hateful, repulsive. " Thou art so *loothly*, and so oold
also."—Chaucer, *W. of Bath's Tale* (*c.* 1386), 244.

LOUR, " or frown, or *lour* " (J.T. 80a), scowl, look discontented.

LOVE, THE PLAY OF—*Text*, pp. 137–190. *Editions*—twice printed by Rastell (1) in 1533; a copy is in the library of St John's College, Oxford; (2) also in 1534; it was likewise (3) printed by Waley (who published between the years 1547 and 1558): a copy of this is in the Bodleian, and is the text now given (see Terminal Essay); and (4) it was reprinted in Prof. Brandl's *Quellen des Weltlichen Dramas in England vor Shakspeare*. This play has been condemned by critics, past and present, as " deadly dull." What play, however, reads with a tithe of the interest that attaches to representation? " Business " counts for much in matters dramatic, and, quite apart from the popularity of the word-contests and scholastic disputations of Heywood's day, there are in this play numerous touches of humour (some of them " broad " enough in all conscience) and many an amusing quibble, which, supported with by-play, must have raised many a laugh. Let it not be overlooked also that the amusement and the fad or craze of to-day becomes a weariness to-morrow. No more notable example of this, in any age, could be found than the spelling-bee of the late eighties! *Variorum Readings*—these are those of the St John's College copy, unless otherwise stated—for my *whole* service (140b), orig. *hoole*, Bodley *hole*; *in* deadly pain (144a), orig. *I*; that sooner may the *suffrant* (147d), orig. *suffret*; that part *rehearse* (149d), *rehearsed*; be ye *sure* (156b), orig. *sewer*; without *mo* words (158b), *no*; shall never *swerve* (161c), orig. *swarme*; your will *outweigheth* (186c), orig. *out wolth*; answereth you *plain* (178c), orig. *playe*; all *errors* or doubts (187d), orig. *errous*; more pleasure than *ye* (188c), orig. *he*.

LURCH, " this *lurch* " (P.F. 23c), cheat, swindle, discomfiture, difficulty: once literary, now usually in phrase to leave in the *lurch*.

LUST, " in good health and *lust* " (F.P. 51b), vigour, lustiness. " To restore the *luste* bothe in plantes and in beestes."—Trevisa, *Barth. de P. R.* (1398), III., viii. 54 (1495).

LYCKLY, " anything *lyckly* " (L. 151*d*), likely.

LYDGER (W. 118*a*), the bedstone, a fixed stone over
which the runner moves : properly *ledger* : Heywood's
use of the word is the earliest given in the O.E.D.
" The molecopstone being always the runner, and the
Darbyshire-stone the *Legier*."—Plot, *Staffordshire*
(1686), 170.

MACULATE, " we may not *maculate* " (P.F. 19*a*), spot,
stain, defile, pollute. " A sensuall prynce . . . pur-
posed to *maculate* this vyrgyn gloryous."—Bradshaw,
St Werburge (1513), i. 2791.

MALES, " he be in such endless *males* " (W.W. 214*a*),
evil, trouble, torment : also as *adj*. " That the dewke
in hys perlement Hym forgeve hys *male* entente."—
MS. Cantab. Ff. ii. 38, f. 181.

MARK, " five *mark* a year " (W. 107*b*), a money of
account, originally representing the value of a mark
weight of pure silver. In England, after the Con-
quest, the ratio of 20 sterling pennies to an ounce
was the basis of computation ; hence the value of the
mark became fixed at 160 pence = 13s. 4d. or two-thirds
of the £ sterling. " Vj *marc* yeerly, to scars is to
sustene The charges that I have."—Hoccleve, *De
Reg. Princ.* (*c.* 1412), 1224.

MARK, SAINT (F.P. 30*c*), " at the Church of St Mark,
in Venice, they pretend to have the body of that
evangelist, which was brought thither by certain
merchants from Alexandria, in Egypt, in the year 810.
Coryat says, that the treasure of this church was of
that inestimable value, that it was thought no treasure
whatsoever in any other place in Christendom might
compare with it, neither that of St Denis in France,
nor St Peter's in Rome, nor that of Madonna de
Loretto in Italy, nor that of Toledo in Spain, nor any
other. See Coryat's *Crudities*, p. 214, and *The Com-
monwealth and Government of Venice*, by Contareno,
translated by Lewes Lewkenor, Esq., 1599, p. 165 "
(Reed).

MASHIP, MASSHIP, " I beseech your *maship* " (F.P. 47*d*)
—" he taketh your *maship* but for knave " (F.P. 48*c*)
—" your *masship* " (J.T. 79*d*)—*et passim*, mastership :

in the last instance, as applied to a cleric, there is obviously a play on *mass*. " I shall gyve your *mashyp* a good reward."—*Hundred Mery Tales* (1526), 16 (1866).

MASTERY, " now have I found one *mastery* " (F.P. 42a), an exercise of skill or power on or against a person. " Ye shul wel seen at eye, That I wol doon a *maistrie* er I go."—Chaucer, *Can Yeom. Prol.* (*c.* 1386), 507.

MEAN, " we shall find *mean* " (W. 117d)—" by *mean* of the length " (L. 144a), means.

MEDDLE, MEDDLING, MEDDLETH (W. 125a and b; L. 162b), Merry Report uses the word suggestively: see *Slang and its Analogues*, s.v., Mell.

MELL, " how that they shall *mell* " (P.F. 24a), meddle with, fight, contend.

MENT, " my love thus *ment* " (L. 169b), made mention of.

METS, " which maketh me *mets* " (L. 164c), mete, fit.

MEVE, " he hath *meved* " (F.P. 58d)—" I would *meve* thee " (J.T. 72b), consult, question, address oneself to, told. " The Florentine will *move* us For speedy aid."—Shakspeare, *All's Well that Ends Well* (1598), i. 2.

MEYNY, " all your *meyny* " (W. 100c), company, crew: also *meyne*. " Whanne al was redy, *meyné* and vitaille, They bide not but wynde for to saille."—*MS. Digby* 230 (xv. Cent.).

MICHAEL (SAINT) (P.F. 7d), the Archangel Michael, whose feast (Michaelmass) is celebrated on Sep. 29.

MINION, " my *minion* seemeth very merry " (L. 155a)—" this *minion* " (L. 168d), a dainty person, darling, favourite, sweetheart: also in an opprobrious sense.

MIST, " ye would not have *mist* " (F.P. 40a), in original *mit*.

MISTER, " shall not *mister* " (F.P. 34a), master, achieve.

MISTRIST, " never more shall he his wife *mistrist* " (P.F. 6d), mistrust.

MIT, " ye would not have *mit* " (F.P. 40a), see Mist.

Mo (*passim*), more. " To them I wyshe even thus, and
to no *mo*, That as they have hys judgement and hys
yeares, Even so I would they had hys fayre long
eares."—*Old Ballad, Bibl. Soc. Antiq.*

Mocks, " he weeneth all is but *mocks* " (P.F. 24*c*)—
" the *mocks*, the fables " (J.T. 80*d*)—" a proud
mock " (J.T. 82*d*)—" cometh of rudeness . . . that
mock " (L. 148*d*), sneer, gibe, taunt : also a trifle, a
wild assertion.

Moder, " we *moder* our sails " (W. 116*b*), moderate,
adjust.

Saint Modwin (J.T. 85*a*), " S. Modwena, an Irish
virgin, who died A.D. 518. She is said to have been
the patroness of Burton-upon-Trent, and Henry
VIII.'s commissioners sent thence to London ' the
image of seint Moodwyn with her red kowe and hir
staff, which wymen labouryng of child in those parts
were very desirous to have with them to lean upon ' "
(P.).

Mot, " so *mot* I thrive " (F.P. 36*b*)—" so *mote* I thee "
(J.T. 87*b*), may : in last example=may I thrive.
" They byed on hym and can hym wrye, In helle
mote they long lye ! "—*MS. Cantab.* Ff. ii. 38, f. 103.

Mother, " the terrible words that *mother* brendered "
L. 158*d*), hysterical passion, anger. " How this
mother swells up toward my heart."—Shakspeare,
Lear (1605), ii. 4.

Muswell (F.P. 30*c*). " Muswell Hill (in the northern
suburbs of London), called also Pinsenall Hill : there
was a chapple sometime bearing the name of our
ladie of Muswell : where now Alderman Roe hath
erected a proper house, the place taketh name of the
well and of the hill, Mousewellhill ; for there is on
the hill a spring of faire water, which is now within
the compass of the house. There was sometime an
image of the ladie of Muswell, whereunto was a con-
tinuall resort, in the way of pylgrimage, growing, as
is (though as I take it fabulouslie) reported in regard
of a great cure which was performed by this water,
upon a king of Scots, who being strangely diseased
was, by some devine intelligence, advised to take the

water of a well in England, called Muswell, which after long scrutation and inquisition, this well was found and performed the cure."—Norden, *Speculum Britanniæ*, p. 36, edit. 1723. " I am informed that the mosaic pavement and other ruins of this well and its chapel were to be seen about twenty-five years ago " (Dodsley, *Old Plays*, edit. 1780).

NAIL, " naked as my *nail* " (W. 124*a*), as bare as may be, stark-naked. " And tho' he were as naked as my *nail*, Yet would be whinny then and wag the tail."— Drayton, *Man in the Moon* (1605), 510.

NAKED, see Nail.

NE, " *ne* suffer other their ears to incline " (P.F. 14*d*, *et passim*), nor.

NETHER (*a*), " the *nether* end is good enough for me " (L. 173*d*), lower end, in the back-ground. (*b*), " to fear *nether* " (J.T. 70*a*), neither.

NIFFLES, " the fables and the *niffles* " (J.T. 80*d*), a trifle. " He served hem with *nifles* and with fables."— Chaucer, *Cant. Tales* (*c.* 1386), 7342.

NOBLE, " I hold a *noble* " (J.T. 69*d*), a coin of the value of 6s. 8d. : to hold a *noble*=to stake or wager it. " I hold a groat ye will drink anon for this gear."— Udall, *Roister Doister* (*c.* 1552), i. 3, 27.

NOCK, " lick my tail in the *nock* " (W. 129*a*)—" beyond the *nock* " (L. 154*a*; L. 182*a*), a slit, nick, or notch : properly the notch of an arrow, or bow where the string is fastened : also *nock* (*nockandrow*)=pos- teriors, tail, whence numerous vulgar allusions in early writers.

NODDY, " I were a *noddy* " (F.P. 42*d*)—" whoreson *noddy* " (F.P. 60*d*; L. 164*c*), fool, dolt. " Ere you came thither, poor I was somebody ; The King de- lighteth in me, now I am but a *noddy*."—Edwards, *Damon and Pithias* (1567).

NONNY, NONNY (W. 128*b*), usually an exclamation, here one of dissent : often found as a refrain to cover indelicate allusions. " These *noninos* of beastly ribauldry."—Drayton, *Eccl.* (1593).

NOTHER, " *nother* for our meat nor for our drink "

(P.F. 4*a*; P.F. 16*b*; J.T. 69*a*; *et passim*), neither:
see Other.

NYCEBYCETERS, " such *nycebyceters* as she is " (W. 123*c*),
apparently a term of contempt: *cf.* " between you and
your Ginifinee *Nycebecetur* " (Heywood, *Proverbs* i.
11. 57): ?Fr. *niaise* = simpleton, fool, and as *adj.*
silly; Eng. *nice* = silly—" he was *nyce* and knowthe
no wisdome (*Rob. of Glouc.*). The word has puzzled
all editors so far; all that seems clear is that Heywood in each case employs the word in contempt of
a woman, as also does Udall—" Merygreeke : ' But
with whome is he nowe so sadly roundyng yond? '
Doughtie : ' With *Nobs nicebecetur miserere* fonde ' "
(*Roister Doister*, I. iv. 12). Gayley says this is ex-
plained by Flügel as a contraction of *Nescio quid
dicitur* = Mistress " What's-her-name."

NYFULS, " I take them as *nyfuls* " (W. 113*d*), see
Niffles.

OAK, " Our Lady that standeth in the *oak* " (F.P. 30*c*),
a shrine to the Virgin Mary standing by the wayside
over against an oak : *cf.* " our Lady of the walnut-
tree," " our Lady of the vault," &c. " Our lady
of the fair *oak* "—Stephanus (trans. by R. C.), *World
of Wonders* (1607), 316.

OBJECT, " thus be *object* " (W. 114*b*), opposed, objected
to. " No thing probable *object* ayenst the same by
the said craft."—*Surtees Misc.* (1485), 43 (1888).

ODD, " too far *odd* " (W. 109*c*), too much at variance.

OFF, " come, *off* quickly " (F.P. 37*c*), lay down, down
with (*i.e.* the money): an elliptical verbal use of the
adverb.

ONES, " for this *ones* " (J.T. 69*b*), once.

OTHER (*passim*), either : *cf.* Outher and Nother.

OUGHT, " mad by love that she *ought* we " (L. 158*a*),
owed. " The devill or els his dame, they *ought* her
sure a shame."—*Gammer Gurton* (1575), i. 3.

OUTHER, " *outher* groats or else pence " (P.F. 6*a*),
either : *cf.* Other and Nother.

OWETH, " that any beast *oweth* " (P.F. 6*c*), possesses, is owner of. " The goode man that the beastes *oweth.*"—Chaucer, *Pard. Tale* (*c.* 1386), 33.

OYEZ (W. 128*d*), " Hear ye ! hearken ! " a call by a public crier or officer of a court to attract attention : generally uttered three times, *Oyez, oyez, oyez!*

PALMER (F.P. *passim*), a pilgrim returned from the Holy Sepulchre, but also an itinerant monk travelling from shrine to shrine under a perpetual vow of poverty. " The difference between a pilgrim and a palmer was thus : The pilgrim had some home or dwelling-place ; but the palmer had none. The pilgrim travelled to some certain designed place or places ; but the palmer to all. The pilgrim went at his own charges ; but the palmer professed wilful poverty, and went upon alms. The pilgrim might give over his profession and return home ; but the palmer must be constant till he had obtained the palm, that is, victory over all spiritual enemies, and life by death, and thence his name *Palmer,* or else from a staff, or boughs of palm, which he always carried along with him."— Staveley, *Romish Horseleech* (1769), 93.

PARDE, PARDIE (*passim*), a form of oath, but often used in a watered-down sense=verily, certainly : *par Dieu.*

PARDON-BOWL, " to kiss the *pardon-bowl* " (F.P. 45*d*), the 'Pothecary has an eye on similar devices for granting pardons : *e.g.* the angelus bell, popularly named *the pardon-bell,* because special pardons were formerly granted to those who on hearing it recited the angelus correctly.

PARDONER (*passim*), a person licensed to sell papal pardons or indulgences. " Pardoners were certaine fellowes that caried about the Pope's Indulgences, and sold them to such as would buy them ; against whom Luther, by Sleydans report, incensed the people of Germany in his time, exhorting them *ne merces tam viles tanti emerent.*"—Cowell, *Interpreter* (1607), Sign. A A A 2. See Palmer.

PARDONER AND THE FRERE, THE. The *text* is given on pp. 1-25. The only copy known, formerly Heber's, is now in the library of the Duke of Devonshire : the title-page is missing. The *date* of composition is unknown. If the reference (9*a*) to Pope Leo Tenth is taken as referring to a reigning pontiff, the play must have been written before 1521, but see Terminal Essay (E.E.D.S., Heywood's *Complete Works*, Vol. III.). *Editions*—(1) printed by Rastell, 5 April, 1533; (2) facsimile reprint, 1820; (3) in *Four Old Plays*, ed. Child, Cambridge, U.S.A., 1848; (4) in Hazlitt's *Dodsley* (i. 1874). " Its chief end appears to have been the exposure of the tricks and impositions practised by wandering friars and pardoners, who bore relics to cheat the unthinking laity of their money. To both these classes Heywood is unsparing in his censure, as he also is in his Four P's."—Fairholt, *Wit and Folly*, li. " This piece . . . is destitute of the allegorical element and . . . is a mere dramatic interlocution, lightly and inartificially constructed, with little or no plot " (Dodsley, *Old Plays* (1874), i. 198).

PARSON, " Master *parson* . . . my mistress, your wife " (W. 104*b*). As (says Pollard) the play was written before 1533 when the clergy were still celebates this is clearly only Merry Report's humour.

PARTLETS (F.P. 36*d*), ruffs or bands for women, worn about the neck and upper part of the chest: originally a neckerchief of linen or the like.

PASTAUNCE, " for dalliant *pastaunce* " (L. 153*d*), pastime. " To have in remembraunce Her goodly dalyaunce, And her goodly *pastaunce*."—Skelton, *Ph. Sparrow* (c. 1500), 1095.

PATERNOSTER WHILE (L. 165*d*), the time it takes to say a *paternoster*. " Al thys was don, as men say, in a *Pater Noster wyle*."—*Paston Letters* (1448), i. 74.

PATRICK'S PURGATORY, SAINT (F.P. 30*b*), " this place, which was much frequented by pilgrims, was situate on a lake called Logh Derg, in the Southern part of the county of Donegal, near the borders of Tyrone and Fermanagh. It was surrounded with wild and barren mountains, and was almost inaccessible by horsemen even in summer time, on account of great bogs, rocks, and precipices, which environed it. The popular tradition concerning it is as ridiculous as is to be found in any legend of the Romish Martyrology. After continuing in great credit many years, it began to decline; and in the 13th of Henry the Seventh was demolished with great solemnity, on St Patrick's Day, by the Pope's express order. It, however, afterwards came into reputation again, insomuch that, by an order of the Privy Council, dated 13th of September 1632, it was a second time destroyed. From this period, as pilgrimages grew less in fashion, it will appear extraordinary that the place should be a third time restored to its original state, and as much visited as in any former period. In this condition it continued until the second year of Queen Anne, when an Act of the Irish Parliament declared, that all meetings and assemblies there should be adjudged riots and unlawful assemblies, and inflicted a penalty upon every person meeting or assembling contrary to the Statute. The ceremonies to be performed by the pilgrims are very exactly set forth in Richardson's *Great Folly, Superstition, and Idolatry of Pilgrimages in Ireland, especially of that to St Patrick's Purgatory,* Dublin, 8vo, 1727. Enough hath been already said on the subject of *Saint Patrick's Purgatory,* I shall therefore only add, that it is often mentioned in Froissard's *Chronicle,* and that Sir James Melvil, who visited it in 1545, describes it as looking 'like an old coal-pit, which had taken fire, by reason of the smoke that came out of the hole.' "—Melvil, *Memoirs,* p. 9, edit. 1683. " It is mentioned in Erasmus's *Praise of Folie,* 1549, Sign. A : ' Whereas before ye satte all heavie and glommyng, as if ye had come lately from Troponius cave, or *Saint Pattrickes purgatorie* ' " (Reed).

PAYMENT-STICK, " her *payment-stick* by her side " (J.T. 70b), the staff or cudgel with which chastisement was to be administered. " Syre launcelot . . . chafe his hede and neck vnto the throte . . . Now hast thou thy *payement* that long thou hast deserued."—Malory, *Arthur* (1470–85), VI. x.

PEASING, " in *peasing* your pains " (L. 187c), appeasing.

PECKING-IRON (W. 118b), an iron with which millstones are dressed. " If thy mill-stones be not worne too blunt for want of *pecking.*"—Harvey, *Pl. Perc.* (1589), 10 (1860).

PEEL'D PRIEST (J.T. 76*b*), shorn, tonsured.

PERCASE, " my *percase* " (J.T. 71*d*), guess, conjecture.

PERFIT, " are you *perfit* in drinking " (F.P. 38*a*), perfect, skilful, seasoned. Also *perfitly*, adv.

PER SE, " I *per se* I " (W. 96*c*), see I.

PHEBE (W. 94*b*), the dispenser of rain : see Saturn.

PHEBUS (W. 94*b*), the dispenser of sunshine : see Saturn.

PIG, " a *pig* in the worse panyer " (J.T. 89*a*), a proverbial phrase : also in Heywood's *Proverbs*, II., xi. " Who that hath either of these *pigs* in ure, He hath a *pig* of the worse pannier sure."

PINCASES (F.P. 36*b*), pins are mentioned in a statute of 1483. " Brass pins," says Haydn, " were brought from France in 1540," but it would seem from this passage that they were really introduced at an earlier date.

PINKING, " my eyes will be *pinking* " (F.P. 38*a*), winking, blinking.

PITH, " hath *pith* sufficient " (L. 184*b*), strength, cogency, weight, importance.

PLUMPING, " *plumping* all manner corn " (W. 115*b*), to swell out.

PLY, " *ply* it " (W. 133*c*), use, employ.

POIGNETS (F.P. 36*d*), " little bodkins or puncheons " (Cotgrave, s.v. *Pinconnet*); but surely wristbands (Fr. *poignet*).

POINT, " *point* us a day " (W. 128*b*), appoint.

POINT DEVICE " at all points, *point device* " (L. 154*d*), to a nicety, exactly : from O.Fr. *à point devis*＝to the very point imagined.

POLL, " I came not . . . to *poll* nor to shave " (P.F. 3*c*), plunder, pillage, rob. " With *polling* and shaving." —Skelton, *Works* (Dyce, ii. 29), d. 1529.

'POTHECARY (F.P. *passim*), an apothecary.

POULES, " Church of *Poules* " (J.T. 71*d*)—" Saint *Powle* " (W.W. 209*c*), St Paul's in London : this was the edifice (which preceded the present Cathedral) commenced in 1087 and totally destroyed in the Great Fire in 1666.

PRATELY, " served thus *prately* " (L. 158*d*), prettily, softly, gently, lovingly.

PREFARDE, " the witty wise worker to be *prefarde* Above th'idle sot " (W.W. 217*a*), preferred.

PREFE, " indifferent *prefe* " (L. 184*c*)—" ye put for *prefe* " (W.W. 209*a*), proof.

PREST, " to find me *prest* " (F.P. 37*d*)—" make them *prest* " (F.P. 41*d*), ready; Fr. *Pret.* " What must be, must be ; Cæsar's *prest* for all."—*Cæsar and Pompey* (1607).

PREVAIL, " nought should *prevail* you " (J.T. 69*a*)— " shall greatly *prevail* you " (W. 103*a*), avail, have effect on, influence over.

PREBENDS, " no *prebends* ne exhibition " (P.F. 19*a*), the stipend or maintenance granted to a canon of a cathedral or collegiate church out of its estate ; a canonry. There are two kinds of prebends : a Simple Prebend is one restricted to the revenue only ; a Dignitary Prebend has jurisdiction annexed to it (*Enc. D.*).

PRICED, " how rain hath *priced* corn within this vii year " (W. 144*c*), " the earliest reference to a dearth of corn in the reign of Henry VIII. which I can find in Holinshed is *sub anno* 1523, when he states that the price in London was 20 *s.* a quarter, but without assigning any cause. The reference here is, I think, clearly to the great rains of the autumn of 1527 and April and May, 1528, of which Holinshed writes that they ' caused great floods and did much harme namelie in corne, so that the next yeare [1528?] it failed . . . and great dearth ensued ' " (Pollard).

PSALTER, " Our lady's *psalter* " (W. 111*c*; W. 134*c*), the Psalms appointed for the " Hours of the Blessed Virgin."

P'SUMING (W.W. 194*c*), presuming.

S

PURLIEU, "*purlieus* and chases" (W. 107*b*), see Chases.

PURSE, "your tongue in your *purse*" (W.W. 201*d*), a proverbial injunction to silence; Heywood, however, does not include it in his *Proverbs*.

PURVEYED, "I am *purveyed*" (W. 128*a*), provided.

QUEAN, "such gross *queans* as thou art" (W. 123*c*), primarily a woman, without regard to character or position; hence slut, hussy, strumpet. A distinction was made in M.E. between *Queen* and *Quean* (*Quein Queyn*): a notable example occurs in *Piers Plowman* (ix. 46): "At church in the charnel cheorles aren yuel to knowe, Other a knyght fro a knave other a *queyne* fro a *queene*."

QUERE, "the organs bear brunt of half the *quere*" (W. 113*b*), choir.

QUITE, "God shall *quite* you well" (P.F. 10*b*), redeem, deliver, release.

RAGEOUS, "*rageous* wind" (W. 114*d*), furious, like a hurricane. "The boystrous wyndes and the *ragious* skie."—Lydgate, *Bochas* (1430–40), i. 2 (1544) 5.

RAGMAN-ROLLS, "publish his *ragman-rolls* with lies" (P.F. 22*d*), a rigmarole, tedious story. *Ragman-roll* or *rageman-roll* was the name given (O.E.D.) to a statute of 4 Ed. I. appointing justices to hear and determine complaints of injuries done within 25 years previously. Concurrent and derived meanings are numerous—a roll, list, contract, official document, discourse, rhapsody, &c.—many of which have apparently been influenced by *rageman* = the Devil.

RATHER, "would God this relic had come *rather*" (F.P. 45*c*), sooner, earlier. "After me is comun a man, which was maad bifor me; for he was *rather* than Y."—Wyclif, *John I.* (1388), 30.

RAUGHT, "Or ever I *raught* them" (W. 131*c*), reached. "*Rawghting* after the empty shadow of blissfull life."—Golding, *Calvin on Ps.* xix. 9 (1571).

RAYED, "*rayed* my clothes" (J.T. 87*d*), bewrayed, soiled.

RECEIVE, " teyse and *receive* on every side " (W. 103*a*), rouse game and call off and kill.

REDBURNE (F.P. 30*b*), within 3 miles of St Albans. " At this place were founde the reliques of Amphiball, who is saide to be the instructour and convertour of Alban from Paganisme, of whose reliques such was the regard that the abbottes of the monasterie of Alban had, that they should be devoutly preserved, that a decree was made by Thomas then abbott, that a pryor and three munckes should be appointed to this holie function, whose allowance in those dayes amounted yearely to 20 pound, or upwardes, as much as three hundred pound in this age."—Norden, *Descr. Hartfordshire*, 22. " Bishop Usher has proved that this saint never existed, and that we owe the honour of his saintship to a mistaken passage in the Legend of St Alban, when the *Amphibolus* there mentioned is nothing more than *a cloak.*"—Dr. Middleton, *Letter from Rome.*

REDE, " I *rede* you beware " (W. 122*d*), warn.

REFORMABLE, " of reason I will be *reformable* "(L. 141*c*) capable of being instructed or informed.

REGENT, THE (F.P. 50*c*). " *The Regent* was one of the largest ships of war in the time of King Henry the Eighth. In the fourth year of his reign, Sir Thomas Knevet, master of the horse, and Sir John Carew, of Devonshire, were appointed captains of her, and in company with several others she was sent to fight the French fleet near Brest haven. An action accordingly ensued, and *The Regent* grappled with a French carrick, which would have been taken, had not a gunner on board the vessel, to prevent her falling into the hands of the English, set fire to the powder-room. This communicating the flames to both ships, they shared the same fate together, being both burnt. On the part of the French 900 men were lost; and on that of the English more than 700 " (See Hall's *Chronicle*, 1548, fol. 21).—Reed.

REHEATING, " ye come in revelling and *reheating* " (W. 109*b*), making merry, rejoicing.

REPARATIONS, " were not *reparations* " (W. 108*d*), repairs, making good defects.

REPREFE, " to their *reprefe* " (P.F. 4*d*), reproof.

REQUIRE, " I thee *require* " (J.T. 79*d*), ask, request, order, call upon. " In humblest manner I *require* your highness That it shall please you to declare . . . whether ever I Did broach this business."—Shakspeare, *Henry VIII.* (1601), ii. 4.

REVERENCE, " saving your *reverence* " (J.T. 78*d*), with all respect : apologetic.

REWARD, " stand at *reward* " (W. 123*c*), as the object of.

RHODES (F.P. 30*a*), an island to which the Knights Hospitallers, now Knights of Malta, retired, on being driven out of Jerusalem. The Knights Hospitallers were a community whose office was to relieve the poor, the strangers, and the sick. They built an hospital at Jerusalem in 1046 which was capable in 1112 of receiving 2,000 guests, and included an infirmary for the sick. The Knights Hospitallers were also called the Knights of St John ; and, on removing to Malta, the Knights of Malta.

RICHARD, SAINT (F.P. 30*c*), probably (says Reed) Richard Fitz-Neale, bishop of London and Treasurer of England in the time of Henry II. His shrine was (Weever, 714) in St Paul's Church ; and as he contributed largely to the building of the church, it is conjectured to have been erected there on that account. Drayton, however (*Poly-Olbion*, xxiv.), speaks of others, " Richard, the dear son to Lothar king of Kent " ; " Richard . . . of St Andrews . . . the bishop . . . for fame his holiness had won " ; and " of Chichester *St Richard*."

RIGHT, " in the self *right* " (W. 106*a*), in the same rightness.

ROCK, SAINT (F.P. 30*c*), St *Roche* (or *Roke*), born at Montpelier in France ; and died in prison at Angleria in the province of Lombardy, where a large church was built in honour of him (Reed).

RONNER, see Lydger.

ROOD, " the good *rood* of Dagenham " (F.P. 30*b*), a cross or crucifix ; *spec.* a representation of the crucified Saviour, or, more generally, of the Trinity placed in Catholic churches over the altar-screen. The *rood* consisted of the three Persons of the Trinity, the Son being represented as crucified. Generally figures of the Virgin and St John were placed at a slight distance on each side of the principal group, in reference to John xxix. 26. Hearne, in his Glossary to *Peter Langtoft*, p. 544, under the word *cross* observes that, although *the cross* and *the rood* are commonly taken for the same, yet *the rood* properly signified formerly the image of Christ on the cross, so as to represent both the cross and the figure of our blessed Saviour as He suffered upon it. The *roods* that were in churches and chapels were placed in shrines, that were styled *Rood-lofts*. "*Rood-loft* (saith Blount), a shrine, whereon was placed the cross of Christ. The *rood* was an image of Christ on the cross, made generally of wood, and erected in a loft for that purpose, just over the passage out of the church into the chancel." But *roof-loft* sometimes also signifies a shrine, on which was placed the image or relics of a saint, because generally a crucifix, or a cross, used likewise to attend such image or relics.

Roost, Roast, "rule the *roast*" (F.P. 43*b*), lead, domineer. "He ruleth all the *roste* With bragging and with boste."—Skelton, *Why Come Ye Not?* (*d.* 1529).

Round, "my mind *round*" (W. 111*b*), roundly, completely.

Runner, "beware your *runner*" (W. 118*a*), the turning stone of a mill.

Saturn, "*Saturn* and Phebus, Eolus and Phebe" (W. 94*b*), "the dispensers respectively of frost, sunshine, wind, and rain" (Pollard).

Saviour's, Saint (F.P. 30*c*), now the Cathedral of Southwark. "In September, the same yeare (says Weever), viz., an. 30 Hen. 8, by the speciall motion of great Cromwell, all the notable images, vnto the which were made any especiall pilgrimages and offerings, as the images of our Lady of Walsingham, Ipswich, Worcester, the Lady of Wilsdon, the rood of grace of our Ladie of Boxley, and the image of the rood of Saint Saviour at Bermondsey, with all the rest, were brought vp to London, and burnt at

Chelsey, at the commandement of the foresaid Cromwell, all the Iewels and other rich offerings to these,
and to the shrines (which were all likewise taken
away, or beaten to peeces) of other Saints throughout
both England and Wales were brought into the King's
Treasurie."—Edit. 1631, p. 111.

SCATH, " and other like *scath* " (W.W. 195*b*), harm,
loss, damage. " For harme and *scathe* by hym done
in Fraunce."—Fabyan, *Chronicle*, lxxv.

SCIO (W. 106*b*), Chios.

SCOURED, " thou has *scoured* a pair of stocks " (P.F.
24*c*), been in the stocks : to *scour* the cramp-rings = to
lie in chains (Harman, 1573).

SCRAT, " *scrat* and bite " (P.F. 22*c*), scratch. " Am-
bitious mind, a world of wealth would haue, So *scrats*,
and scrapes, for scorfe and scornie drosse."—*Mirrour
for Magistrates*, p. 506.

SEELED, " hath *seeled* such perfection " (W.W. 198*c*),
sanctioned, attested, established. " *Seal* the title with
a lovely kiss."—Shakspeare, *Taming of the Shrew*
(1593), iii. 2.

SEEN. See Well-seen.

SELDE, " her *selde* presence " (L. 145*d*)—" right *selde*
or never " (W. 111*d*), rare, scarce, seldom ; *cf. seld-
shown* (Shakspeare, *Cor*. ii. 1) = rarely seen in public.

SENSE, " *sense* the sheriff with your heels " (W. 126*d*),
swing to and fro before the sheriff as a censer is
swung by a thurifer (Pollard) : *sensen* = to incense
(Mandeville, *Travels*, 174 ; Hollyband, *Dict*. [1593],
s.v. *Encenser*).

SEVEN SINS, " forgiven for the *sins seven* " (P.F. 13*d*),
pride, covetousness, lust, gluttony, anger, envy, sloth.

SEVEN SLEEPERS (F.P. 44*c*), " these *seven sleepers* are
said to have lived at Ephesus in the time of the
Emperor Decian. Being commanded to sacrifice according to the Pagan manner, they fled to a cave in
Mount Ceylon, where they fell asleep, and continued
in that state 372 years, as is asserted by some, though
according to others only 208 years. They awoke in
the reign of the Emperor Theodosian, who, being informed of this extraordinary event, came from Con-

stantinople to see them, and to satisfy himself of the truth of the relation. Having communicated to him the several circumstances of their case, they all, as the *Legenda Aurea* expresses it, ' enclyned theyr hedes to th' erth, and rendred their spyrites at the commaundement of our Lorde Jesu Cryst, and soo deyed.' "—See *Legenda Aurea*, 196 (Reed).

SEVEN YEAR, " within this *seven year* " (W. 114*c*), see Priced.

SHALL, (*a*) " no *shall* " (J.T. 68*a*). Elliptical (*cf.* J.T. 87*a*) : " And had ye no meat, John John? no had? " (*b*) ⌐ whither I *shall* " (L. 139*c*), so in orig. ? *shall* be.

SHATTER, SHATTERING (W. 110*c*), scatter, blow about : hence *shattering* = flying apart.

SHAVE, " I come not . . . to poll or to *shave* " (P.F 3*c*), to strip, to fleece, to extort. " Then haue you Brokers yat *shaue* poore men by most iewish interest . . . Then haue you the *Shauing* of Fatherlesse children, and of widowes, and that's done by Executors." —Dekker, *Seven Deadly Sinnes* (1606), 40 (Arber).

SHERIFF, " sense the *sheriff* with your heels " (W. 126*d*), see Sense.

SHITTEN SAIL, " shatter the *shitten sail* " (W. 110*c*), worthless : generic abuse. Here " the wind is hardly strong enough to stir the torn bedraggled rags of a woman's gown."

SHOOTER'S HILL (W. 100*a*), near Greenwich.

SHORN, MASTER JOHN (F.P. 30*c*), " who (says Reed) this John Shorn was, I can give no account. In the preface to *The Accedence of Armorie*, 4to, 1562, a story is told of one who had been called to worship in a city within Middlesex, and who being desired by a herald to show his coat (*i.e.* of arms), ' called unto his mayd, commanding her to fetch his coat, which, being brought, was of cloth garded with a burgunian gard of bare velvet, well bawdefied on the halfe placard, and squallotted in the fore quarters. Lo, quoth the man to the heraught, here it is, if ye will buy it, ye shall have time of payment, as first to pay halfe in hand, and the rest by and by.

And with much boste he said, he ware not the same since he came last from Sir John Shorne,' &c." Latimer (p. 186 b) says, " Ye shall not thinke that I will speake of the popish pilgrimage, which we were wont to use in times past, in running hither and thither, to *M. John Shorne*, or to our lady of Walsingham. No, no, I will not speake of such fooleries." Possibly, from his being called Sir John, we may conjecture that a priest of Shorne in Kent is alluded to.

SHORTER, " tied *shorter* " (W. 109c), given less freedom.

SHORTLY, " I go *shortly* " (J.T. 75c), " in the French farce *Pernet qui va au vin* " (Pollard). There are similar false starts and returnings, but in that case Pernet keeps coming back to watch his wife and her lover.

SHOT, " while the *shot* is tinking " (F.P. 38a), the reckoning, share of expense. " There he bestowed cheare and ipocras vpon them, drinking hard til the *shot* came to a noble."—Green, *Notable Disc.* (1591). " I'll to the alehouse with you presently; where for one *shot* of five pence, thou shalt have five thousand welcomes."—Shakspeare, *Two Gent.* (1595), iii. 5.

SHOT-ANCHOR, " his ointment is even *shot-anchor* " (F.P. 46d), a sheet-anchor : orig. and properly *shoot*-anchor, *i.e.* an anchor to be shot out or lowered in case of great danger. Here, fig. the last refuge or resort for safety.

SHREW, " I *shrew* thy heart " (P.F. 21c, *et passim*), beshrew, curse.

SHYT, " the door to her she *shyt* " (L. 158b), shut.

SIGHT, " I have some *sight* in singing " (F.P. 38b), to read at sight=to read a piece at first sight without previous knowledge.

SIMPER DE COCKET (W. 122d), wanton ; Mdlle. Simper de Coquette. " An affected mealy-mouthed girl " (Cotgrave).

SIMPLE, " *simple* office " (W. 129^a) foolish, mean, of little account.

SIPERS (F.P. 36b), *i.e. Cyprus*; thin stuff of which women's veils were made. So in Shakspeare's *Winter's Tale*, A. 4, S. 3—"Lawn as white as driven snow, *Cyprus* black as any crow." Again, in *Twelfth Night*—"A *cyprus*, not a bosom Hides my poor heart" (Steevens).

SIR JOHN (J.T. *passim*), generic for a priest: familiar or contemptuous. "From *Sir* as rendering L. *dominus* at the Universities" (O.E.D.). Also Mass (or Mess) John, and in Wyclif Sir Jack.

SISTREN, "brethren and *sistren*" (P.F. 19a), an old pl. of sister: this inflexion is now obsolete except in *oxen, children*, and *brethren*, the last named being now unusual save in poetry.

SITH, "*sith* God were bore" (P.F. 13c, *et passim*)— "*sith* it is so" (J.T. 87d)—"*sith* he is gone" (L. 180a), since; and as conj. seeing that.

SKILLS, "what *skills* our apparel" (W. 97c)—"what the devil should *skill* though all the world were dumb" (W 108b), what (what the devil) matters, signify: in Shakspeare, "it *skills* not."

SLIDDER, "the way to heaven is very *slidder*" (P.F. 12d), slippery: *slyder*, glissant (Palsgrave).

SLOUCH, "thou *slouch*" (P.F. 21c), a term of contempt: in a MS. glossary (quoted by Halliwell) *slouch* is defined as "a lazy lubber, who has nothing tight about him, with his stockings about his heels, his clothes unbutton'd, and his hat flapping about his ears."

SLOUGH, "where that thou *slough*" (P.F. 23b), killed, slew.

SMOKE, "beaten her till she smoke" (J.T. 67d), *i.e.* till a dust is raised by beating: *cf.* dust one's jacket. "I'll *smoke* your skin-coat an I catch you right."— Shakspeare, *King John* (1596), i., 139.

SOLICITOR, "I beseech you be my *solicitor*" (W. 109d), in the old sense of one who asks or begs with earnestness.

SOMER, MASTER (W.W. 194c), a jester attached to the Court of King Henry VIII. Full accounts of this

buffoon will be found (a) in a tract, printed in 1676,
and reprinted in 1794, entitled " A Pleasant History
of the Life and Death of *Will Summers* : how he
came to be first known at Court, and by what means
he got to be King Henry the Eighth's Jester : with
the Entertainment that his Cousin *Patch*, Cardinal
Wolsey's Fool, gave him at his Lord's House ; and
how the Hogsheads of Gold were known by his
means " ; and (b) in the Shakspeare Society's reprint
of Armin's *Nest of Ninnies* (1608) ; also see Sot *infra*.
Armin thus describes Somer's personal appearance
and traits :—

" Leane he was, hollow eyde, as all report,
  And stoop he did, too ; yet in all the court
  Few men were more belov'd then was this foole
  Whose merry prate kept with the King much rule.
  When he was sad the King and he would rime :
  Thus Will exiled sadness many a time."

His popularity with the King is corroborated by contemporary anecdotes, and he used the power he
possessed for the best purpose. Armin says—
      " He was a poor man's friend
  And helpt the widow often in the end,
  The King would even grant what he would crave,
  For well he knew Will no exacting knave,
  But wisht the King to doe good deeds great store,
  Which caus'd the court to love him more and more "—
in view of which Heywood's diatribe against Somer
is curious (see Sot). One of his last acts of kindness
is recorded by Granger. He says, that Somer was
at one time a servant in the family of Richard
Farmer, Esq., of Eston Weston, in Northampton-
shire, ancestor to the Earl of Pomfret, who was found
guilty of a præmunire for sending eightpence and a
ccuple of shirts to a priest in Buckingham gaol who
had denied the king's supremacy ; he was deprived
of all his property and reduced to a state of miserable
dependence ; but Somer in Henry's last illness dropped
some expressions, which so affected the king's
conscience that he restored the dismembered estates
to Will's old master (Fairholt, with additions).

SONG, " devoutly *song* every year " (P.F. 19a), sung.

SOOL, " *sool* possessed " (W. 134a), solely.

SOON, " abide till *soon* " (P.F. 17*b*), the evening.

SOOTH, " in *sooth* " (P.F. 6*d*), truth.

SORT, " the whole *sort* of my craft " (W. 110*b*)—" such another *sort* " (W. 128*c*), assembly, set, company (or lot) of people. " Remember whom you are to cope withall,—A *sort* of vagabonds, rascals, and runaways."—Shakspeare, *Richard III.* (1597), v. 3.

SOT, " admit all *sots* " (W.W. 193*d*)—" Somer is a *sot* " (W.W. 210*d*), a fool : in the old signification of the word (=natural fool, idiot) there was no implication that lack of sense arose from drunkenness : *cf.* " saith the *sot*, the natural fool call'd, or th' idiot " (W.W. 193*d*). Fairholt holds that " the term is not fairly applied to Somer," and Heywood certainly seems to have been either splenetic towards, or jealous of, the king's favourite jester (see W.W. 210*d*–211*b*). Collin, in his introduction to the *Nest of Ninnies,* says :—" he was a jester of a different character to the others, inasmuch as he was an artificial fool—a witty person, affecting simplicity for the ·to the sake of affording amusement." Much ·to the same effect will be found s.v. Somer, *supra.*

SOTHERY BUTTER (F.P. 54*c*), sweet or fresh made : *sote* = sweet.

SOUTHWELL, OUR LADY OF (F.P. 30*c*), the church dedicated to Saint Mary at Southwell, in Nottinghamshire.

SOWNE, " fall in a *sowne* " (J.T. 87*b*), swoon.

SPEED, " in despair of *speed* " (L. 147*c*), luck, fortune, success in an undertaking. " Happy be thy *speed*."—Shakspeare, *Taming of the Shrew* (1593), ii.

SPIN, " more tow on my distaff than I can well *spin* " (P.F. 25*c*), proverbial for more in hand than can well be undertaken. The phrase occurs again in the *Proverbs.*

SPITAL, " in some *spital* " (W. 126*a*), lazar-house, hospital.

SPRINGING, " *springing* . . . all manner corn " (W. 115*b*), quickening, causing to vegetate, grow.

SQUIRE, " *squire* for God's precious body " (W. 99*c*), originally a *squire* of the body was an attendant on a knight, but subsequently the meaning was debased to designate a pimp.

STARK, " *stark* dead " (J.T. 68*d*), " so *stark* a knave " (W. 126*c*)—" a *stark* fool " (L. 153*d*), wholly, absolutely, entirely : the original sense=stiff, rigid as in death ; now mainly confined to the phrase *stark* naked.

STATIONS, " gone the *stations* all a-row " (F.P. 29*d*), the stages or regular places of rest for pilgrims between London and Rome, or the Holy Land, of which there is a map in a MS. of Moth. Paris Roy. Libr., 14 C. vii., and Benet. Coll., c. ix. and Pl. VII. *Brit. Topog.*, i., 85, G. (Reed) : see also *Stacyons of Rome* (E.E.T.S., ed. Furnivall) : " And forasmuch as ther be many that hath wrytten of the Holy Lande of the *stacyons* & of the *Iurney* or way, I doo passe ouer to speake forther of this matter." —Borde, *Intr. Knowledge* (1542).

STEWS, " a haunter of the *stews* " (J.T. 74*c*), a brothel, or street of brothels ; " a place for comen women " (Palsgrave). " These abominable *stew*-houses were kept in Southwark . . . being whited houses, painted with signes to know them. These bawdy houses were tollerated, and had lawes and orders made for the *stew*-holders to observe."—*Proclamation* (1546) [MSS. note by R. Smith quoted by Hearne, *Diary*, October 12, 1713]. " [They] shal breake downe thy *stewes*, and destroy thy brodel houses."—Coverdale, *Bible* (1535), Ezek. xvi., 39.

STICK, " *stick* not for a penny " (P.F. 21*a*), scruple not. " I know a younker that will ease you . . . . That will not *stick* to marry you within this hour."— *Marr.*, *Wit and Science* (1569) (E.E.D.S. Anony. Pl., 4th Ser.).

STOCKFISH, " *stockfish* in Thames Street " (J.T. 70*c*), now rough fish, such as cod, ling, &c., split open and dried in the sun without salting : formerly, however, and probably in this case it was salted so hard that it had to be softened by beating before cooking.

STOCKS, "scoured a pair of *stocks*" (P.F. 24*c*), see Scoured.

STONES, "both thy *stones* in my purse" (W. 125*b*), here the meaning both of *stones* and purse is obscene : *stones* = testes ; *purse* = pud. mul. "*Damp.* Your ladyship sets too high a price on my weakness. *Han.* Sir, I can distinguish gems from pebbles ——. *Damp.* Are you so skilled in *stones?* [*Aside.*] "— Jonson, *Silent Woman* (1609), v. 1.

STYNTE, "to *stynte* the debate" (J.T. 79*a*), *i.e.* stint or lessen : *stynte* in original is misprinted *stynk*. *Thought* in next line is likewise misprinted *though*, *my* two lines lower down misprinted *me*.

SUDBURY (W. 100*a*), there are two Sudburys—one in Suffolk and another in Middlesex.

SUFFICIANCE, "meat for my *sufficiance*" (J.T. 87*d*), need, sufficiency.

SUNDAY (SAINT), "sweet *Saint Sunday*" (P.F. 7*a*), like All Hallows and Holy Trinity, a piece of humour on the part of the Pardoner.

SUPPORTATION, "your patience and *supportation*" (P.F. 5*b*), support, countenance.

SUSPECT, SUSPECTION, "in *suspect*" (J.T. 72*c*), suspicion. "And draw within the compass of *suspect* Th' unviolated honour of your wife."—Shakspeare, *Com. of Er.* (1593), iii., 1.

SWATHBANDS (F.P. 36*b*), rollers in which infants were *swathed*. So, in *Timon of Athens*, "Had thou, like us, from thy first *swath*," &c. (Steevens).

SWEETING, "his own *sweeting*" (W. 97*d*)—"my *sweeting*" (L. 154*a*), (*a*) a mistress, *pour le bon motif*; and (*b*) a wanton.

SYNDE, "where men will have her *synde*" (W. 133*a*), sent.

TAKE (TAK in orig.), "and th' auditor's wit who shall *take* th' account so clear" (W.W. 206*b*), give : A.S. "And alle that they aske scho wylle them *take*, For drede of theym, swylke boste they make." —*MS. Harl.* 2260, f. 59. "But *take* hur an oolde stede."—*MS. Cantab.* Ff. ii. 38, f. 72.

TAIL, see Feofed.

TAIL-PIN, " fiddling with the *tail-pin* " (F.P. 37a), there is probably a double meaning here : see *Slang and its Analogues,* s.v. Tail, subs. 2.

TALLEST, " the *tallest* man within this town " (F.P. 50a), *tall,* in old colloquial usage, is generic for worth. Thus *tall* (=seemly) prayers ; a *tall* (=valiant) man ; *tall* (=fine) English ; a *tall* (=courageous) spirit ; a *tall* (=celebrated) philosopher ; to stand *tall*=to rely boldly ; *tally* (=becomingly or finely) attired ; a *tall* (=great) compliment, &c. " One of the *tallest* young men."— *Paston Letters* (1448–60), 224.

TAMPION, " I thrust a *tampion* in her tewell " (F.P. 50b, &c.), " the allusion is to gunnery. *Thampion* (*tampon,* Fr., a bung, cork, or plug of wood) is now written *tampion,* and signifies the stopper with which the mouths of cannon are closed up, to prevent the admission of rain, or sea water, whereby their charges might be rendered incapable of service. A *tewel* (*tuyau* or *tuyal,* Fr.) is a pipe ; and is here used (for the sake of continuing the metaphor) for bore or calibre. Moxon, in his *Mechanick Exercises,* defines the tewel to be that pipe in a smith's forge into which the nose of the bellows is introduced ; and in a MS. fragment, said to be written by Sir Francis Drake, concerning the stores of one of the ships under his command, the word *tewel* is applied to a gun " (Steevens).

TASTED, " so far *tasted* " (W. 120a), *i.e.* decayed : the author's eye was probably on the proverb, " a new moon is made of green cheese."

TEN BONES (or COMMANDMENTS), " by these *ten bones* " (F.P. 58c)—" thy wife's *ten Commandments* " (F.P. 59a), the ten fingers : spec. of women. By these *ten bones* was a common oath of the time, in punning reference to the Mosaic Decalogue. " By these *bonys ten* thei be to you vntrue."—*Digby Myst.* (c. 1485), 4 note (1882). " I'd set my *ten Commandments* in your face."—Shakspeare, 2 *Henry VI.* (1594), i., 3.

TEWELL, "I thrust a tampion in her *tewell*" (F.P. 50*b*), properly *tail*, and hence fundament, which is still good Norfolkese as regards a horse. "And whan this sike man felte this frere About his *towel* gropen ther and here, Amid his hond he let the frere a fart." —Chaucer, *Cant. Tales* (*c.* 1386), 7730.

TEYSE, "both *teyse* and receive" (W. 103*a*), rouse the game and call off after bringing it down.

THAN (*passim*), then.

THANK, "knaves rob away my *thank*" (F.P. 33*d*), gratitude, thanks.

THOROUGH, "I have been *thorough*" (F.P. 57*c*), through.

THOROUGHOUT, "*thorough out* the world" (F.P. 55*c*), throughout.

TICKLE, "the waist . . . was *tickle*" (L. 153*b*), wanton. "For she is *tikel* of hire tail. . . . As commune as a cartway."

TILL, "if I stick no better *till* her" (W. 118*c*), until.

TIPTREE (W. 99*d*), in Essex.

TONE, TOTHER (*passim*), once (1180–1600) literary, *tother* now vulgar—the one, the other : *the*=thet, the old neuter article. "The *toon* yeveth conysaunce, And the *tother* ignorance."—Chaucer, *Rom. of Rose* (1360), 5559 ; Tyndale sometimes, like his enemy More, uses the old form, "the *tone*, the *tother*."

TONGUE IN PURSE (W.W. 201*d*), see Purse.

TOO TOO, "I love thee *too too*" (J.T. 72*d*), old literary : now colloquial : an intensive form of *too* : over-and-above, more than enough, very good, extreme, utter ; spec. (modern but obsolete) of exaggerated æstheticism. "It is often nothing more in sense than a strengthening of the word *too*, but *too-too* was regarded by our early writers as a single word" (Halliwell).

TORMENTRY, "not in pain but in *tormentry*" (L. 163*b*), torment.

TOTHER, see Tone.

TOUCH, " play me such another *touch* " (P.F. 21*c*), dirty trick, ill-turn, dodge : *i.e.* if you continue your annoyance and interruption.

TOW, " more *tow* on distaff," &c. (P.F. 25*c*), see Spin.

TOYS, " the *toys*, the mocks " (J.T. 80*d*), whims, fancies, idle talk, jokes, gibes, &c. " I never may believe these antique fables, nor these fairy *toys*."— Shakspeare, *Midsummer's N. Dream* (1592) V. 1 3.

TRAIN, " *train* her by the hair about the house," to drag, trail. " In hollow cube *Training* his devilish enginery."—Milton, *Paradise Lost*, vi. 553.

TRESTLES, " on the *trestles* " (J.T. 76*c*), the frames or bars with divergent legs, used as supports for the " board " of the table.

TRIACLE, " one box of this *triacle* " (F.P. 46*a*), *triacle* is not unfrequently used for a balsam, or indeed any kind of infallible or powerful medicine (Collier); an antidote. " Is there no *triacle* in Gilead? "—Wyclif, *Jer.*, viii. 22.

TRICK, " so *trick* it is " (W. 122*b*), neat, spruce, trig.

TRICKEST, " the *trickest* and fairest of you all " (W. 123*d*), smartest.

TRIFLES AND KNACKS (J.T. 87*a*), *i.e.* trifling, tricky treatment.

TRINDLE (W. 108*d*), wheel.

TRISE, " to trip or *trise* me " (L. 154*b*), pull up : *i.e.* get the better of.

TRUNNION, SAINT (F.P. 30*a*), the following mention of *Saint Tronion* occurs in Geffrey Fenton's *Tragical Discourses*, 4to, 1567, fo. 114 b : " He returned in haste to his lodgynge, where he attended the approche of his hower of appointment wyth no lesse devocion than the Papistes in France performe their ydolatrous pilgrimage to the ydoll, *Saynt Tronyon*, upon the mount Avyon, besides Roan " (Reed). " Nay, softe, my maisters, by *saincte Thomas of Trunions*, I am not disposed to buy of your onions." —*Appius and Virginia* (1575), E. 2.

TRY, " *try* from port to port " (W. 112*c*), sail.

TURDS, "my *turds* in . . . thy teeth " (F.P. 59a), a
contemptuous address : Go to the deuce ! "A *turd*
in thy little wife's teeth."—Jonson, *Barth. Fair*
(1614), i. 1. "A *turde* in thy mouth, the devyll take
thee "—Harman, *Caveat* (1567), 86.

TWENTY DEVIL WAY, "in the *twenty devil way* " (P.F.
18d), *i.e.* in the name of the devil : *twenty* = an in-
definite number, hence, in the twenty devil way = an
intensified form of a common oath.

TWIGGED, "each day be *twigged* " (W.W. 209a),
whipped.

UNCUMBER, SAINT (F.P. 30a), see Brand, *Pop. Antiq.
Gt. Britain*, ii. 136.

UNIVERSAL, " be ye so *universal?* " (F.P. 37d), *i.e.* such
an all-round man, such an out-of-the-ordinary person.

UNNETH, " so pale that *unneth* I " (L. 166c), scarcely.
" *Uneath* may she endure the filthy struts."—Shakspeare, *2 Henry VI.* (1594), ii. 4.

UP, " *up* shall this pack " (F.P. 37d), elliptical : *i.e.
up* on my back.

URE, (a) " in *ure* " (F.P. 54a), chance, destiny, fortune. " So pitously gan cry On his fortune and on
ure also."—Lydgate, *Complaint of the Black Knight.*
(b) " in *ure* " (L. 156c), use, practice. " For in the
time that thieving was in *ure*."—Taylor, *Penniless
Pilgrimage.*

VAILABLE, " for speed most *vailable* " (W. 105c), avail-
able.

VARIORUM READINGS, see the different plays by name in
this Note-Book.

VARYING, " her shrewd *varying* " (J.T. 80b), badly-
disposed temper, vixenish goings-on.

VICE (*passim*). For an exhaustive and admirable essay
see Gayley, *Representative English Comedies*,
xlvi.-liv., from which the following extract must
suffice—" A general view of his history shows that
the Vice is neither an ethical nor dramatic derivative
of the Devil ; nor is he a pendant to that personage,

T

as foil or ironical decoy, or even antagonist. The
Devil of the early drama is a mythical character, a
fallen archangel, the anthropomorphic Adversary.
The Vice, on the other hand, is allegorical,—typical
of the moral frailty of mankind. . . . The functions
were gradually assimilated with those of mischief-
maker, jester, and counterfeit-crank. . . . It was only
gradually, and as the conflict between good and evil
was supplanted by less didactic materials,—in other
words, as the moral became more of a play,—that the
Vice grew to be farcical, a mischief-maker, and
ultimately jester."

WAG, " I will hold ye *wag* another way " (W.W. 203*b*),
tell another story, hold a different opinion.

WALK, "*walk* her coat, John John " (J.T. 68*c*), beat
her, drub her, dust her jacket : *walk* = to full cloth.

WALKED. "*walked* them well " (J.T. 88*d*), beaten,
drubbed.

WALSINGHAM (F.P. 30*b*), in Norfolk, " where was
anciently an image of the Virgin Mary, famous over
all Europe for the numerous pilgrimages made to it,
and the great riches it possessed. Erasmus has given
a very exact and humorous description of the superstitions practised there in his time. See his account
of the Virgo parathalassia, in his *Colloquies*
(Gibbings, 1890) entitled *Peregrinatio Religionis
Ergo.* He tells us the rich offerings in silver, gold,
and precious stones, that were there shown him, were
incredible ; there being scarce a person of any note in
England, but what some time or other paid a visit,
or sent a present, to our *Lady of Walsingham.* At
the dissolution of the monasteries, in 1538, this
splendid image, with another from Ipswich, was
carried to Chelsea, and there burnt in the presence of
commissioners." See Percy's *Relics of Ancient
Poetry,* vol. ii. p. 79. In his *Vision concerning
Pierce Plowman,* W. Langland says—" Heremites on
an heep, wyth hoked staues, Wenten to *Walsyngham,*
and here wenches after " (Reed). See also Weever,
Fun. Mon., 131, and the next entry.

WALSINGHAM RING (W.W. 194*d*), see previous entry, in connection with which, it may be noted, that it was usual for pilgrims to bring away with them from these shrines leaden signs or some other token of their visit. These were generally of little or no intrinsic value, and were rudely executed in lead stamped with the figure of the saint, and carried in the hat of the male pilgrim as a " sign," or on the breast of the female as a " brooch." In the very curious museum of C. Roach Smith, Esq., F.S.A., is preserved one given to the pilgrims who visited the shrine of St Thomas à-Becket, at Canterbury, which has been engraved in the *Archæological Album,* as well as in Mr. Smith's *Collectanea Antiqua,* along with many other curious specimens, British and foreign. Other examples are engraved in the *Journal of the British Archæological Association,* vol. 1. Mr. Smith possesses a very curious leaden brooch of our Lady of Walsingham ; and in Miss Wood's *Letters of Royal and Illustrious Ladies of England,* is one from Elizabeth Newhouse, to her son, Roger Wright, on the eve of the Reformation, telling him she had been this pilgrimage, adding, " I have no good token to send you at this time but a *Walsingham brooch.*" Mr. Smith, in a later number of his *Collectanea,* notices that *rings* and other objects appear to have been manufactured in vast numbers, and sold to pilgrims and others who resorted to the shrine of the three kings of Cologne. One in brass found in London, reads, IASPAR. MELCIOR. BALTAZAR ; another, in the possession of Mr. E. J. Carlos, has the two names only, IASPAR. BALTASAR : these are believed to be *cramp rings* (see Pettigrew *On Superstitions connected with the History and Practice of Medicine and Surgery,* p. 87). The *Walsingham ring* was similar to these (Fairholt).

WALTER, " your stomach sore to *walter* " (F.P. 46*c*), feel sick or squeamish.

WALTHAM (F.P. 30*b*), the holy cross of Waltham, which tradition says was erected in the reign of Canute : see Lambarde, *Dictionarium* (1730), 431.

WAN, " no man hath *wan* " (F.P. 61*d*), won.

WARE, (a) " which she *ware* " (P.F. 7c), wore.

WARE, " or I were *ware* " (J.T. 75a), aware.

WARK, " a pretty piece of *wark* " (L. 163c), work : still good Scots.

WARRANTYSE, " shall make *warrantyse* " (W.W. 201c), warranty, assurance.

WASTER, " nother staff nor *waster* " (J.T. 69a), cudgel : " *Wasters* or cudgels used in fence-schools."—Florio, *Worlde of Wordes*, 95.

WAWLING, " leave this *wawling* " (J.T. 70d), cat-calling.

WAYT, " such a *wayt* she took " (L. 157c), care.

WEALTH, " I do it for your *wealth* " (J.T. 78a), prosperity, success.

WEATHER (THE PLAY OF THE)—*Text*, pp. 91–135. There are four known copies, two of which are incomplete : (1) a copy in the Pepys Collection, Magdalen College, Cambridge, 1533, printed by William Rastell ; (2) in the library of St John's College, Oxford : this copy wants the last leaf, containing twenty lines of the text and the colophon with the printer's name, but it is identical with that in the Pepys Collection ; (3) another imperfect copy at the University Library, Cambridge (it lacks sixteen lines of text and the colophon), which has been identified as printed from Rastell's edition, and to come intermediate between his edition of 1533 and the next entry ; (4) a perfect copy in the Bodleian, obviously printed by Kitson from No. 3 : the colophon reads " Imprynted at London in Paules Churchyearde at the Sygne of the Sunne, by Anthonie Kytson," who was publishing between the years 1549 and 1579. *Reprinted* (5), as far as a few extracts go, by Fairholt in his introduction to *A Dialogue Concerning Witty and Witless*, published by the Percy Soc. (1846) ; included (6) in Gayley's *Representative English Comedies*, and also (7) in Prof. Brandl's *Quellen des Weltlichen Dramas in England vor Shakspeare. Variorum Readings*—the var. read. are those of the St John's College copy, except where otherwise stated—*The* ancient estate (93b), *That* ; *Solely* to honour (93d), *Wholly* ; *we* shall say (94a), *well* ; cold and *hoar* (94c), *hote*; their *powers* be denied (94*d*), *poures*; these *four* in no manner (95*a*), iiii; wholly *surrendered* (95*b*), *sundred*; *shew* quickly (96*c*), *shew me*; in *thy* light behaviour (96*d*), in *the* light behaviour; *of too much* lightness (96*d*), *of much*; my *manner* (97*a*), *name*; *nor* my name (97*a*), *not*; *husband* departed (97*d*), *husbandes*; *thanked* me heartily (97*d*), *thanketh*; have *taken* it (97*d*), *take* in St J. copy; thine *indifferency* (97*b*), *indifference*; *in* my conscience (99*c*), *on*; *in* Lombardy (99*d*), *at*; Welbeck (99*d*), *at* Welbeck; *at* Westchester (99*d*), *and at*; half *thus much* (100*b*), half *so much*; a *goodly* hearing (100*b*), *good*; pointeth to the *women* (101*c*), *woman*; comfort *the* cry (102*c*), *thy*; shall *make way* (104*c*), *make a way*; right humbly *beseecheth* (104*d*), *beseeched*; we may be *partakers* (105*c*), *parte takers* (Bodleian copy); the *wind* measureable (105*c*), *winds*; next *to go* (106*a*), *to go to*; come again *hither* (106*c*), *thether*, *hether*; at *this* meeting here (106*d*), *his*; And if *I* cannot get (107*c*), *we*; For, I *see* (107*d*), I *see well*; as I found *ye* (108*a*), *you*; touching *ourselves* (108*c*), orig. *ourselfes*; which is right small *and* (108*d*), *as*; our *millstones* (108*d*), *millstone*; wheel with her *cogs* (108*d*), *cog*; *pricked* me hither (109*a*), *pycked*; even *boldly* (109*a*), even *bodily*; *must be* tied shorter (109*c*), *shalbe*; with *no nother* man (109*d*), *none other*; my *solicitor* (109*d*), *solyter*; *Here entereth* (110*b*), *Entreth*; time *of* beginning (110*c*), *to*; let *that* gear pass (111*a*), *this*; as ye say (111*b*), *you*; be *lords* over all (111*c*), *lord*; mean of *our* craft (111*c*), *your*; *but* then by your license (112*b*), *and*; for a time shall *hang* (112*b*), *stande*; both *mast* and shroud (112*d*), *man*; we spake of *wind* (113*c*), *mind*; afore *we* were born (114*c*), *he*; it *were* impossible (115*a*), *were* is omitted; springing and *plumping* (115*b*), *pluming*; *thing* of necessity (115*b*), *things*; for *scouring* (115*b*), *showring*; may grind *all times* (116*b*), *at all times*; help to *those* (116*c*), *chose*; I think *it* meet (116*c*), *ye*; *Entereth* Merry Report (117*a*), *Here entreth*; *tell* by experience (117*b*), *tell ye*; *gate is no* sooner open (117*c*), *gates not*; *setting your* stones (118*a*), *setting of*; stick *no better* (118*c*), *not the better*; *to* pass time (121*b*), *of*; so *fet* it is, so *neat* it is (122*a*), so *far* it is, so *near* it is; I pray *you*

(122*b*), *ye*; have ye *alway* (122*c*), *always*; your
simper de cocket (122*d*), *simper the cocked*; pick not
your *pocket* (122*d*), *pocked*; little *or* much (123*a*), *of*;
not *thy* beauty (123*d*), *the*; is all *the* joy (124*a*), *thy*;
devil shall have the *tone* (124*d*), *one*; more ye *bib*
(125*c*), *byd*; will do *no* worse (126*c*), *no* omitted;
unto such *rich* (126*d*), *tyche*; sense the *sheriff* (126*d*),
street; greatest friend ye have (126*d*), *you*; how they
flicker (127*c*), *flytter*; all *this* time (129*a*), *his*; to
wait for *mo* (129*a*), *me*; I *come* now (129*b*), *to me*;
trees to tear (129*d*), *tree*; to make *snowballs* (130*b*),
balls; wide from the *tother* (130*d*), *other*; Such
debate (131*b*), *debates*; pressed *to* your presence
(131*d*), *as*; not *in* your sight (131*d*), *is*; *on hills we*
(132*c*), *the, hills he*; fair *women* (132*d*), *woman*; full
of some (133*b*), *of the some*; no one craft (133*b*),
none.

WELBECK (W. 99*d*), in Nottinghamshire. Welbeck
Abbey is now the seat of the Dukes of Portland.

WELL-SEEN, " ye seem *well-seen* in women's causes "
(F.P. 36*c*), well-informed, fully cognisant.

WENEFRED'S WELL, SAINT (F.P. 30*b*), " Saint Wenefrid's well, near Holywell, in the county of Flint, is
a spring which rises at the foot of a steep hill out
of a rock, and is formed into a beautiful polygonal
well, covered with a rich arch supported by pillars;
the roof exquisitely carved in stone. Over the fountain
is the legend of St Wenefrid on a pendent projec-
tion, with the arms of England at the bottom.
Numbers of fine ribs secure the arch, whose inter-
sections are coupled with some sculpture. To this
place the resort of pilgrims was formerly very great;
and though considerably diminished, there are still
to be seen in the summer a few in the water in deep
devotion, up to their chins for hours, sending up their
prayers, or performing a number of evolutions round
the polygonal well; or treading the arch between
well and well a prescribed number of times. The
legend of St. Wenefrid is well known. Those who
desire more information on this subject may be referred to *The Legenda Aurea*, Bishop Fleetwood's
Works, or Mr. Pennant's *Tour in Wales*, p. 28 "
(Reed).

WENT, "I had *went*" (J.T. 76d)—"I *went* it had been" (W. 100c), thought, weened.

WHIPPER, "here is a *whipper*" (F.P. 44b), something out of the common : still colloquial.

WHIT, "the devil speed *whit*" (J.T. 68a), the devil a bit.

WHORESON, "a *whoreson* drivel" (P.F. 17c, *et passim*), a generic reproach.

WIFE (W. 104b), "as the play was written before 1533, the clergy were still celibates, and this is only Merry-report's humour" (Pollard).

WILLESDEN (F.P. 30c), in Middlesex, the church dedicated to St Mary : see Saint Saviour.

WIST, "this would be *wist*" (J.T. 68c), known.

WITHAM (W. 100a), in Essex.

WIT, "ye shall all *wit*" (P.F. 5d)—"I will *wit*" (F.P. 53c), know, ascertain.

WIT AND FOLLY, see *Witty and Witless* : Collier, in his *Annals of the Stage*, gave this name to the B.Mus. MS., but Heywood's title is now restored.

WIT, WITLESS, WITSAFE, WITTY (W.W. 193–217, *passim*), *wit*=knowledge, wisdom, "every-dayness" : so the reverse in negative.

WITTY AND WITLESS (A DIALOGUE CONCERNING), sometimes called *Wit and Folly.*—*Text*, pp. 191–217. *Editions.*—(1) Original manuscript in British Museum. (2) Printed 1846 for the Percy Soc. from the original MS., edited by F. W. Fairholt, F.S.A.

WO, "won his own *wo*" (W. 133b), woe, sorrow.

WOOD, "then be they *wood*" (F.P. 37a), mad, furious, or violent. "Howe will you thinke that such furiousness, with *woode* countenaunce and brenning eyes, with staringe and bragging, with heart redie to leape out of the belly for swelling, can be expressed y tenth part to the vttermost."—Ascham, *Toxophilus* (1545), 56 (Arber). "To wax so wild and *wood*."— Churchyard, *Worth. of Wales* (Evans, 1776), 103.

WOODCOCK, " a very *woodcock* " (J.T. 82*d*)—" Master
Woodcock " (L. 148*a*), a fool, simpleton. " O this
woodcock ! what an ass it is ! "—Shakspeare, *Taming
of Shrew* (1593), i. 2.

WOE, " I would be *woe* " (F.P. 34*b*), sorry. " I am *woe*
for it."—Shakspeare, *Tempest* (1609), v. 1. " I
wolde be *wo*, That I presume to her is written so."
—Chaucer, *Court of Love.*

WONDERS, " *wonders* well " (F.P. 57*a*), wonderous.

WOT, WOTEST (*passim*), know.

WRABBED, " so wayward and *wrabbed* " (F.P. 57*b*),
? rabid, but so spelt to look more like a rhyme to
crabbed (Nares).

WRAWLING, " she will never leave her *wrawling* " (J.T.
78*c*), brawling.

WROKEN, " on the walls was *wroken* " (F.P. 51*a*), properly wreaked, revenged : here=hurled, shattered.

WYST, " this wolde be *wyst* " (J.T. 68*c*), *i.e.* this
question must be answered.

YER, " *yer* full intent " (W.W. 194*c*), your.

YNGE, see Jayberd.

YNOWE, " well *ynowe* " (J.T. 67*d*), enough.

Printed in the United States
126279LV00003B/25/A

9 781436 522472